1938

Adoption
and the
Jewish Family

*For Shaare Shamayim —
Beth Judah's
Family

B'Shalom
Shelley
Rosenberg*

Adoption
and the
Jewish Family:
Contemporary Perspectives

by

Shelley Kapnek Rosenberg

The Jewish Publication Society
Philadelphia and Jerusalem

Library of Congress Cataloging-in-Publication Data
Rosenberg, Shelley Kapnek
  Adoption and the Jewish Family/Shelley Kapnek Rosenberg.
     p.   cm.
  Includes bibliographical references (p.   ) and index.
  ISBN 0-8276-0653-2
  1. Adoption—Religious aspects—Judaism. 2. Adoption—United
States—Psychological aspects. 3. Jewish Families—United States.
4. Adoption (Jewish law) I. Title
HV875.25.R67   1998
362.73'4'089924073—dc21   98-20879
                                                                              CIP

Designed by Sasgen Graphic Design
Printed by R. R. Donnelley

To

Michael and Jessica

my two miracles

and

Ken

my husband, my love, and my best friend

The publication of this book was assisted
by a generous grant from
THE KORET FOUNDATION
(San Francisco)

Contents

Acknowledgments

Researching and writing this book has been one of the most emotional, and one of the most rewarding, experiences of my life. I learned an immense amount from all those who shared their personal stories and professional expertise with me; I learned about adoption and I learned about myself. Many were the interviews I conducted with tears streaming down my cheeks, grateful for the privacy provided by long distance telephone. My hope is that by retelling these experiences and sharing the collected wisdom of the many experts who have been working in this field for years, I can help other members of the adoption triad and, by doing so, repay the kindness and trust of those who shared their very lives with me.

I owe an incredible debt of gratitude to the over one hundred people who made time and space for me in their busy lives. Some were adoptees, some adoptive parents, some birth parents; when people shared their personal stories, their hopes and fears, dreams and struggles, I changed their names and disguised their identities to protect their own privacy and that of their families. The adoption professionals I interviewed patiently explained theories, shared case histories, and recounted experiences gathered from many years in this field; I have acknowledged their contributions throughout the text.

Some of those professionals have gone even further, reading and critiquing chapters, making invaluable suggestions regarding both content and language. We sought always to be cognizant of the sensitive nature of this material and the powerful feelings it calls forth. I want to thank Claude Riedel, Michael Colberg, Deborah Siegel, Roseann Michelson, Deborah Silverstein, Sharon Kaplan Roszia, Lucy Steinitz, Myra Hettleman, Gail Lipsitz, Jane Tausig, Sharon Schanzer, Carol Demuth, Rabbi Sherry Shulewitz, Besie Katz, Beverly Bernstein, Molly Wiener, Robin Allen, Julie Bulitt, Janice Bershad, Helene Tigay, and Rabbi Richard Fagan. Special thanks are owed to Abby Ruder and Linda Yellin, who shared their unique and sensitive professional and personal wisdom, guiding me always toward a better understanding of the issues facing each member of the adoption triad and how to best address them. Any shortcomings are mine alone.

My editor, Ellen Frankel, understood from our first conversation why this book needed to be written and how it should be approached. She is any writer's dream editor, empathetically guiding my thinking and astutely suggesting precisely the appropriate revisions that both respected my ideas and helped me make the most of them. Christine Sweeney was always helpful and patient, guiding this writer, new to book publishing, through every step of the process. Copy editor Nancy Peske made careful and skillful suggestions that greatly enhanced the existing material.

Family and friends have been my mainstay, patiently listening to my ideas and concerns about both the content and the process of writing the book. Colleagues at the Auerbach Central Agency for Jewish Education, in Melrose Park, Pennsylvania, especially Drs. Sharon Schanzer and Jane Tausig, were always available with insightful and thought-provoking ideas. They were also always ready to share a joke and a laugh when things got rough. Fredda Sacharow, my first editor at the *Jewish Exponent*, in

Philadelphia, is both my mentor and my friend; she encouraged my writing and taught me with style and grace. She is the consummate professional.

My family—my parents, Lewis and Arabelle Kapnek, my in-laws, Roslyn and Lester Cohen, and my sister, sisters-in-law, and brothers-in-law—have been my Gibraltar. They are the best family anyone could have and lovingly supported me, not only during the writing of the book, but throughout our entire journey through infertility and adoption.

And, of course, my two miracles—Michael and Jessica—and my dearest friend and partner, my husband Ken, have taught me all there is to know in life about love.

To all of you—heartfelt and enduring thanks.

Introduction

"Like a branch transplanted" into new and fertile ground, every adoptee has been plucked from one existence and rerooted into another. He or she has been transplanted into a new family, a new community, a new life. The branch, the psalmist writes, has been "made strong," and this is the desire, and expectation, for the adoptee. *Ametz*, the word for adoption in Hebrew, comes from these verses. It means "strengthen," and it echoes and reinforces the hope that this child will invigorate his or her family as the family and community empower the child.

Just as a vine demands nurturing and care, with appropriate amounts of water, sun, and fertilizer, so too a child requires concern and attention to his or her basic developmental needs. Food, shelter, clothing, and attention to safety and physical well-being are the basic rights of all children. Educational opportunities appropriate to the child's talents and interests, structured and lovingly applied discipline, and empathic concern for the child's emotional needs lay the groundwork for every child's healthy growth. An adopted child is no different.

But just as the transplanted vine must accustom itself to new soil, an adopted child must become acclimated to an environment different from the one in which he or she would have grown. No matter how careful the uprooting, how rich the soil, how bright the sun, how appropriate the amounts of water and fertilizer, this vine may require additional attention in order to thrive. So, too, the adopted child may require special attention in order to flourish. The soil, while rich, is different. The transplanting, however delicate, shocks the roots. By virtue of being adopted, this child faces additional challenges and issues that are different from those other children face. At each stage in the child's development, there are questions—normal questions—but ones that are unique to adoption. For a Jewish adoptee and adoptive family, an additional lens filters each event, encounter, and question through thousands of years of history and generations of traditions, as well as through the experience of contemporary American Jewish life.

It was once widely believed that if the child were young enough, the placement smooth enough, and the adoptive family did everything "right," adoption was "just like having a baby of one's own." If no one talked too much or asked too many questions about biology and birth parents, no one, including the adoptee, would notice that adoption, not birth, had brought the child into this family. If an adoptee did notice that he or she was somehow different from siblings or friends, love, it was assumed, would conquer all. Adoption was the answer to three problems: It provided a home for a child who needed one, a child for parents who couldn't produce one biologically, and a solution for people who couldn't raise the child they had. It was meant, and believed, to be a "happily ever after" story.

Sometimes, however, life does not match theory. Adoption *is* a good answer to real problems, yet adoption creates challenges of its own. Raising an adopted child *is*, in many ways, like raising any child, yet adoption is a different way of entering a family, which creates differences within and for that family. These differences are neither positive or negative; they simply are.

What matters is how people react to them. If confronted openly, their power can be diminished and people can deal with them. Secrets, however, can be destructive; they may acquire the power to cause pain, shame, and self-doubt. Children often assume what their parents fail to say, what is not discussed, must be too awful to mention.

Adoptees have long harbored questions and feelings about themselves and the missing pieces of their heritage. They have longed to know about their birth families in order to better understand themselves and the differences between themselves and their adoptive families. Some have not been able to simply adopt the family and heritage that has adopted them without filling in the missing pieces of their personal puzzle. They need to know who they would have been and integrate that with who they are in order to become who they want to be. However, adoptees often feel unable to ask their questions or express their feelings for many reasons; chief among them is usually the desire not to hurt the adoptive family they love.

Medical, mental health, education, and even some adoption professionals have not recognized that what they considered a "benign" adoption, that of a healthy infant into the same race family, could be a cause for concern. They did not understand that adoption, by its very nature, raises questions. And new situations create new, and more complex, issues for which many people are not prepared. The number of transculturally and transracially adopted children and adoptions of children with visible disabilities has grown. Adoption has been recognized as a risk factor for a variety of invisible disabilities. Open adoptions have increased in popularity, and greater numbers of adoptees in closed adoptions are seeking their birth parents. Singles, gays, and lesbians are adopting in greater numbers.

Adoptive parents, anxious to believe what they have been told, often have not recognized that their children harbored unspoken questions. They may have hoped that the curiosity would fade, or worried about the effect that a discussion about adoption might have. Would it stir up painful feelings for themselves and their child? Could it ignite a desire to search for birth parents? Would it highlight the child's difference from the rest of the family and community? Might the child think he or she is not loved? Would he or she love less?

Adoptive parents do well to remember that questions about the past and its meaning dwell in their child's heart and mind. Some feel only the faintest stirring of curiosity, while others confront many troubling concerns. Adoptive children who deny these questions deny their very selves. Their adoptive parent's love is a crucial beginning, but does not answer these questions. Giving an adoptee permission to ask, and helping him or her find answers, is an adoptive parent's gift of love. Recognition that the adopted member has questions about the missing pieces of his or her life does not detract from the love that members of an adoptive family feel for one another. The willingness to face difficult questions together is a tribute to the unswerving power of that love.

Within the Jewish community, adoption has always engendered conflicting responses. Family is honored as a key to Jewish existence. The Torah's first injunction is "be fruitful and multiply." Most life-cycle events and holidays are family-centered occasions. Adoptive families have only to look to the Torah and Talmud to understand that adoption has long been a respected way to build a family. Yet in biblical times, these were not actual adoptions, and no such legal institution, conferring all the rights of relationship, existed. Moreover, Judaism has always maintained its emphasis on the bloodline, according primacy to biology in the rights of religious and tribal status. Under traditional Jewish law, adopted children must be officially converted to Judaism, yet are not accorded precisely the same status and privileges as their nonadopted siblings. Through its ancient religious practices, Judaism has recognized what has become understood as a universal truth about adoption: Adoptees can not erase their past; it is there and it is theirs, and they must acknowledge it and incorporate it into who they are.

Jewish adoptees are a minority within a minority. Should a Jewish adoptee also have a disability, be of a different race or culture, or have single, gay, or lesbian parents, he or she becomes a member of an even smaller subset. Each additional identity raises questions that overlap the others, layer upon layer, creating heretofore unrecognized, but not unfelt, stress on adoptive Jewish families. Families often do not know where to turn with this stress. They may hesitate to acknowledge a concern or hesitate to consult an adoption specialist, because they are embarrassed to be less than the perfect family with whom their child presumably was placed. Jewish professionals do not often think about adoption as an issue necessitating their concern. They do not understand the complexities of adoption or the added uncertainties that Judaism, with its conflicting messages, creates.

While it is true that adoptive families confront additional complexities that other families do not, it is also true that adoption is a miraculous way to build a family. Most adoptees ultimately do well; they and their families face the challenges and prevail. These adoptive parents treat challenges as opportunities to strengthen the family, and the rewards are sweet, perhaps sweeter for having been more difficultly won. Love, respect, and dedication supersede genetics; they grow as the family builds a life together. That life is a blessing that Jewish families can share with their community.

This book arose from my experiences as a parent of two children, one who was adopted and one who was not. It arose from my life as a Jew who is committed to my people, my tradition, my heritage, my community, and to enabling both of my children to feel comfortable with that heritage and in that community. And it arose from my experiences as an educator in both the Jewish and secular communities. I had slowly—too slowly—

realized that adoption brought different challenges to parents, family, and community than did parenting a birth child, and that I had been ill prepared to meet them. I also realized that the uniqueness of our life experiences as Jews was an additional lens through which we needed to examine adoption. I became determined to explore these challenges and to help other Jewish adoptive families by sharing what I have learned.

This book is largely the result of over a hundred interviews with Jewish members of all parts of the adoption triad—birth parents, adoptive parents, and adoptees—as well as adoption professionals, in both the Jewish and non-Jewish communities. I have distilled and summarized the experts' opinions, as well as those of the triad members with whom I spoke. My own experience has informed my discussion of adoption, most specifically as it relates to the Jewish community.

The book discusses such questions as:

• How does an adopted child become a Jew?

• How do adoptees feel about their search for and reunion with birth parents? How do Jewish adoptees feel upon finding Jewish, or non-Jewish, birth parents?

• How are transcultural and transracial adoptees faring in Caucasian families? How do Asian, South American, or African American adoptees relate to being Jewish? How do those adoptees relate to their birth heritage?

• What effect do disabilities have on adoptive families? What does a disability mean in the context of a Jewish family?

• What are the challenges of being a gay or lesbian adoptive parent? How does the Jewish community support these families?

• Are there different challenges for single adoptive parents? What is the Jewish community's response?

• How are families involved in open adoptions faring? What impact does open adoption have when birth parents are not Jewish?

- What difference does it make when one sibling was adopted and another wasn't? How do other members of Jewish families support the adopted member of the family?

- What could and should educators, doctors, therapists, and other members of the helping professions do to support adoptive families? What could synagogues, Jewish schools and youth groups, rabbis and Jewish educators do to support Jewish adoptive families?

There are no right or wrong answers, but I do know that had I known in the beginning of our adoption journey what I know now, both from experience and from the research for this book, my family and I would have navigated the rapids of adoption very differently. The Jewish community has much to offer its adoptive families, and they in turn have much to offer their community. The intention of this book is to illuminate the issues facing Jewish adoptees and their families, and to permit people to give voice to their questions and answers, fears and joys, challenges and triumphs. Then adoptees and their loved ones will truly be able to rejoice in the miracle of the family they have created and greet each day with a blessing, thankful for being able to celebrate it together. I write this book to celebrate the opportunities that lie ahead.

CHAPTER 1

The Halakhah of Adoption: What Jewish Law Says

≈

*J*ewish tradition emphasizes the importance of adoption in creating a Jewish family; it also teaches that adoption alone does not create a Jew. While Judaism affirms that raising a child, establishing a Jewish home, and teaching Torah are the acts of a Jewish parent, it also recognizes the tension between nature and nurture inherent in adoption. The laws and ceremonies of Jewish tradition assert that, although an adoptee becomes a Jew, he or she never loses his or her personal history.

The Talmud speaks eloquently to adoptive parents. "He who brings up a child is to be called its father, not he who gave birth" (Exodus Rabbah 46:5). "Whoever raises a child in his home, it is as if he had begotten him. . . . Whoever teaches Torah to the son of his companion, Scripture considers it as if he begat him" (Sanhedrin 19b). These are welcome and comforting sentiments for Jewish adoptive parents, many of whom are unable to fulfill the Torah's injunction to "be fruitful and multiply" (Genesis 1:22). Emphasizing interconnectedness through commitment, not genetics, they acknowledge the ongoing responsibility of parenting throughout a lifetime, and the contribution adoption makes to Jewish families and the Jewish community.

Jewish tradition has, since biblical times, informally recognized the role of adoption in the formation of Jewish families. Jacob provided inheritance for his grandsons, Joseph's sons,

1

Efraim and Menashe. Batiah, the daughter of Pharaoh, saved Moses from the Nile and reared him as her own. King David's wife, Michal, raised her sister Merab's five sons. Mordechai became foster father to his orphaned cousin Esther, and Naomi helped to raise her daughter-in-law Ruth's son. These, however, were not legal adoptions, because the institution was unrecognized by halakhah [Jewish law]. In fact, there was no word for "adoption" in biblical Hebrew. Modern Hebrew uses the word *ametz*, "to strengthen," a reference to the verse from Psalm 80: "be mindful of this vine . . . which Thy right hand *has planted*, and the branch that Thou *madest strong* for Thyself." This word and this verse imply the honor attributed to adoption; many see it as a mitzvah [good deed], as adoptive parents take on the responsibility of raising a child whose life's journey is radically different from what it would have been had he or she not been placed for adoption, especially adoption by a Jewish family.

Many adoptive Jewish families, unaware of the traditional Jewish legal doctrine, wrongly assume that the action of civil law, coupled with their emotional and familial connection to their child, confers Jewish identity on that child. Halakhically, it does not. There are also variations in the laws concerning conversion among the four branches of Judaism. This is critical to understand, for the decisions adoptive parents make about conversion can have lifelong repercussions within the Jewish community for their children. The import of these decisions, following so close on the heels of the adoption itself, may be overwhelming, and even frightening, to some adoptive families. They should consider carefully which of the options open to them fits comfortably with their personal convictions and beliefs. They should also seek guidance from rabbis within their own communities regarding individual situations. When adoptive families understand the halakhah, they are able to make informed decisions that can help children feel strongly connected to and supported by their adopted community.

Was I Born Jewish?

A child is Jewish, according to traditional halakhah, if the child's birth mother is Jewish. Reform and Reconstructionist Jews also recognize patrilineal descent, that is, that the child of a Jewish father, who is raised as a Jew, is Jewish. When Jewish adoptees begin to search for their roots, the first question many ask is "Am I really Jewish?" They mean, says Rochelle Sanders, MSW, manager of adoption services for the Paths to Parenthood Program of Jewish Family and Children's Service of Greater Philadelphia, in Pennsylvania, "Was I born Jewish?" Many adoptees do not quite believe what they have been told throughout their lives—that they were, in fact, born Jewish. Learning that they were Jewish by birth seems to be reassuring to many adoptees, she says. Many express relief, as if this confers authenticity upon their Judaism. It confirms them as part of a people who put great stock in bloodlines and shared history.

Some people, including adoptees themselves, accept the myth that Jewish children are not placed for adoption. They believe that Jews do not face out-of-wedlock pregnancies or the termination of their parental rights due to incompetence, abuse, or neglect. However, most children placed for adoption with Jewish families prior to the 1970s were born Jewish, explains Shirley Sagin, MSW, ACSW, former director of adoption for JFCS in Philadelphia. There was no abortion and scant possibility of keeping a child born out of wedlock; Jewish agencies quickly placed these children with Jewish families.

"It was a *shandeh*, a disgrace," recalls Sandra, recounting a story similar to that of many Jewish birth mothers. "I was nineteen years old, in college, and very much in love with the baby's father. I had a strict moral upbringing in a middle-class Jewish home. We didn't use birth control—and I know it sounds ridiculous now—because we thought it couldn't happen to us. It just didn't happen to 'nice Jewish girls.'

"The father left me. I didn't tell my parents until I gave birth.

I couldn't. I mean, it was the kind of thing they used to talk about over dinner: 'Guess whose daughter got pregnant?' When I told them, they just wanted to know whether I'd told anyone else. I hadn't, so they said that we'd never discuss the matter again. The prevailing attitude was that girls who got pregnant were tramps. I even heard one of the operating room nurses say it. I knew I had to go back to school and couldn't keep the baby. Placing him for adoption with a Jewish agency was the only thing to do."

Knowledge and increasingly liberal attitudes about birth control and abortion have seriously limited the number of Jewish children placed for adoption since the 1973 Roe v. Wade Supreme Court decision legalizing abortion. Greater acceptance of single parenthood has also lessened the number of children available to adopt. Although there are still Jewish children being placed, most have special needs or disabilities.

Adopting a Jewish child can present thorny issues for adoptive parents. Questions about an adoptee's parentage arise if he or she wishes to marry a traditionally observant Jew or chooses to make *aliyah* to Israel, where religious ceremonies such as weddings and divorce are under the jurisdiction of Orthodox authorities. A child who is the product of a halakhically illegitimate relationship, that is, the offspring of a woman who has a Jewishly legal marriage to one man and produces the child of another Jewish man, is considered a *mamzer* [illegitimate]. A *mamzer* is forbidden to marry a Jew of legitimate birth. There is also a possibility, slim though it might be, that a Jewish adoptee might, inadvertently, marry a biological sibling. Thus, some traditionally observant Jews refrain from adopting Jewish babies.

With the popularity and acceptance of open adoptions, however, it is possible to know exactly who a child's birth parents are. Thus, says Vicki Krausz, founder and director of the Jewish Children's Adoption Network, a Jewish adoption exchange in Denver, Colorado, many observant Jews who wish to adopt

Jewish children can do so. She advises prospective adoptive parents who are concerned with halakhic issues to consult a rabbi knowledgeable about the halakhah of personal status and adoption. They should seek specific genetic and familial information about the child they wish to adopt, because this can be difficult and distressing for the adoptee to track down later in life.

Paula was adopted as an infant and raised in a Conservative home, and felt very affiliated and identified as a Jew. She became engaged to an Orthodox man who wanted to be married by a hasidic rabbi. Upon learning that she was adopted, the rabbi required proof that she had been born a Jew. "I had never thought about it. I assumed I was Jewish and I didn't care how. When the rabbi said I had to prove I was Jewish, it threw my whole identity into question," she remembers. "My dad said that they hadn't converted me because the Jewish adoption agency told them I was Jewish. Now, all these years later, I needed verification in writing. I contacted the agency; the adoption professionals were sympathetic and got me a statement. Next, the rabbi wanted to know if my Jewish birth parents had been married. I got a letter, which I had to get notarized, that I was born of an unmarried Jewish woman. However, the stress involved destroyed the relationship with my fiancé. He didn't understand why having to prove my identity upset me so much."

The man Paula eventually married was also Orthodox, and he, too, was anxious to be married by an Orthodox rabbi. This rabbi accepted Paula's letter, but needed to know if her birth mother had been previously married. Although the agency could only assume, but not prove, that she was never married, this was acceptable to this rabbi. Most important, Paula says, was her husband's attitude: He was sympathetic and concerned about her feelings.

If a child is the Jewish birth mother's firstborn son, not born by cesarean section, and neither of his birth parents is a descendant of *kohanim* or *levites* [members of the priestly tribe], he

should have a *pidyon ha-ben* [redemption of the firstborn] ceremony on the thirty-first day after his birth, regardless of the status of the adoptive parents or whether they have older sons. The
laws for this are complicated, and the family should consult a
rabbi.

Once parents have assured themselves that no halakhic problems exist, it is a mitzvah to adopt a Jewish child, says Rabbi
Steven Dworken of the (Orthodox) Rabbinical Council of
America's Commission on Gerut [Conversion]. This makes certain that Jewish children remain within the Jewish community.
To some adoptive parents, there is also a sense of comfort in
adopting a Jewish child. "It wasn't an issue," explains Marc, who,
with his wife, Dina, had been preparing to adopt transculturally.
"But it felt like Divine Providence" when the first Jewish child
ever placed by their agency suddenly became available for adoption. This may be, says Shirley Sagin, because there is "a sense of
fit, a feeling of adopting within extended family, or at least within the community."

The Transformative Rituals of Conversion

When an adopted child is not born Jewish, conversion is necessary in order that the child be unequivocally accepted as a Jew
in any Jewish community. Knowing this, many adoptive parents
express the desire "to do everything Judaically possible" so that
their child, and the world, will know that he or she "is really
Jewish." "We didn't want any questions later on," one adoptive
father explained. "In our eyes, and in the eyes of God, there
should be no doubt," an adoptive mother said.

Life-cycle rituals are meaningful markers in an individual's
Jewish existence and for the Jewish community. They help many
adoptive parents lay spiritual claim to their adopted children,
welcoming them into their family and the Jewish people. Rituals
demonstrate the importance of the event itself and, by celebrating it Jewishly, the importance of Judaism to the celebrants.

"When we converted our daughter, we had an enormous sense of changing her destiny and her future," explains Sara. "We believe that she was meant to be Jewish, that she has a Jewish soul, and that this is the way things were supposed to work out. It was *bashert* [meant to be]. We explain to her that [with the ritual] we made her a Jew."

Ordinarily, Jews do not perform conversions without the express and knowing consent of the convert. How, then, is it possible to convert an infant or toddler? The answer is found in the assumption that being a Jew is a *z'khut* [privilege], and that one can perform a meritorious act on a person's behalf without the individual's consent.

The powerful and transformative rituals of *milah* [circumcision] and *tevilah* [immersion] for a boy and *tevilah* for a girl are the heart of classical halakhic conversion ritual. Like all Jewish boys, an adopted boy should have a *brit milah*. Unlike the *brit* of a boy who is born a Jew, it does not have to take place on his eighth day of life. When possible, however, performing the ceremony on the traditional day can be moving and meaningful. Susan remembers the phone call informing her of her child's birth. "Call the *mohel* [the person who performs ritual circumcisions]," the [Jewish] adoption counselor announced. In this way, Susan learned that the long-awaited baby was a boy.

The call to the *mohel* "was the first official thing we did to make him ours," Susan recalls. Because Joel came home from the hospital when he was four days old, his *brit* was held on the traditional eighth day. Adoptive parents should inform the *mohel* that their son is being adopted. The circumcision document must indicate this, and the blessing, altered for the occasion, declares, "Blessed are You, Lord our God, Ruler of the Universe, Who has sanctified us with Your commandments and commanded us to circumcise proselytes."

Michael, an adoptive father and a rabbi, invited his entire congregation to his son's *brit*, holding it in the sanctuary of his synagogue with "Brit Buses" to shuttle the attendees from an over-flowing parking lot. "After all the years of naming other people's children, the *simha* [joyous occasion] was finally ours," he explains. "Everybody came to reciprocate." Although the ceremony was not held on the baby's eighth day of life, it was held, symbolically, on his eighth day in his new home. In a gesture that presaged the positive confirmation of his child's Jewish identity, Michael announced his son's future Bar Mitzvah date.

If a child has already been circumcised, a symbolic circumcision is required. Called *hatafat dam brit* ["the drop of blood of the covenant"], it involves taking a drop of blood from the side of the penis. The technically simple procedure can be performed by a *mohel* in front of a single additional witness instead of at a public ceremony. However, the ritual can be emotionally trying for parents and children, and the Jewish professionals involved should be sensitive to their doubts and fears.

Sharon's son was already four by the time his adoption was final and it was appropriate to begin conversion proceedings. She needed to convey the message that, just this once, it was all right for him to allow a strange man to touch, and even cut, him on his penis. She explained that all Jewish boys have this ceremony, which she planned as a private event at home. The *mohel* gained Josh's confidence by showing him the Freon spray that would be used as a local anesthetic, and encouraging him to gather the *kiddush* [prayer over wine] cup, wine, and *kipot* [skullcaps]. Josh cried at the actual cut, Sharon recalls, but recovered more quickly than did she and her husband.

Bill's son, Matt, was almost eleven when Bill discovered the necessity of having a *hatafat dam brit*. Matt had been circumcised in the hospital as a newborn, and Bill never realized that a second ritual would involve drawing blood. "I thought that the circumcision was enough and that we would have a ritual to give him a Hebrew name that would be purely ceremonial. I never asked, and our rabbi, who knew Matt was adopted, never said anything. I really fault myself because there are things in life that you can't leave to assumption. If you don't know, you should ask, and putting it off just makes it harder."

Bill says that once he learned what was involved, he desperately wanted to avoid drawing Matt's blood "because of the potential psychological trauma." He explored the possibility with his rabbi, who explained that the ritual was required if Matt wanted to be recognized as a Conservative Jew. Bill, who had been raised in an Orthodox home, but "drifted away," says that "a certain amount of ritual remained ingrained." He believed, and explained to Matt, that the ceremony was necessary for Matt to officially become a Jew. Matt, who had grown up completely involved in Judaism, at home and at his synagogue, agreed; he wanted no barriers to being fully Jewish.

Because they always do things together, Matt asked Bill if he would undergo the ritual too, and Bill agreed. "I felt that if my son was willing to go through this, I could do it with him," Bill explains. When the day arrived, Bill, Matt, the rabbi, and the *mohel* gathered in the rabbi's office, and Bill explained his promise. The rabbi and *mohel* objected immediately; Bill had already been circumcised and there was no ritual reason for him to have a *hatafat dam brit*. Bill was devastated, and felt obligated to let Matt rethink his decision. Matt asked Bill's advice, and Bill replied that he hoped Matt would go through with the ceremony. He knew that Matt wanted to be able to say, without reservation, that he is Jewish. Matt decided to continue, and asked only that Bill hold his hand.

"I looked into his eyes, and his love for me, his trust that I would never do anything to hurt him, and his sense of wanting a place in the Jewish community all combined to overcome his fear," Bill recalls. "To see an eleven-year-old do this without crying was overwhelming. I felt so proud of my son, yet such inadequacy, remorse, and guilt that I hadn't dealt with this sooner, and that my negligence had put him in this situation. My son saved me because of the way he went through it. Afterward, the first thing he said was, 'Dad, it was just like you said.' I never lie to him and I'd told him it would hurt a little, like a pinprick when they take blood from your finger. He said to my heart, 'It's okay. We'll go through this together no matter how we got here.'"

Increasingly, Jewish families are adopting children from countries that do not routinely perform medical circumcisions on infant boys. *Hatafat dam brit* is not an option, and this child must undergo a circumcision, usually with the proviso that it pose no serious health risks. Rabbis and *mohelim* should be especially sensitive when counseling an adoptive family regarding the circumcision of an older child, since it can be a difficult and potentially traumatic time for parents and child.

Noam was adopted from El Salvador when he was two and had a circumcision at age three. "Our feelings were mixed," his mother Pat recalls. "We asked ourselves how we could put our child through this, but felt it was necessary if we were going to raise him as a Jew." The procedure was performed by a urologist in the operating room under general anesthesia, with the *mohel* present to draw the ritual drop of blood. The blessings were recited in the recovery room, with the family and godparents present.

Tevilah is required for both boys and girls, at any time prior to Bar or Bat Mitzvah. Many people wait until the child is comfortable in water and doesn't mind being completely immersed. The ceremony should take place in a *mikvah* [ritual bath] before a *bet din* [religious court]. The child must be naked, and a very young child can be accompanied into the water and held by a parent so that he or she can be dunked completely under the surface. Two blessings are recited: "Praised are You, Lord our God, Ruler of the Universe, Who has sanctified us with Your commandments and commanded us on the immersion," and "Praised are You, Lord our God, Ruler of the Universe, Who has kept us alive, sustained us, and allowed us to reach this season."

Michael scheduled the *tevilah* immediately following the civil procedure finalizing his son's adoption. "We went to court on Friday and the *mikvah* on Monday. This provided civil and religious closure; one wasn't sufficient without the other," he explains. Sara remembers Malka's *mikvah* as "the most wonderful day. I laughed the hardest I'd laughed in a long time when I saw her come out of the water sputtering and my dad said, 'She's Jewish!' It was a release of tension and emotion." Meryl remembers the "*mikvah* lady" telling her that "being in the waters of the *mikvah* was like being in amniotic fluid and being reborn." She entered the water with her daughter and says, "It gave me a feeling as if I had given birth, of what it might have felt like emotionally. I was very glad to have done it."

The rabbis presiding over the *bet din* may question the adoptive parents or the child, if he or she is old enough, about the family's link to Judaism, their motives for the conversion, or the child's understanding of his or her Jewish identity before proceeding to the *mikvah* itself. Because Josh's adoption is open and his birth parents are not Jewish, the rabbis wanted to explore the type and amount of contact he would have with them. Sharon and her husband Sam explained that they felt it was their job to make being Jewish so joyous and so much a part of Josh's life that the interactions he would have with his non-Jewish birth parents would not be a problem. They added that, even with a biologically Jewish child, a parent never knows whether a child will choose to practice Judaism as an adult. The rabbis then turned to Josh. "What special food did you just eat on Passover?" they asked. Sharon recalls her nervousness when, with typical four-year-old shyness, he didn't answer immediately. Her relief was obvious, she reports, when he finally responded, "Matzah."

Differences in Conversion Laws and Rituals

The problem that arises for parents planning to convert their adopted children to Judaism is that the traditional and liberal branches of Judaism have different requirements for conversion. Moreover, the Orthodox and traditional Conservative movements do not accept other rabbis' authority in this area. The decision adoptive parents make about conversion can have lifelong consequences for their children. Some rabbis require proof of Jewish lineage before they will enroll a child in a Jewish school, permit synagogue membership, or conduct a Bar or Bat Mitzvah or wedding. They may request the certificate from a child's *brit* and/or *mikvah* to determine where and by whom these rituals were performed. Parents need to consider that, regardless of their own level of observance, they have no way of predicting their child's future interest in and observance of Jewish ritual. It is devastating for an adopted person who has been raised as a Jew to be told that he or she "isn't really Jewish." Some adoptive parents, therefore, choose the most traditional path. They should seek rabbis within the halakhic community who are sensitive to adoption issues, says Rabbi Richard Fagan, an educational consultant at the Auerbach Central Agency for Jewish Education, in Melrose Park, Pennsylvania. Others select a more liberal procedure, while anticipating how they and their child will handle whatever future complications might arise. Whatever their decision, it is critical that adoptive parents have accurate information. Because the laws are complex, they should consider consulting a rabbi who is well versed in the halakhah relating to adoption.

Reform Judaism

Reform Judaism takes a liberal approach to Jewish law, maintaining that halakhah is no longer binding and should be changed or modified to meet the needs of modern Jews. Reform Judaism does not require the formal conversion of a child born to a non-

Jewish mother, if the child is to be raised as a Jew. However, many of the traditional rituals, which were eliminated or modified as Reform practice developed, have since been brought back as people's needs have changed. Recognizing the differences among the branches of Judaism, and the difficulties this can cause adoptees later in life, some Reform rabbis suggest that people may wish to comply with more traditional practice (Alexander, 1993, p. 4). Others, like Rabbi Simeon Maslin, Rabbi Emeritus of Reform Congregation Keneseth Israel in Philadelphia, Pennsylvania and past president of the Central Conference of American Rabbis, do not recommend conversion, but do suggest that all children have a *brit* ceremony, at home or in synagogue, that formally marks their entry into the community.

Reconstructionist Judaism

Reconstructionist Judaism holds that the traditional halakhah "has a vote, not a veto." By defining Judaism as the evolving civilization of the Jewish people, Reconstructionism endorses the value of observing traditional laws and rituals, but maintains that they are not binding. The movement requires conversion, unless the birth mother or father was Jewish. (Patrilineal descent is not generally accepted by more traditional Jews. Such a person, adopted or not, may be asked to convert if they want to involve themselves in the more traditional branches of Judaism.) The traditional rituals are seen as "imperative parts of the conversion process," and it is recommended that "their meaningfulness and transformative potential" be emphasized (Gluskin and Levy, 1993, p. 4). Rabbi Sherry Shulewitz, associate executive director of the Jewish Reconstructionist Federation, explains that in the Reconstructionist view, "conversion is a gateway to membership in the Jewish people and a gift that the Jewish people offer new members." The conversion itself is considered only the beginning of Reconstructionist Jewish life; like all groups, the movement encourages lifelong Jewish learning, synagogue membership, Shabbat and holiday observance, and involvement in home and family rituals.

Conservative Judaism

Conservative Judaism accepts the authority of halakhah, but also maintains that modern life necessitates some modifications of certain laws. To be acceptable, these modifications must be made by authorized rabbinic authorities and supported by halakhic reasoning. For a child to be considered Jewish by most Conservative rabbis, he or she must be formally converted to Judaism under their authority, or one that is more rigorous. Discussion concerning the details of conversion under Conservative authority can be found in a document entitled "On the Conversion of Adopted and Patrilineal Children." With the Certificate of Conversion, the Conservative Rabbinical Assembly provides a "Parental Statement on Conversion" in which parents pledge "to rear their child according to the [teachings of the Torah and the] Jewish faith" by providing "a [comprehensive] Jewish education, bringing the child [regularly] to synagogue, establishing Jewish observance in the home, and surrounding the child with the warmth and joy of the Jewish religious practice in the home."

"A conversion is required by Jewish law and is a beautiful ceremony and a celebration," says Rabbi Michael Gold of Temple Beth Torah of Tamarac, Florida and author of *And Hannah Wept: Infertility, Adoption, and the Jewish Couple*. "Although a Conservative ceremony may not be recognized by some Orthodox rabbis, I recommend that people try to maximize their observance while doing the best they can within their reality."

Orthodox Judaism

Orthodox Judaism holds that the Torah was given directly to the Jewish people by God. Therefore, only strict adherence to traditional halakhah, as expounded in the Torah and interpreted in the Talmud, is permissible. Since performing these rituals is seen as a direct act of obedience to God, they have to be performed in the most proper manner. Accordingly, most Orthodox rabbis will not accept anything other than an Orthodox conversion, not out of prejudice, but because they believe that any deviation would be disobedience of God's will. The Rabbinical Council of America's Commission on Gerut, "Standards for Conversion of Adopted Children," requires that both adoptive parents be Jewish, keep a kosher home, be affiliated with an Orthodox synagogue, have a sponsoring rabbi with whom they will continue to be in contact, have knowledge of basic halakhah, and promise to provide a Jewish day school education. The rabbis who comprise the *bet din* must be Orthodox and the *mikvah* must be kosher according to Orthodox standards.

In Actual Practice

In addition to the differences among the movements, rabbis within each movement exercise considerable discretion in determining how the rituals will be performed. Many adoptive parents, unaware of the subtleties, may believe they are fulfilling certain traditional requirements when, in actuality, they are not.

Although they know it is not required by their movement, some Reform Jews, like Harvey and Donna, want a "full-blown traditional conversion" to give their child "the most solid Judaic grounding possible." Thus, they arrange for a *bet din* and a *mikvah*. But with the *bet din* composed of, in their case, a Reform, a Conservative, and an Orthodox rabbi, like other conversions that do not comply with the requirements of the Orthodox Rabbinical Council of America, it is unlikely to be acceptable to most Orthodox authorities. Other Reform, Reconstructionist, and Conservative Jews find Orthodox rabbis who will conduct a *bet din*. However, fewer Orthodox rabbis are willing to do this, explains Rabbi Gold, because they believe that it is better not to convert a child who will not live a traditionally observant Jewish life. And even if such a rabbi is found, his signature on conversion documents may be unacceptable to other rabbis.

Shoshana's daughter was converted by a rabbi who, although he was ordained at an Orthodox yeshiva, was the rabbi of her Traditional/Conservative synagogue. The other two rabbis on the *bet din* were Conservative. When Shoshana attempted to enroll her daughter in the local Orthodox yeshiva for kindergarten, she was asked to produce the certificate signed at the *brit* and the *mikvah*. She was told that while her child would be accepted because both her family and the rabbi were well known in the community, the school strongly recommended another conversion by "a more acceptable, fully Orthodox *bet din*." Although it was "traumatic" at the time, Shoshana complied, in order to ensure her child's future acceptance in any Orthodox community.

Carol's Conservative rabbi conducted her son Jeff's conversion at a community *mikvah*. It serves the entire Jewish community of her city, except for the Orthodox who have their own separate *mikvah*. Two Orthodox friends were witnesses. She recognizes that this conversion would not be acceptable to Orthodox authorities and her feelings are mixed. She agrees with her rabbi, who counseled her against bowing to the pressure of having an Orthodox conversion for fear that her own movement's conversions will never be recognized. She is also concerned for her child's future in the Jewish community, and doesn't want him to suffer for her beliefs. Thus, she contemplates providing Jeff with the opportunity to have another, Orthodox, *mikvah* prior to his Bar Mitzvah, but worries that she would be sending a message that their family's and synagogue's observance "is not good enough."

Joyce and Alan planned a three-part ceremony for their daughter, Melanie. The *bet din* and *mikvah* were conducted by Orthodox rabbis. This, Joyce explains, leaves all of Melanie's options open, and connects her to Jews throughout the world and throughout history. They also had an *aliyah* at their Conservative synagogue, connecting with the local Jewish community of which they are a part. And they fashioned a creative naming ceremony which they held at home, bringing together all of the diverse people involved in their lives and continuing their involvement in constructing Jewish rituals to meet their personal religious needs and beliefs.

Some Jews do not accept classical halakhah as binding and, therefore, choose other ceremonies that are meaningful to them. Susan and Carl, while knowing that a Reconstructionist conversion would not be universally recognized, chose to have Joel's conversion conducted by a Reconstructionist *bet din*. "These are our rabbis and this is our belief system," Susan explains. "We wouldn't have felt good about what we were doing if we hadn't been true to that. We wouldn't lie to an Orthodox rabbi about our observance or our future plans for our child to get him to perform a conversion. If Joel wants to marry a girl who is more observant than we are, we'll help them deal with it at the time."

Other liberal Jews, like Jane, who considers herself "an observant Reform Jew," are "resentful about doing something that is not part of our tradition." She chose not to have any special ceremony at all, and is raising her child in her Reform synagogue. Ken, the adoptive father of twins, describes himself as a liberal Jew who was raised in a secular context. He "dislikes bloodline Judaism," believing that Jewish identity belongs to anyone who wishes to affirm it, and was unwilling to convert his children, resisting what he considers "submission to the Orthodox norm, which is like saying that they're the 'real' Jews."

On the other hand, he is actively involved with a liberal congregation, and wants his children to grow up with a strong Jewish identification, "even if it isn't the standard one." When his children were four, he and his wife, in consultation with their rabbi, planned a tree planting ceremony as a public affirmation of the children's adoption. Based on a tradition in ancient Israel in which a cedar is planted for a boy and a cypress for a girl (BT Gittin 57a), they crafted a ceremony that reflected their feelings and sensibilities about adoption and raising their children as Jews. Family and friends brought meaningful things to plant with the trees, such as stones from Israel, offered blessings, and recited a prayer by Reb Nachman of Bratslav that affirms nature. The ceremony was beautiful, he reports, and felt exactly right.

What's in a Name?

A rose by any other name would smell as sweet, but it wouldn't be a rose. Names are important markers and claimants of identity. In her book *Raising Adopted Children: A Manual for Adoptive Parents*, Lois Ruskai Melina suggests that selecting their child's name is particularly important for adoptive parents. It is a way of claiming this child as their own and demonstrating that he or she belongs to their family and their people (Melina, 1986, p. 11).

In Jewish tradition a child is often named for a beloved and special family member or friend. In Ashkenazic tradition a child is named for someone who has died; in Sephardic tradition it can be for someone who is alive. Adoptive parents should select both English and Hebrew names, or a Hebrew name that is used for both, one that will be meaningful to them and their child. This custom provides a special opportunity to bind the child to the family, community, and heritage of the Jewish people. "We had all of these grandparents that we wanted to memorialize," Michael, the rabbi, explains. "It's a way to reach back and forward, a powerful way to maintain the link." All children love to hear stories about how and why their names were selected, what they mean, and the people they commemorate. Adopted children understand the special significance that their names convey: They are part of this family and this people.

Most Jewish boys receive their Hebrew names at their *brit*. For girls, a naming ceremony called a *simhat bat* [celebration for a daughter] has become popular. Either ceremony can include creative readings, songs, and personal comments from the new parents and grandparents or from other family members and friends. Many parents explain the origin of their child's name and some speak about their gratitude to their child's biological parents and the gift they have received from them. Shoshana spoke about her struggle with infertility and wished the best for those who are still struggling. Childless friends carried Sara's daughter, Malka, into the synagogue, a custom indicating the hope that they, too, will receive the blessing of having a child. Cindy read a poem about adoption, and her mother read a prayer that she had written about her hopes for her new Jewish grandchild. Adoptive parents who do it say that creating their own ceremony was meaningful; it connected their child to their new family and their new heritage, and emphasized the importance of Judaism in the family's life.

Sharon and Sam held Josh and Leah's joint naming ceremony at their synagogue, where they were honored with an *aliyah* during the Torah service. The children joined them on the *bimah* [raised platform from which the service is conducted], and the rabbi recited the blessings which officially bestowed on them their Hebrew names. Then, Sharon and Sam spoke about the names they had chosen, reflecting both the children's connection with their new Jewish family and their own gratitude to the birth parents who had given their children life. They expressed their hope that Josh and Leah will bring their genetically endowed talents and abilities to their adoptive family. Peter, Josh's birth father, attended the ceremony, and Sharon and Sam "felt happy that he heard that part."

Nancy and Bob held Aliza's naming ceremony in their yard, on a lovely spring afternoon. With just their rabbi, immediate family, and friends present, they conducted a brief ceremony that they had designed themselves. It included a candlelighting and the *kiddush*, which was recited by their eight-year-old son, as well as prayers for the parents and grandparents. After the rabbi recited the blessings, they explained Aliza's Hebrew and English names.

In some cases, adoptive parents will find that their child has already been named by his or her birth parents. Leah had been given "a very Christian-sounding name," one that Sharon and Sam didn't like. Since she was only days old when they brought her home from the hospital, they were comfortable changing her name to Leah, a more Jewish-sounding name. Lois Melina recommends caution, however, if the child has already learned to respond to his or her birth name, since a name is an important part of a person's identity. She also reminds adoptive parents that changing a child's name does not change or erase the child's past. Pretending otherwise, she says, indicates unrealistic expectations about who this child is and will become.

In Jewish tradition names also indicate religious lineage; people are identified as the son or daughter of their father. Liberal Jews also identify the mother. This is the way in which a person is called up to the Torah and identified on a *ketubbah* [marriage certificate] or a *get* [divorce document]. Converts, however, are identified as the "son or daughter of Abraham our father [and Sarah our mother]," the first Jews.

Some rabbinic authorities insist that an adopted person be treated like any other convert, in order to avoid halakhic problems that might arise when not identifying a person properly. However, this constant reminder that a person was adopted can be distressing to both child and parents. Other rabbis permit the adoptive father's name to be used if it is followed by the word "*hemegadlo*" ["who raised him"]. Still others allow an adoptee to be called by his or her adoptive parents' names, with the proviso that the person make his or her status known if necessary. Michael, the rabbi, uses his and his wife's Hebrew names to identify his son, explaining "we are his parents." Sara says that her rabbi permits Malka to be known as "the daughter of

Yitzkhak and Sara," although her *ketubbah* will indicate that she was adopted.

As the Adopted Child Grows

Adoptive parents have the same obligations as other Jewish parents to provide a proper Jewish home and education for their child. The child has the same obligations, as do other children, of "honoring his [or her] father and mother," of sitting *shivah* [the ritual period of mourning], and reciting *Kaddish* [the prayer for the dead]. The Jewish tradition of "he [or she] who raises a child" prevails.

However, Judaism's insistence on the primacy of blood still has authority, even after a child has been adopted and converted to Judaism. Although there are ways in which he or she is treated like any other Jew, there remain ways in which his or her position is different. Under traditional halakhah, an adoptive father's status as a *kohen* or *levi* [member of the priestly tribe] does not transfer to his adopted son. The child remains a *yisra'el* [one of the common people], and cannot be called to the Torah for one of the first two *aliyot* [blessings after the Torah reading], which are reserved for *kohanim* and *levites*. Among the people a *kohen* cannot marry are women who were adopted and are Jewish by virtue of having been converted. Bloodlines can never be replaced; biology gives a child his or her religious status, not a court proceeding (Gold, 1987, p. 443).

To some people, these are painful reminders of the different status an adopted person holds. Jews who observe classical halakhah may be troubled by these laws, but say there is little they can do. Shoshana simply hopes that her daughter will not want to marry a man who is a *kohen*. Aaron "swallows hard" when his older son, who was adopted, receives an *aliyah* as a *yisra'el*, while his younger son, who was not adopted, can join him for the more prestigious *aliyah* reserved for the *kohanim*. Liberal Jews have removed these biological categories and do not consider this a problem. They do, however, demonstrate the Jewish regard for blood relationships and the importance accorded to ancestry.

An adoptee who was converted as a child retains the halakhic right, upon reaching the age of religious majority (Bar or Bat Mitzvah), to renounce the conversion and Judaism. Rabbis differ on how this difficult and controversial issue should best be handled. Some rabbis advise that a child must be informed of the situation and consciously choose Judaism. Others believe that this is too difficult and open-ended a choice to offer a teen, who is often in the throes of adolescent identity crisis and rebellion. Most Jewish adoption professionals agree that this is too emotionally charged a decision to present to so young a teen, and is likely to offer a rebellious adolescent a convenient target. They recommend that any real decision making be left for adulthood when religious affiliation will be one among many choices that adults make.

Diane and Richard are members of an Orthodox synagogue and their daughter Marla's original *bet din* was conducted by Orthodox rabbis. They were told, however, that the conversion "wasn't complete" until, at the age of twelve years and one day, Marla took responsibility for herself as an adult Jew and "reconfirmed" her commitment to Judaism. At that time, the same rabbis conducted a second *bet din*, asking Marla herself questions about her commitment to Judaism, and she, again, immersed in the *mikvah*. Diane and Richard explained to her that they believed it was important and right for her to accept this responsibility for herself, and they made the ceremony special by giving her a *hai* [the Hebrew symbol for "life"] pendant. Marla herself, however, says that she felt a great deal of anxiety about this event, especially since other children in her day school told her that she wasn't really Jewish until she had reconfirmed her Judaism. Sometimes, she says, she felt like saying, "If I'm not really Jewish, then never mind."

Sara and Shoshana, who are also Orthodox, say that their rabbis have advised them that such a step is unnecessary because the children have been converted to Judaism, and raised as Jews, and "the minute they start doing mitzvot [good deeds] it is as if they have accepted Judaism." Michael, the Conservative rabbi, says that while the conversion must be confirmed by "a positive Jewish act at the age of majority," any positive Jewish step will suffice.

Many rabbis and adoptive parents consider the Bar or Bat Mitzvah itself a reaffirmation of an adoptee's conversion, says Rabbi Michael Gold, and find particular significance in the ceremony for this reason. Susan and Carl helped Joel select a number of meaningful rituals to incorporate into his Bar Mitzvah ceremony, as specific acts of reaffirmation. While not providing him the choice of rejecting his Judaism, they presented the positive idea of reconfirming an act that he was, originally, too young to understand. He selected a *tallit* [prayer shawl] on a pre-Bar Mitzvah family trip to Israel and his grandparents presented it to him and helped him to put it on at the ceremony. During the point in the Torah service when their Reconstructionist congregation's tradition is to hand the Torah from generation to generation, Susan, Carl, and each grandparent read a portion of a poem about passing on their Jewish heritage. As Joel accepted the Torah from them, he recited lines acknowledging his acceptance of this heritage as his own.

CHAPTER 2

Building Jewish Identity

Jewish identity is a feeling of affiliation with a group, of kinship to a people, of oneness with Jews throughout time and throughout the world. It is more than the sum of its parts: Life's experiences shape Jewish identity, and Jewish identity shapes life. For many adoptees, forming a personal identity with which they are comfortable is a major life challenge; for many Jewish adoptees, forming that identity with Judaism included complicates the task. Some adoptees question their connection to their adoptive family. For Jewish adoptees, that adoptive family includes an entire community, with thousands of years of history, with whom they are expected to bond. Many question their right and their ability, if not their desire, to belong.

People who are not adopted—who have never had to wonder "Who am I?"—can not fully appreciate the import of this question. Adoptees can not imagine not asking this question of themselves. Most adoptees are Jews by choice—except that they haven't really chosen. Rather, Judaism was chosen for them by their adoptive parents. While some adoptees seem readily willing to adopt the people that have adopted them, others struggle to feel connected. Some adoptees feel they are forever missing pieces of their past, and so it may be difficult for them to connect to the present or the future. They have difficulty forging an identity from a personal history that is a mystery. Not knowing who and what they were and where they came from, they are unable to define for themselves who they are and where they are going. Others know their birth identity, that they were not born Jewish, and have to struggle to develop an emotional connection to Judaism despite being brought up with Jewish rituals and religious education.

When adoptive parents discover that their child is struggling with identity issues, it can make them wonder about their parenting skills. When Jewish adoptive parents, especially those who identify strongly as Jews, realize that their adopted son or daughter does not share that identity, they may be disappointed, hurt, or shocked. They have probably assumed, and hoped, that their child would find Judaism and the Jewish community a safe harbor sheltering them from the prejudice and cruelty found in the rest of the world. Instead, the child appears to be rejecting the essence of who and what the adoptive parents are. These parents cannot help but wonder why.

If adoptees believe that they are not fully accepted by the Jewish community, it can cause them to reject that community in turn. There may be several reasons for feeling such rejection. For one, halakhic issues may make them feel not "really" Jewish. They may also feel uncomfortable because they lack the physical attributes that commonly mark one as Jewish; in other words, they might not "look Jewish." Hearing negative references to "goyim" or "goyishe" traits may make them question their adoptive community's respect for the community of their birth. And the community's judgments about out-of-wedlock birth may distress them, as they would any adoptee.

Furthermore, if adoptive parents are ambivalent about their own attitudes toward Judaism, it is nearly impossible for them to communicate a positive Jewish identity to their children. Whereas Jews by birth know they are Jewish regardless of their family's level of connectedness to the Jewish community, adoptees, who are struggling with their identity, need a connection that is active and engaging. If such a connection is lacking, they may assume that their parents are not integrating them into the Jewish community because, as "goyim" who have been "given up" by their "real families" they are, somehow, "not good enough" to be Jews!

Many questions confront all adoptive parents as they wrestle with helping their child forge a confident and comfortable identity. Jewish parents have additional questions to incorporate into their deliberations: Do I have the right to force my adopted child to be Jewish? After all, she could have been a member of some other religion, not a minority. How should I react when he says he doesn't "feel" Jewish? Is this just youthful rebellion—he knows exactly what to say to provoke me—or is it perhaps something more? How do I recognize and honor her birth religion while still building a strongly identified Jewish family? If I acknowledge a different birth religion will she feel less connected to our family and the Jewish community? Adoptive parents question the messages the Jewish community gives adoptees. Is there subtle, or not so subtle, prejudice?

It is helpful if parents bring these questions into the open and deal with them honestly. Although it can be difficult to discuss these sensitive issues, parents who do so have the opportunity to reassure their children, to help them to recognize who they are, and to free them to choose who they want to be. Few, it seems, will ultimately turn their backs on Judaism.

Adoption and Identity

"Identity is perception of the self in the world," explains Roseann Michelson, an adoptive parent and director of education at Temple Or Elohim in Long Island, New York (Michelson, 1993, p. 30). "Identity consists of how we view ourselves, how others view us, and how we think others view us. . . . It is how we see ourselves in relation to other people such as family, friends, peers, co-workers, or those having authority over us. Identity is how we perceive ourselves in conjunction with institutions such as school, as well as attitudes about ourselves stemming from our ethnic background including race, religion, and country of origin."

The formation of a stable identity is one of the main challenges of the adolescent years. This means, according to adoption experts Kenneth W. Watson and Miriam Reitz, that teenagers "must define their values, beliefs, gender identification, career choice, and expectations of themselves" (Hochman and Huston, 1995, p. 2). They do this by trying on a variety of personae, imitating and possibly rejecting various role models. They may shun or embrace family values, traditions, ideas, and beliefs. Ultimately, they must come to terms with the big questions: Who am I? Where do I belong?

Psychoanalyst Erik Erikson described eight common stages of identity formation, marked by a crisis at each transition point: Basic Trust versus Mistrust; Autonomy versus Shame and Doubt; Initiative versus Guilt; Industry versus Inferiority; Identity versus Role Confusion; Intimacy versus Isolation; Generativity versus Stagnation; and Ego Identity versus Despair. In each stage, as a crisis or turning point is encountered and resolved, the possibility exists for gaining new identity strength. Erikson's theory explains the difficulties that can occur during the normal course of maturation. The adoptee faces these ordinary challenges, as well as the particular challenges inherent in being adopted. As a result, the development of a positive self-image may be a more complex and difficult process for people who are adopted (Michelson, 1993, p. 46).

Seven additional issues particular to adoptees have been identified by Deborah N. Silverstein, MSW, an adoptive parent and a licensed clinical social worker specializing in adoption issues, and Sharon Kaplan Roszia, co-author of *The Open Adoption Experience* and executive director of the Kinship Center in

Tustin, California. These issues surface regardless of the child's age at the time of the adoption, the adoptee's ethnic identification, or other circumstances surrounding the adoption, creating "additional hazards" for the adoptee. The issues are: loss and separation; rejection; guilt and shame; grief; identity; intimacy; and mastery/power. Despite confronting these issues, it is important for adoptive parents to remember that many adoptees successfully weather stormy teen and young adult years and emerge with positive identities intact (Silverstein, 1985, p. 322).

Some adoptees eloquently express the difficulties and pain they experience in confronting these seven issues. Others vehemently deny ever thinking about adoption, a form of denial that many adoptive parents are willing to accept, even as their children are buffeted by challenges that are likely to be related to adoption. These parents recognize only the positive aspects of adoption. They do not acknowledge that each adoption has its genesis in pain: the pain that they endured when they were unable to conceive a child, the pain that birth parents endured when they acknowledged that they were unable to parent their child, and the pain that the adopted person endured in losing his or her birth family and identity. This pain may not be identified by therapists, educators, doctors, religious leaders, and others in the helping professions who have not worked specifically with adoption, and do not understand the depth or pervasiveness of these issues.

Samuel, an adoptive parent and rabbi who volunteers to work with troubled teens, says that adoption "is like an elephant in the living room that everyone is pretending not to see." He admits that while his own children were growing up, the family didn't talk about adoption. They assumed it didn't matter. They did not join an adoption support group because "they [the group] were talking about the elephant I wanted to ignore. I thought they were seeing issues where there weren't any. Now, I see there are issues. I have come to believe that adoption creates additional identity issues for teens who have identity issues anyway. They can't talk about it to their parents, and the parents aren't aware that it is an issue. And, if the parents do pick up on it, the kids often deny it."

"Adoption doesn't go away," adds Gail, an adoptive sister and parent. "I'd been exposed to it my whole life and I still didn't know. I thought you told the story once and then lived happily ever after. No. You deal with it your whole life and need to be prepared for that. There will be issues, and not admitting that is hiding your head in the sand. People want to hear that they'll be just like everyone else, and in some ways they will be and in some they won't. Adoption is more difficult; that doesn't mean you shouldn't do it."

Adoptees experience their first loss at the initial separation from their birth mother. Bonding with the birth mother is a biological phenomenon that happens at a level prior to and, therefore, beyond language, explains Marcy Wineman Axness, an adoptee who is a writer and adoption educator. On the most primal level, she says, even an infant knows that it is being separated from its mother, a loss which can not be disallowed or smothered by love, no matter how quickly and how excellent a substitute is presented.

Awareness of this loss is inevitable, Deborah Silverstein agrees, and it is "a potentially traumatic and life-altering event." Rhonda remembers, "I first realized what adoption meant and sensed the loss when I was in second grade. I went through a period of grieving, which, at the time, came out in acting-out behaviors like stealing and doing other things to draw attention to myself. I didn't know what to do. Fortunately, my parents got me help, and I had a pretty normal childhood after that."

Subsequent loss and separation become more difficult for adoptees, and can cause feelings of grief. Every additional loss can bring back the pain of the first loss, Marcy Wineman Axness says. "We make other people's responses to us fit the slots of our own experiences. Adoptees have a template for being rejected, so they see rejection in other people's actions, even when no rejection is intended. If someone even cancels a lunch date, adoptees may interpret it as an intentional rejection. It creates a challenge just to take people as they are."

Lisa, an adult adoptee, agrees. "The worst thing is being rejected. I've struggled with this a lot. I have friends who have ceased being friends for no apparent reason and it really hurts. Other people seem to move on more easily."

Adoptees may deal with rejection in one of two ways: They either avoid it at all costs or provoke it in order to validate their self-perceptions, Deborah Silverstein explains. "'Good' adoptees [this is the term adoptees themselves use over and over], compliant adoptees, are over-achievers and become whatever other people want them to be in order to justify their existence and avoid rejection," Marcy Wineman Axness says. Noncompliant adoptees constantly push the boundaries. "We seem to be testing to see how much it takes before someone else [in addition to our birth parents] rejects us, too," Amy, an adult adoptee, explains. "I tried so hard to make them [my adoptive parents] get rid of me. I tested them so, but somehow, no matter how bad I was I couldn't make them stop loving me."

Their sense of deserving rejection leads to tremendous guilt and shame, Silverstein continues, which is validated in the secrecy that surrounds many adoption proceedings. What parents don't, won't, and can't talk about—especially the story of their birth, something that other children hear all the time—is assuredly quite terrible. At least, that is the adoptee's interpretation, Axness explains.

In addition to problems of accepting their own self-worth, some adoptees have lifelong issues with intimacy, especially in relationships with members of the opposite sex, Silverstein says. All of the difficulties in dealing with loss, grief, rejection, and guilt can lead to fears about establishing relationships that might put them at risk of re-enacting those issues. "I tend to keep relationships at bay; they're too threatening," Lisa says. "I don't know if I can do the family thing. I feel very alone in the world." Other adoptees are "relationship junkies," forming and discarding many liaisons without ever becoming truly involved. They may be dealing with questions and feelings about their birth mother's pregnancy—probably unplanned and perhaps unwanted—and wonder if they will follow in these footsteps. In addition, they do not know their genetic heritage and often wonder if they carry any inheritable diseases or conditions. This may also interfere with forming healthy sexual relationships.

Adoptees may also have issues about power and control. Because they were not part of the decision-making process that led to their adoption, they may feel powerless, Silverstein says. They had no control over the loss of their birth family or the selection of their adoptive family. "I'm not really their child, but I am," Carly says, expressing the confusion many adoptees feel. "I could have been with another family." In response, some adoptees rebel against authority, seeking control any way they can, even in ways that are self-destructive or hurtful to those who love them.

"I knew it hurt them [my family] when I took off, and I enjoyed hurting them. I enjoyed them not having any control, because I didn't have any control over being adopted. I always wanted to make the choice and have the control. I wandered through many different families, and when they asked me to stay I left the next day so I would be in control," Amy explains. "My family was angry, but they always gave me a place to come back to. The less they reacted, the less reason I had to push."

Some adoptees may feel that they are exempt from the societal rules that apply to other people, Axness explains. Because no one will discuss their birth, they "have a sense of never having been born." "I had no information; I felt I happened instead of being born," agrees Rhonda. They have, instead, almost a "magical sense of just having come from nowhere," says Axness. And, since the most basic rule of all—that people are born—doesn't seem to apply to them, they have a sense that other rules don't apply either. Society's laws may feel insignificant when the laws of nature don't apply, she says.

Lack of access to information about their birth, their medical history, their genetic predispositions, or any religious or cultural background, may impede adoptees' formation and integration of identity, Silverstein concludes. Ultimately, impaired or incomplete identity causes difficulty in integrating all of the previous steps of development and precludes a sense of belonging to society. Yet belonging to a specific and special segment of society is at the heart of Jewish identity. Thus, it is not difficult to understand how being Jewish puts a different and more difficult spin on these core issues of adoption.

What Is Jewish Identity?

Jewish identity is a complicated combination of religious, national, ethnic, and historical components, according to Jewish sociologist Bernard Reisman. The religious element includes prayer, rituals, faith, spirituality, synagogue affiliations, and a variety of interpretations of Judaism that range from traditional to liberal. The national element centers around Israel and the degree of attachment one feels to it, from making *aliyah* to providing financial and/or moral support. The ethnic element includes food, holidays, language, friends, customs, jokes, and the general feeling of being Jewish. The historical element is the connection to generations of Jews and the sense of having a shared destiny. Reisman believes that the modern Jew selects various combinations of these four elements to form a personal Jewish identity (Michelson, 1993, p. 61).

Jewish adoptees face multiple issues as each works out a personally satisfying answer to the question "Who am I?" They encounter the normal developmental issues that everyone confronts in the formation of a whole persona. Their development is additionally complicated by the seven issues that specifically affect adoptees. And, as they determine the particular religious, national, ethnic, and historical elements of Judaism that form their Jewish identity, the task of integration becomes even more complex.

The least problematic component of Jewish identity for adoptees seems to be the religious component—the prayers, rituals, laws, and synagogue or denominational affiliation. In adolescence, people seem to realize that religious belief is a matter of personal choice, says Lois Ruskai Melina. Many adoptees, adds Roseann Michelson, consider religion "learned, rather than inherited, behavior." In interviewing adult adoptees for her master's thesis, she discovered adoptees who believe "that a person is a member of the faith in which he or she has been raised." As one adoptee, who was converted to Judaism, said to her, "Jesus is not waiting in one of my genes to flower one day and make me into a believer." Adoptees seem to feel that once they learn the prayers, laws, and rituals, they can choose to accept them, or not. On the other hand, Michelson says, many consider ethnicity to be inherited and an unchangeable part of their identity.

The ethnic component of identity—that overall sense of "feeling" Jewish—and the historical component—the recognition that sharing thousands of years of history means sharing a common destiny—seem to be closely related and are often the most troublesome for adoptees. Adoptees usually don't say, "I don't believe in Judaism," although that may be true. Rather, they may say, "My birth mother wasn't Jewish and I don't feel Jewish." Because they weren't born into it, they don't feel part of the group.

"I'm so into Jewish history, but there's a separation," Amy explains. "I connect to the ancestry, but I don't. When [as a child] I was asked where my grandparents came from I'd give the answer for my adoptive family, but inside me there was a red flag.

I knew it wasn't so and I always wondered."

Selma Gwatkin, MA, of the Bellefaire Jewish Children's Bureau in Shaker Heights, Ohio, confirms that clients often want to find out whether their birth parents were Jewish. Her colleague, Beth Brindo, LSW, who facilitates the agency's adoption support groups for both parents and teens, says that the teens ask many questions about the Jewish identity of their birth families. "They are wondering if they are 'really' Jewish, and express their lingering doubts that one is only really Jewish if one is born Jewish."

"Allison asked whether her birth mother was Jewish when she was about twelve," Gail remembers. "It wasn't easy for me to tell that her birth mom wasn't Jewish, because it made her seem less like me and I wanted her to be completely mine. I cried and she remembers that. A few years later, she rejected Judaism. She just never felt the attachment."

Sheryl has three children, the oldest of whom, Jason, she adopted. "He's picked up somewhere that his relationship to Judaism is slightly different than that of his siblings," she says. "There is a sense of choice that he has that is different. It's internal, not external. He feels ready to reject Judaism, which isn't usual for people who are raised in a strictly Orthodox Jewish environment."

Harvey, on the other hand, found out as an adult that he was born a Jew. "I always wanted to know," he says. "I thought it would be incongruent with who I am if I wasn't [born Jewish], because I'm so active in my Jewish community. Finding out that I was gave more meaning, more credibility to everything that I had been doing with my life."

Maryanne, who was adopted into a non-Jewish family and became a Jew by choice as an adult, explains the feeling of not belonging by birth to a particular ethnic group. "Adoption informed my ability to choose; not knowing a bloodline gave me permission to choose. The whole notion of ethnicity is foreign to me, so why not think about and choose a religion that is meaningful. The boundaries feel looser because I'm adopted. I don't know if I'd have broken a tie that I'd been born into, something that was a part of my family for hundreds of years."

Membership in the clan is at issue for any adoptee, confirms Lois Melina. They ask themselves what claim they have to their name and to their family. When membership implies roots that can be traced through generations of history, as it does with Judaism, it adds layers of significance. Ethnicity is the sense of affinity with the group, the feeling that what happens to Jews anywhere affects each Jewish individual. What makes someone feel that affinity, if not genetics? she asks. It is an answer each person must find on his or her own, and will be different for each person.

Individuals who feel secure in their ethnic identity and do not try to deny that heritage are more likely to be at peace with and feel good about themselves, observes Roseann Michelson. Self-acceptance is an important part of emotional health. People who deny their Jewish identity are failing to accept a part of themselves, which can lead to inner conflict. Adoption gives a person "an out;" the adoptee realizes that he or she would not have been Jewish if not for being placed for adoption with a Jewish family. For the adoptee then, even more than for other Jews, identification as a Jew must include experiences other than birth. And, Lois Melina says, the extent to which a person is comfortable with his or her ethnicity is the extent to which it is integral in that person's life. Many issues, experiences, and attitudes concerning adoption affect the adoptee's comfort level with Judaism and Jewishness. Jewish adoptive parents hope that their religious community will be a safe haven for their child.

I Don't Look Jewish

One issue that can affect adoptees' feelings about their Jewish identity is their appearance. Does the adoptee "look Jewish?" Thoughtless comments about their "non-Jewish appearance" have upset and offended many adoptees. Since there is nothing adoptees can do about their appearance, telling them that they don't look Jewish can be truly destructive. In fact, Deborah Silverstein claims, because of this, "the bond between Jews and the adoptee may never cement."

For adopted children, frequent reminders that they do not resemble their parents can reinforce their feelings of not belonging to the family, Roseann Michelson explains. Such comments can also become a self-fulfilling prophecy, and have a detrimental effect on adoptees' emerging Jewish identity. If they are told often enough that they do not look Jewish, this fact may become a part of their self-image. While such comments can sometimes also be directed to people who are born Jews, they are aware of their biological heritage and secure in the knowledge that they are physically descended from Jews. For adoptees, on the other hand, such comments only confirm their alienation and reinforce the separateness some already feel.

"I was brought up Jewish in a small, tight Jewish community," Amy recalls. "And although my parents weren't sure, I always felt that I wasn't born Jewish. I look very different from my family and people said that I look Irish. I always wondered, and I later found out that I am Irish. But I don't connect to it. I do connect to a Jewish identity; it's a strong identity. But at the same time I separate myself from it. The line is where the physical comes in. I feel like I'm no religion and all religions.

"I always felt like I didn't belong to anybody," she continues. "I wanted to go off by myself and not be connected to anybody. I would get close to people and then leave. I would touch base with my family and then leave. It was a symbolic flight alone, to wander the world and get in touch with my own identity without the identity that my adoptive family was giving me. I felt completely displaced, like a clean slate."

Lisa, who also never believed she was born Jewish because of her appearance, recalls her teenage anger at her adoptive mother because they didn't have the same physical appearance. "I still get a lot of comments about my looks and I don't like to explain. Body image was always a big deal," she says. Even as an adult, were she to meet her birth mother, her first questions would be about her physical appearance. "I want to know what size bra she wears and what color eyes she has."

Some adoptees go out of their way to enhance their already obvious physical differences from their adoptive family, and perhaps, their lack of connection to the community. "I'm different from my family, especially physically," Carly says. "I don't look Jewish. I do some things because I like to be original."

"She feels different and she deals with it all the time," agrees Cynthia, Carly's adoptive mother. "It's a wound on her mind all the time. She once told me, 'I close my eyes and I don't know who I look like.' She needs to play up and explore her differences, and we let her as long as what she's trying is safe," she says, recalling the time that a teenage Carly dyed her hair purple.

Some Jewish adoptive parents believe that comments by Jews about their children's "non-Jewish appearance" seem to reflect a "Jewish inferiority complex." "My daughter looks very Nordic, and we've been told, 'She's so beautiful; she doesn't look Jewish,'" Lois says. "I'm blonde, too, and I've grown up hearing this my whole life and I wonder why Jews have an inferiority complex."

Are Parents Ambivalent?

Comments about their adopted children's appearance can fuel negative self-images and ambivalence in parents who themselves have questions about Jewish identity. Especially in the post-Holocaust era there seems to be Jewish self-hatred and Jewish identity that is formed from negative images, Deborah Silverstein says. "There are Jews who rebelled against Judaism, and don't have enough information about Judaism to know what they are passing on to their children. Parents need to have a positive image of what they are giving and why they are raising their children Jewish. We are all Jews by choice; we decide what form of Judaism to practice, how much Jewish activity we will partic-ipate in, etc. There are a lot of choices, and those choices have implications to ponder."

"When adoptive parents say they feel guilty about making their child Jewish, because of the problems there are in being Jewish and fears that their child will be exposed to anti-Semitism, I tell them to look at their own feelings about Judaism," says Shirley Sagin, MSW, ACSW, former director of adoption services for Jewish Family and Children's Service in Philadelphia, Pennsylvania. Building an adopted child's Jewish identity depends a great deal on how the family feels about its Jewish identity, she explains. Is it a joyous thing? Does the family enhance the positive aspects about being Jewish within the family? Is the family proud of being Jewish and do they convey that to the child?

There seem to be two main schools of thought about Jewish identity and adoption, adds Dina Rosenfeld, DSW, director of the undergraduate social work program at New York University. One says to provide a strong Jewish identity so that a child who is struggling with his or her identity can feel grounded. The other is based on ambivalence about Judaism, with the idea that the parents are imposing something on the child.

"This [the feeling of ambivalence] shows who the parents are; it shows their questions," Rosenfeld continues. "It is in the child's best interest for the parents to provide a strong positive sense of identification with Judaism. Kids want to be like their families; they take to it enormously. Adoptees feel it as an extreme rejection if their adoptive parents don't raise them in their religion." They believe that there is something wrong with them, that they aren't "good enough" to be Jewish—not that their parents are protecting them.

Added to this common ambivalence about Jewish identity is the lingering social prejudice about adoption, which can further erode an adoptee's self-esteem. "No one told me, but I knew I was just like my birth mother and that's why I was evil," Marla explains. "I was confused about what people in the Jewish community wanted me to be. I always wanted to make them happy, but I always felt I could never fit into the community, even when I tried really hard. They were all doctors and lawyers, and I felt I was abnormal, messed up, the wrong one. I had to find me in myself, and to like myself, before I could feel part of the Jewish community."

Selma Gwatkin recalls a client who caused such conflict in her adoptive home that, as a teenager, she had to be removed from the house. She "knew" that "Jews were upright people and that I, as a product of a 'bad birth mother,' was not good enough to be Jewish," Gwatkin explains. As a young adult, she learned enough about her birth mother to know that the woman was neither irresponsible nor reprehensible. Only then was she able to accept herself as a Jew and become part of the Jewish community.

Acknowledging Difference

When adoptive parents do not encourage their children to practice Judaism, the children may believe the fault lies in their birth religion, especially when their Jewish parents find it difficult even to acknowledge that their child was born into a different religion. "There is a certain ethnocentricity and stereotyping that goes on in the Jewish community which implies that non-Jews aren't as good," says Karen Rosenberg, LSW, a clinical social worker in private practice in Ohio.

"I have a lot of unresolved conflicts for myself about being born Jewish," admits Elaine, an adoptive parent of a child who was not born Jewish. "There's something about Jewish people that's different from other people; there are certain abilities that we have that are very special. That isn't to say that others don't have it. Part of my feeling connected is knowing that I belong genetically and spiritually to this race of people. But I'm moving toward the notion that if you are called to be Jewish, then you are, and that who you are is based on what you do as a person. But this is my conflict."

"I have never spoken with my daughter about her conversion," Miriam, an adoptive mother, says. "She knows she's adopted and even that she's from another culture, and I'm very comfortable talking about that. But I'm not comfortable talking about her having been born into another religion. Shira was about eight years old when she asked whether she was born Jewish. I told her that she was born with a Jewish soul," Miriam recalls. "I told her the midrash that there were other souls at Sinai who wanted to accept the Torah. God told them that it wasn't the right time for them, but that there would be a time for them in the future. That satisfied her."

Adoption specialists, however, caution parents about trying to ignore or wipe out their child's birth heritage. Adoption counselor and adoptee Linda Yellin, MSW, ACSW, of Farmington Hills, Michigan, calls the coming together of religious backgrounds in adoptive families a "transreligious issue," and likens its importance to transcultural and transracial issues for families who adopt children from other countries and cultures. "Adoptive parents may be threatened by this. They may discount the child's questions about his or her birth family and religion. But these questions are natural and normal for children to ask, and it is important for parents to acknowledge that their adopted children weren't born Jewish," she says. "The child has feelings of loss and wonders what life would have been like with his or her birth parents, or if he or she had been adopted by a different family. This is reality, and it creates problems if the parents discount the child's feelings or get into a power struggle over whether the child is 'really' Jewish.

"If the parent discounts the child's heritage or there are negative feelings around the non-Jewish community, what does that say to a child?" questions Yellin. "How the non-Jewish commu-

nity is discussed, who the parents' friends are, implies something
to a child. Children may not make the connection immediately,
but they will feel that they weren't acceptable and their parents
had to wipe it [their birth heritage] out."

"My parents said they didn't know the religion of my birth
parents. They didn't acknowledge that I came from non-Jewish
blood, which was probable," Barbara, an adult adoptee, says.
"My adoptive father was a *kohen* and my parents instilled in me
how great Jews are and how lucky I was to be adopted and to be
Jewish. I had an identity crisis as a teen and my mom got some
information about my birth mother. It clarified for me that she
was a slut. That's what I was taught. I became very opinionated,
unaccepting, and unforgiving about 'goyim.' I overreacted
against Christianity; I couldn't even go into a church. But I never
acknowledged that everything my parents put down is what I
am. When I had my own daughter, I became severely depressed.
During Pesach that year, I was reading the haggadah and realized
that it wasn't me. It was very upsetting. I'm not comfortable in
shul anymore. I used to be so certain about how I felt, but I
never knew who I was; I was only playing a role."

Clinical social worker Karen Rosenberg says that adoptive
families that acknowledge differences fare much better than families that deny differences and insist that their children are blank
slates. One of her clients, who knew that he wasn't born Jewish,
says he never felt that he fit in with his [adoptive] family, but says
that they pretended that he wasn't adopted. He recalls hearing
derogatory comments throughout his life about "goyim." One
day, he realized that "my origins are those people" and that that
is who he is. It was very painful for him, Rosenberg says. "We
[the Jewish community] need to be more pluralistic. If a child
has biological origins that are different, we need to acknowledge
and explore them. Otherwise, the child has to keep splitting off
parts of him- or herself that aren't acceptable to his or her family or peers."

"Most children don't know what they'll believe as adults, so parents should not be so nervous," Linda Yellin adds. "Children search for identity and religion is a part of it. Adoptive parents can incorporate the value of other religions into their thinking, and give children the feeling that people who practice differently are okay. Show them that they can value, appreciate, and see a connection between religions, and acknowledge that each religion has positive values." However, she continues, adoptive parents should also explain to their children why they are Jewish and that our heritage can be shared, not only through blood, but through family tradition and choice.

Doing Jewish

The more families are involved in Judaism and Jewish life, the better, many Jewish adoption specialists believe. People who are born Jewish take this identity for granted, regardless of their level of ritual observance. Adoptees who were not born Jewish feel more connected to Judaism and the Jewish community when their families actively "do Jewish things," both at home and in the synagogue. Reuben Pannor, MSW, one of the authors of *Adoption Triangle,* has worked with Jewish adoptive families for many years, and interviewed parents whose children are grown. If the children were raised in a Jewish home, where the parents observed important aspects of Jewish life, the children either continued their Jewish identification or explored other religions for themselves but then returned to Judaism, he says. "This is predicated on being raised in a family that observed. If not, the children were adrift. Children should be told honestly that their birth parents weren't Jewish—this avoids any issues later—but that they will be raised as a Jew, and that they can make choices later in life. It is very confusing and destructive for a child to be raised with differences between them and their parents."

"We were not observant Jewishly; it didn't play a major role in my life," Rhonda, an adult adoptee, says. "I remember feeling that I really wasn't Jewish. My husband isn't Jewish, but we decided to raise our son, who was adopted, as a Jew. We celebrate Christmas and Hanukkah. I'm kind of confused about religion now."

"When adopted children are raised so that Judaism is not central to their lives, it is more difficult for them," agrees Sharon Kaplan Roszia. "They have less to hold onto. They know they would have been someone else, and that they've been shifted into a borrowed identity. As they work on identification issues, their job is to cement an identification onto who they've become and whence they've come." Her advice to adoptive parents is to "create a Jewish holding environment. Be who you are to the Nth degree. Don't be wishy-washy. Your child will make choices of his or her own, but he or she can't do that unless you give them something solid."

Adoptees who were given a solid Jewish background speak eloquently of its benefits. "I came from a Conservative home that practiced Judaism, and I feel very affiliated and identify very much as a Jew," says Paula. "I always assumed that I was Jewish, and it didn't matter whether I was born Jewish or converted; I never questioned that identity."

Miriam's daughter, Shira, wrote this testimony to her belief in her adopted religion when she was seventeen years old: "With all my heart and soul I believe that it was no coincidence that I was adopted into a Jewish family. It was God's will that I was brought into the Jewish religion. It was part of His master plan. He saw in me the potential to be a Jew who will view the Torah and its commandments not as a burden but as a privilege, one who will take her role as a Jewish woman with a sense of seriousness and dedication. Every day I work harder and harder to bring out the potential that God sees in me. Every day I pray that when I go up to heaven I can say to God, 'You didn't make the wrong choice. I was the best Jew I could be.'"

But They Still Want to Celebrate Christmas

When Joel was about eight years old, Susan recalls, they were doing their Hanukkah shopping at a large suburban mall, which was thoroughly decorated for the holiday season. Joel spotted the line of children waiting to sit on Santa's lap and asked if he could join them. Susan carefully explained that Christmas is not their holiday, that they were preparing to celebrate Hanukkah, and that, while they could enjoy the decorations, Joel couldn't sit on Santa's lap. Joel's answer was: "I wasn't born Jewish; I can sit on Santa's lap."

This scenario strikes at the very heart of one of most Jewish adoptive parents' worst fears: that, despite everything they do, their children may not feel Jewish and may not choose to remain Jewish. "It's part of a larger issue, that he'll choose not to be part of us," explains adoptive mother Elaine. "The fact that he's adopted highlights what is a possibility for any child." Whether it arises at age eight around celebrating Christmas, or at age eighteen over dating someone who isn't Jewish, many parents, adoptive or nonadoptive, deal with their child's wish to be like the predominant culture. For adoptive parents, however, whose child may actually come from that culture, the request holds additional poignancy and considerable emotional baggage. Is it the beginning of rejection of the adoptive family and all it holds dear, or is it a natural phase that will soon pass? How should adoptive parents react?

There is a natural process of separation that all parents and children experience, and "a natural process of separation for adopted children," explains Lois Melina. "Adoptees step back from the people they are like because of their shared environment and begin asking who they are. They have to realize that they can be like their adoptive parents in many obvious ways, and yet be unique. They also have to separate from their birth parents, often with little or no information about those parents. Adoptive parents need to give children room to rebel safely. The more fearful parents are, the more restrictive they are. And the less productive that is for themselves and their adopted child. On the other hand, every family has basic rules, and children need to be clear about what is important to their family. Certain things may be nonnegotiable."

"It's important for adoptive parents to validate that their children's past history is true, but so is their current history," adds Joyce Maguire Pavao, Ed.D., founder and director of both the Adoption Resource Center in Cambridge, Massachusetts, and the Pre and Post Adoption Consulting Team (PACT) at the Family Center in Somerville, Massachusetts. "They need to honor and respect the birth parents and culture, but not to diminish the current culture. People who are adopted often feel a divided loyalty, that part of who they are is who they were in the beginning. If it is cut off, they may need to over-acknowledge it, instead of giving it a healthy recognition." Pavao has found that when adoptive parents both respect their child's birth culture and hold onto their beliefs, allowing their child to work through the process of finding his or her identity, the child often feels free to choose Judaism.

Adoptive parents as a group seem conflicted over their children's requests to explore their birth religions. They appear to handle it in three very different ways.

Vivian's daughter, Shayna, requested a Christmas tree, explaining that she wanted it because she knew she was born Christian. Because they are not an observant family, Vivian and her husband decided to allow Shayna to have a small tree, which she decorated herself. Vivian believes that she will have to "choose her battles," and says that this was one she did not choose to fight.

Charlotte, who considers her family very Jewishly identified, recalls her daughter Samantha saying that she wanted to celebrate Christmas because that is what she would do if she were with her birth family. Samantha told Charlotte, "I'm not asking you to be a Christian, but since I was born Christian, it's part of our family." Charlotte decided that they could celebrate Christmas with Christian friends, both at the friend's home and church. They did not, however, bring Christmas into their home.

"Samantha felt supported in her sense of wanting to be connected to her birth heritage and explore it, yet it felt foreign to her. She was testing it out and needed information about it. If I'd said no, I'd be asking her to deny her reality," Charlotte explains. "It's her birthright to know about it. It's part of her search for herself, and I have to let her explore it so that she won't feel truncated. I don't think it will mean that she'll want to be Christian. It's a cultural exploration, not a repudiation of what I'm giving her. In the same way that I'm asking her to adapt to my family, I'm adapting to her gifts. I can weather her exploration and not feel threatened. I can tell she's connected to me when we do Jewish things. It's more difficult because we [Jews] are a minority people. But I have a sense that I can acknowledge and include this, and not feel frightened by it. I have a feeling of being expanded, not diminished."

Other adoptive Jewish parents feel strongly that their children should not actively explore or participate in the celebrations or rituals of their birth religion. They prefer that their children, especially while they are young, concentrate on learning about and living their Judaism, although they do acknowledge that their children were born into another religion. They are comfortable explaining to their child that, while he or she will be free to make choices about religion some day, this is what their family does and the child is part of the family.

"We tell our adopted children that they are as Jewish as the rest of the family, and that Jews do certain things and don't do other things," explains Bruce. "We believe that religion is different from nationality or culture and that, if our children had been adopted from another country, we would help them learn about the culture of that country. In fact, we can see helping them learn about the country that their birth ancestors came from. But we don't see any reason for them to explore Christianity; our Jewish heritage is their heritage."

"And, certain things are nonnegotiable," Jennifer, his wife, adds. "In our house, religion is one of them. And if we aren't ambivalent about it, they'll know that this isn't a way to push our buttons."

Michael, a rabbi, agrees and says that he tries to be a role model of how to live Jewishly and wants his children to be proud to be Jewish. He considers it a conflict to introduce his children to the religion of their birth families. "Adoptive parents need to be confident enough of their own identity to know that they are doing the right thing," he says.

It is helpful if adoptive parents can express their feelings on these subjects without any overload of guilt or emotionality. Naturally, they want to avoid, if possible, alienating their child and producing the opposite of what they are hoping for. That does not mean, however, that they should abandon their convictions or their family's standards. All children eventually make choices; providing a strong and nurturing Jewish environment that is pleasurable to be a part of is the best way of keeping all children connected to the community.

Jewish identity exists beyond words and explanations. Rochelle reports that when Amanda was about eight years old, she asked her [Jewish day school] teacher, "How do I know I'm Jewish?" The teacher suggested to Amanda that she try to think of ways herself, and Amanda spent the day telling her teacher many things that made her Jewish. Each one was acknowledged as a good answer, but not *the* answer. Finally, the teacher acquiesced to Amanda's pleas to provide her with an answer and said, "You know you're Jewish because you can feel it in your heart." "Then," Amanda replied, "I know I'm Jewish."

CHAPTER 3

Roots and Branches: Searching for Birth Family

An adoptee's search for roots and branches—for the missing family tree—is, in reality, a search for self. Adoptees may search for people to whom they are biologically connected, or for information about them. They may search for reasons why their birth parents could not parent them and why they chose adoption. They may seek to understand what adoption has meant to them, their adoptive family, and their birth family over the intervening years. What they are searching for are the missing pieces of the adoptee's "Who Am I?" puzzle. They are on a journey to discover who they were and might have been, so that they can better understand who they are. What such a search most often is *not* is a search for a substitute family. Such searches are about the adoptee, not his or her adoptive family. What they are doing is reaching out, not shutting out. They seek inclusiveness, not exclusion.

Although not all adoptees feel a desire to search actively, those who do are following a natural and healthy impulse: the need to feel themselves complete. If adoptive families can respond in this spirit, with encouragement and support rather than discouragement and defensiveness, they will be better able to provide a positive response that can strengthen the family as the adoptee strengthens him- or herself. If they understand that the adoptee who shares his or her desire to search is purely expressing trust, love, and commitment, adoptive families will find a way to help the person they love.

In the days of closed adoption, secrets and anonymity were the norm. Few adoptees expressed a desire for information about, let alone a desire to search for, birth family. Doing so was likely to hurt their adoptive family and label them at the least ungrateful, and at the worst maladjusted. Adoptive parents believed that, if they did their parenting job well, their child would not need or desire to seek his or her birth family. With such attitudes, it is little wonder that an adoptee's desire to search so often has surprised, saddened, and frightened the adoptive family. Most were never prepared for it.

At the same time, those facilitating adoptions were likely to have promised birth parents anonymity and a chance to put the past behind them; they were told they would forget. Yet most have not forgotten. Some birth parents have initiated searches, clearly not waiting to be found. Others have not chosen to search but have been pleasantly surprised when they have been found. Some have built relationships with their adult child and, at times, with his or her adoptive family, a connection that they never dreamed they'd have. Still others have been unable or unwilling to establish a relationship with the adoptee, preferring to continue uninterrupted the lives they created for themselves after the adoption. And some are never found.

Adoptees who search do so despite certain risks. Most realize that they may learn information that is unpleasant or painful about their birth parents, or that they may learn nothing about them at all. They also face the possibility of a second rejection. Yet most adoptees say that these are risks worth taking. The search itself provides a sense of control that many adoptees have never before experienced. Even if they learn nothing, at least they know they have tried. Information, even if negative, fills holes and answers questions. Even if they learn nothing about their birth parents, they may learn a great deal about themselves.

Jewish adoptees may have different and additional questions as they prepare to search. Most want to know if either of their birth parents was Jewish. They wonder how they will feel about their Jewish identity, and their connection to the Jewish people, if they discover they were born Jews—or discover that they were not. They may want to know if their placement with a Jewish family was purposeful. They may wonder what kind of a difference it will make to learn these facts. Will it matter to anyone else? To many who have not received information or have doubted its authenticity, the information they receive now justifies a feeling they have had throughout their lives. To others, identifying their birth parents' religion seems less significant than all that has come after and shaped their lives. What does make a difference is knowledge; that, many adoptees say, has changed their lives.

Adoptees who decide to search benefit from preparing themselves and their adoptive family emotionally. Adoptees need to clarify for themselves just what they are and are not seeking. Discussing their motives and goals with their adoptive family can allow family members to be more emotionally available. It is also important to consider the long-term ramifications of their search: What will it mean for the rest of their lives? Some adoptees focus only on the reunion, hoping that meeting their birth parents will answer all of life's questions. They need to recognize that it won't, and that it may even raise new and different questions. This experience is laden with potential for all members of the triad; the challenge is to use the possibilities it offers for healing and growth.

Why Search?

When asked why they are searching for birth families, adoptees often react with surprise. Their voices, as they answer, imply that the answer should be obvious. "I search," says one adoptee after another, "to know who I am. I search to find the missing pieces of me."

The vast majority of adoptees who search want information that they need to integrate into their sense of self, explains Lois Melina in *Raising Adopted Children* (Melina, 1986, p. 148). "Search answers questions and gives closure," says Barbara Tremetiere, Ph.D., an adoptive parent and adoption professional with Tressler Lutheran Services in York, Pennsylvania. "Part of who you are is who you were in the beginning," adds Joyce Pavao, Ed.D., of the Adoption Resource Center in Cambridge, Massachusetts. "In every single case I have handled," agrees Bradford Blauer Jones, JD, president of The Adoption Forum and an expert in petitioning courts to unseal adoption records, "the adoptee has said, 'I need to know where I come from.' It is essential, in the literal sense of the word 'essence.'" Adoptees who search are seeking the essence of themselves.

The need to search isn't related to whether a person loves his or her adoptive family, explains Linda Yellin, MSW, ACSW, of Farmington Hills, Michigan, a therapist specializing in services to triad members and professionals and an adoptee who has had a reunion with her birth parents. "No matter how loving and close a family is, no one can provide the missing pieces to the puzzle for the adopted person that the birth family can." People who are not adopted, even the adoptive family—perhaps most especially the adoptive family—may have difficulty understanding the need to fill in these missing pieces. They would like their heritage to be sufficient to fill in the gaps, their history to become the history of the adopted member of their family, their love to be enough to assuage a pain that they can never truly comprehend. But often, it isn't enough. "The adopted family's love can't replace the love of that other family," Yellin says. "There are two different cups that need to be filled. The adoptive parents feel that there's something wrong with their relationship with their child if they don't fill the cup. But they can't do it; it isn't theirs to fill. Their cup can be overflowing, but the other cup remains empty."

Some adoptees seek medical and genetic information, a need arising out of the frustration of years of being unable to answer routine questions on medical forms, or fears engendered by advances in medicine indicating the formerly unknown genetic connection of many diseases. While this may be an initial, and often a major, motivation, many adoptees have or develop other questions they want to explore. To some people, however, locating pertinent medical information is the only reason that justifies a search, says Debra Goldstein Smith, former director of the National Adoption Information Clearinghouse and author of *Searching for Birth Relatives* (Smith, 1995, p. 2).

Many adoptees are seeking someone who speaks, walks, and gestures as they do. They want to look into another person's face and see familiar features looking back, Smith says. "I wasn't aware of wanting to search, but when I heard about it I wanted to do it immediately," Marshall, an adult adoptee, explains. "When you look at your adoptive parent, if they look like you it's strictly coincidental. I wanted to see someone who looked like me and see if she acted like me." They may seek the source of other traits: their talents, sense of humor, athletic, musical, and intellectual abilities. "I'm really different from my adoptive parents, so I was extremely interested to see who my birth parents are," Maryanne says. These adoptees want to know themselves better, agrees Annette Baran, MSW, a psychotherapist in private practice and one of the authors of *Adoption Triangle*. They want to "add arms and legs to their tree," she says, because "generational connectedness, a history, is of great importance to people."

Many adoptees also want to know the why behind their adoption—the reasons underlying it and how their birth parents felt about it and them. Moreover, they want to know it firsthand, from their birth parents directly, not filtered through someone else. Even when information is appropriately given by the adoptive parent, some adoptees still need to hear it from the birth parent. They need, Bradford Blauer Jones says, to take control of their lives and are angry at having been denied information that they believe is rightfully theirs. "Searching is a really basic human drive," says Maryanne, who has not yet found her birth parents. "It's a clear pure example of mental health, of striving for connectedness and truth. It's a really good instinct." Adoptees need to look backward before they can go forward, confirm David Brodzinsky, Marshall Schechter, and Robin Henig in *Being Adopted: The Lifelong Search for Self.* The authors believe that all adoptees engage in a search process that is meaningful in terms of integrating the adoption into the adoptee's sense of self (Brodzinsky et al., 1992, p. 79).

A Search for Meaning

Adoptees conduct this search for meaning in a variety of ways throughout their lives. As preschoolers, they begin to sort out who is family and how their family fits together as a unit. Those who become aware that there is something different about them, regardless of what they've been told, want to know what their story is, says Holly van Gulden of Minneapolis, Minnesota, an adoptive parent, therapist and author of *Real Parents, Real Children: Parenting the Adopted Child.* These are the children who realize that there are no pictures of mommy pregnant with them, or hospital pictures, and they are the only ones, she says, who need to ask if they came from mommy's tummy. A simple version of their story in a baby book, that shares the stories of both their biological and adoptive families and emphasizes the feelings each must have had about the adoption and toward the adoptee, can help them integrate their stories. It is less confusing for preschool children, she believes, if birth parents are identified by first name (when possible and if adoptive parents are comfortable) and the word "parent" is reserved for the adoptive parents, the ones doing the parenting.

By age three, most children have developed two fundamental psychological constructs. The first, *object permanence,* is the knowledge that even if a thing or a person is not visible, it still exists. Object permanence enables the child to know that his or her parents still exist, even when they are not visible to the child, explains Claude Riedel, MA, of Minneapolis, Minnesota, an adoptee and a licensed psychologist who conducts individual and family therapy and facilitates groups for all members of the adoption triad. This knowledge takes the form of an image of the parent that the child carries within, and with which the child can comfort him- or herself when necessary. *Object constancy* is the knowledge that things remain the same, even when they change in appearance or effect. This understanding allows children to know that their mother is still the same loving mother, even if she is wearing a different dress, or glasses, or is angry with them. Such knowledge is crucial to the development of a person's sense of self and to a person's relationships with other people in the world. The problem, Riedel and van Gulden agree, is that many adoptees don't develop these essential building blocks. Why? Because adoption itself, no matter how early or how benign, can disrupt this development, Riedel says. It can happen for several reasons.

For one thing, says Marshall Schechter, MD, professor emeritus at the Medical School of the University of Pennsylvania in Philadelphia, and co-author of *Being Adopted: The Lifelong Search for Self,* adopted children come into their adoptive homes without the frame of reference that other children develop intrauterinely. Scientists now recognize that from conception on, the interplay between mother and child is powerful. It is so strong that babies even react to sounds and smells that were introduced during pregnancy. Severing this "birth bond" creates what Nancy Verrier, MA, MFCC, a therapist in Lafayette, California, who has both an adopted and a biological child, calls *The Primal Wound,* in her book by the same name. It can be con-

fusing or even terrifying for a child, she says, to be given to someone who isn't "the right person," whose smell, sound, and energy
is unfamiliar.

The adoptive environment, Schechter and Verrier agree, doesn't
duplicate these familiar senses and may not be a match to the
sensibilities of the adoptee. Some of these children don't, therefore, have a sense of comfort and well-being, and become hyper-
vigilant to prevent a similar trauma from happening again. The
trauma is severe because it happens when a person is most vulnerable, Verrier explains. Some children, Holly van Gulden adds,
are able to make the transition to the new environment, successfully form comfortable connections and thrive, while others have
much more difficulty, and some may never do so. No matter
how much their adoptive parents love them, and they love their
adoptive parents, these adoptees never feel they belong, Verrier
explains. Their first trauma is continually retriggered and reen-
acted. They are terrified to allow themselves to connect with and
trust someone who can disappear, just as their birth mother did.

Confusion can also arise as children hear their own stories and
try to make sense of them, van Gulden continues. They discover that, unlike other children, they have two sets of parents and,
although the first set could not, would not, and did not parent
them, the second set could, would, and did. She calls this "the
dichotomy of adoption," and explains that adoptees have to find
a continuity of meaning within these two stories. "They have to
determine whether they are valuable enough to keep or not," she
says. Some children convince themselves that they are; others
don't. Thus, Claude Riedel adds, when adoptees search for their
birth parents, they are yearning to learn whether they were loved
and wanted, because it is difficult "to hold a sense of being lov-
able when this [adoption] has happened to them."

Circumstances can be especially difficult when the poor fit
between adoptive parents and child takes over the family, Holly
van Gulden explains. A poor fit can work when the parents rec-

ognize and claim all of the talents and characteristics that the child brings to the adoptive family. But if an adoptee never becomes truly incorporated into the adoptive family, he or she will never really feel accepted. So, for example, if a family values scholarship, as is often the case in Jewish households, and the child, though gifted in sports or a technical field, does not shine academically, the parents need to acknowledge and value these other gifts, too, and make them part of the family's lifestyle. Although most mean well, Linda Yellin points out, some adoptive parents have difficulty with this. Parents need to make peace and become comfortable with parenting a child who may not be like them. Yet sometimes, even with the parent's best efforts, a child may not recognize that his or her gifts are being valued. Sometimes it's easier if adoptees can ground their special talents in the reality of being like a birth relative's talents, van Gulden adds.

Jewish adoptees, however, are often searching for something more, confirms Rochelle Sanders, MSW, manager of adoption services for the Paths to Parenthood Program of Jewish Family and Children's Service of Greater Philadelphia, Pennsylvania. "There's a reassurance in knowing the past that helps predict the future. I even had a fifty-eight-year-old woman come in to try to find out her background because her children wondered. It isn't only the adoptee who loses this knowledge; each succeeding generation has lost something."

Wondering about their Jewish identity is an additional dilemma for adoptees, Holly van Gulden agrees. Adoptees may question whether their identity matches that of their birth family or of their adoptive family, or neither or both. They recognize that they have both a past heritage and a present life, and it is important that they blend the two together and make sense of them. "It's very meaningful for adoptees to know and connect with their ethnic identity," Annette Baran confirms. "How they then feel about being [raised] Jewish depends on the quality of their environment, and whether they were allowed to feel that they belonged. It also depends on the birth identity. Some cultures feel that you can't take away who you are, that self-identity comes from the genetic family, but that one can gain pride from the adoptive family. Both are important."

An Undeniable Need

What motivates an adoptee to undertake an actual search? What impels a person to overcome his or her hesitation or fear and disregard "rational"' advice to begin a tangible process that may result in meeting one or both of his or her birth parents? It may be one's journey through life's normal passages, or there may be a specific event that triggers an adoptee's desire to search, explains Linda Yellin. It may be a loss, such as a death or the inability to produce a child biologically themselves, that brings hidden feelings about other losses to the surface. Or it may be a pregnancy, theirs or someone else's, that raises feelings about genealogical connectedness and identity. It may be impending marriage, their own aging or their parents', or simply a discussion about adoption with someone who affirms feelings that the adoptee never allowed to surface that kindles a spark of desire. Once the need to search strikes, for some, it becomes undeniable and can not be ignored. Others, Yellin says, dance around it. It may surface strongly, but they may feel frightened and back off, at least for a time.

"I was a 'good' adoptee; I was profoundly loyal to my parents for 'saving' me and didn't think I had any questions about my adoption, until I was thirty-five," Stan remembers. "I went to a conference on adoption and heard someone speak about the grief many birth mothers feel. I asked the speaker if adoptees also grieve, and when she said 'of course,' I burst into tears. I had never allowed myself to feel the loss—it wasn't safe—but I couldn't deny it any longer."

"I didn't think about adoption when I was growing up; it was terrifying to think about trying to find out," Esther remembers. "I was totally shut down to adoption issues until my first child was born. I recycled through all the pain. I felt so disconnected. That began my own journey of reconciliation. I began to reconnect with a loss that no one could help me hold. When my [adoptive] mom died, my tears at her loss brought back the grief of that first loss, which I hadn't grieved."

"My dog gave birth to puppies on my lap," Julie, an adoptee and adoptive mother, says. "It was so meaningful; I had a sense of going through the birth process from the mother's and baby's sides, but it also made me feel I'd been exiled from the world of reproduction. I knew I was adopted and I'd always wanted a pregnancy in our family. I wanted to search, but a social worker told me that I'd be reopening old wounds. So I looked forward to having a child whom I would look like. But when it became clear that I wouldn't get pregnant, I began to want to search again."

"I was a 'good' adoptee, and I never thought about searching," Maryanne recalls. "Then in graduate school, I began working in an obstetrics unit. I was always very anxious—wanting to please my adoptive parents and prove that my birth parents were wrong to give me up—and I became much more so. But I didn't see how this was affecting me until I got some help from someone who understood about adoption. I was so in denial; I never allowed myself to think about the reality of pregnancy and motherhood. But suddenly, I was knee-deep in needing to search. It was imperative."

The Importance of Preparation

The issues surrounding a search for and possible reunion between adoptees and their birth parents are complex, but hold incredible potential for healing, says Carol Demuth, LMSW, ACP, an adoptee, author of *Courageous Blessing: Adoptive Parents and the Search*, and executive director of Life Matters, a counseling agency in Dallas, Texas. Their potential can best be realized if people are able to prepare for a variety of possible outcomes. Those who undertake the search should recognize that the search process itself may be time-consuming, frustrating, and emotional; that the reunion, if one occurs, can be disappointing or exhilarating and can permanently affect the lives of many people; and that the aftermath of the search may prove ultimately affirming, as the adoptee, birth parents, and adoptive family integrate what has happened into their identities and determine how to live with its effects for the rest of their lives.

Some adoptive parents are supportive and recognize that their adult children need to make choices and decisions for themselves, says Linda Yellin. When they don't, their attitude may drive adoptees to keep their search a secret, making adoptees feel guilty and driving a wedge between them and their family. Depending on the circumstances of the initial adoption, some adoptive parents may be more informed and prepared for the search and may, therefore, find it easier to be supportive than others who were not well prepared. However, intellectual knowledge about the search does not prepare one for the raw emotions that come up when an adoptee actually chooses to search. Adoptees may still wonder, even when their family members voice support and understanding, whether it really is all right. It is best that they begin a search on their own timetable, neither restrained nor pushed into someone else's agenda.

Some family and friends, usually invoking guilt and/or fear, may attempt to convince an adoptee that it is a bad idea to search. Stan's adoptive parents told him they'd never see him again if he attempted to find his birth mother, and it wasn't until his adoptive mother's death that he felt able to approach his father a second time to discuss the possibility of conducting a search. Other adoptive parents, friends, or family members may be more subtle, but still convey disapproval or incredulity that someone would willingly undertake something they perceive as risky with little positive to offer. However, most adoptees who have searched, regardless of the outcome, are glad they did. They recommend that adoptees or birth parents who want to search do so, but only if they prepare themselves for whatever they may find, or for not finding anything at all.

When to Search

Is there a "right time," or even a "best time," to undertake an active search? Is there an age or a stage of development during which it will be more appropriate and easier for an adoptee to integrate new information into his or her personality? Adoptive parents often assume that their child will not wish to search until he or she is a young adult. In reality, the desire may arise long before.

By middle childhood, Holly van Gulden says, most adoptees crave information of all sorts about their birth families. They want to know about the appearance, hobbies, schooling, extended family, and religion of their birth parents. It is helpful for an adoptee's development to form as complete a picture of the original family as possible. Children at this stage are very concrete; if they can't see, feel, or hear something, it isn't real to them, Carol Demuth explains. It is difficult for adoptees to think about and relate to birth parents who are not real to them; it's rather like relating to ghosts, she says.

Middle childhood may also be an appropriate time to visit a birth country, in the case of an international adoption, or to open a closed adoption, van Gulden advises in *Real Parents, Real Children*. This timing coincides with a child's natural interests and allows the child to process the information while still centered on the family (van Gulden and Bartels-Rabb, 1993, p. 202). If they have not yet been struck by the tension inherent in their story, most children will begin to understand and struggle with it at this point. Although they may have been told their adoption story before, it now takes on new meaning, and they want to know it in a different way. If, however, an adoptive parent is not acknowledging the struggle, the child may be painfully aware of what his or her parent isn't saying. When an adoptive parent does not help the adoptee discover positive information about his or her background, the adoptee may assume the information is negative, says van Gulden. Joyce Pavao agrees, and says that learning positive, and accurate, information can help an adoptee accept who he or she is now.

Adolescence may be the most difficult time to search, many adoption experts say. The developmental task of adolescence is to separate from parents and individuate, and this can be doubly difficult for adopted teens who must separate not only from the parents they know, but from parents they don't know. If they have not yet formed well-rounded images of their birth parents, it can be more difficult to separate from them, van Gulden says. Many adoptees have preconceived images of their birth parents, and some act on those images, engaging in behavior they assume, rightly or wrongly, to be similar to their birth parents'. They may be choosing highly risky behavior to imitate; for examples, teens may engage in indiscriminate sexual behavior. When adoptive parents help their children acknowledge and incorporate a wide range of behaviors and traits that may belong to their birth families into themselves, before setting out to find them, children can choose appropriate behaviors to imitate.

Before it is safe to separate, adoptees must have a sense that they are wanted by their parents. Search during adolescence can strain that sense, van Gulden says. Some teens may interpret a search, if initiated by their adoptive parents, as proof that their adoptive parents don't want them, especially if there has been conflict between them. Sometimes, however, adolescent acting out may be more dangerous than searching, Joyce Pavao says. And some teens need that "gigantic dose of reality" that a search provides, Barbara Tremetiere adds. If teens indicate that they want to search, it is important that parents send clear messages to their children that they are loved, wanted, and will always be a part of their family. Parents should also create a safe place to hear and process information that may be difficult and painful.

Adoptive parents should also realize that not every adoptee will feel the need to search, Holly van Gulden points out. The objective of search is "to heal: to grieve the loss, find resolution, and come out of it all with a positive sense of self" (van Gulden and Bartels-Rabb, 1993, p. 229). Some adoptees can do that without a reunion and even without a search. And some are not able to heal, even after finding their birth families.

How to Search

Brodzinsky, Schechter, and Henig suggest that an active search can take many forms, which may or may not include direct contact with birth parents (Brodzinsky et al., 1992, p.113). It may involve visiting places where birth parents lived or worked, the hospital where the adoptee was born, or the agency that placed the adoptee. Contact with other birth family members or friends is sometimes possible. The information an adoptee gathers during this phase of a search can lay the emotional groundwork for a reunion, providing a picture of what the birth family's life was like and allowing the adoptee to absorb that information before moving on. There are support groups for members of the adoption triad who want to search, individual counselors who specialize in adoption, and books and articles to read. Thoughtful preparation can make a difference in how a reunion turns out, both in the short and long terms.

"I felt that my daughter needed to search for her birth mother, and I let her know we'd be willing to help her," Jean says. "We had the name, and she just wanted to show up at her birth mother's house. I told her that before she could search she had to go to at least two meetings of a support group. I wanted her to be prepared for anything, positive or negative."

"Contact a support group, for both technical and emotional

support," advises Charles, a birth father who found Emily, the daughter he and his then-girlfriend had placed for adoption twenty years before. "Don't go it alone and don't do what I did— show up on the doorstep. Use the phone and break it to the person easily."

"My father got the historical information as a gift to me to make peace between us," Stan says. "It was very helpful to know some things before I went to actually search."

"I had several sessions with my counselor, who tried to discourage me from searching at that time," Brian recalls. "He felt I was too young—I was eighteen—and not emotionally ready— I was busy with college—and that a reunion should be more gradual, not like opening a floodgate. But I was stubborn and determined to do it as soon as I was legally able. In hindsight, he was right. That reunion is a blur, but I think I said some things that were quite cruel and immature. And then, I mostly cut off contact with my birth mother for five years."

Preparation for a search and reunion covers much psychological ground for each member of the adoption triad and his or her loved ones. It is helpful, Linda Yellin recommends, for the one who is searching to put him- or herself in the shoes of the other triad members, and imagine what this exploration feels like to them. There are different emotions for each, she says, but the one who is initiating the search is probably the most well prepared. Carol Demuth suggests that preparation for a reunion might include meeting other members of an adoption triad. Sometimes, for example, an adoptee or adoptive parent has never met a birth mother or father, or a birth parent has never spoken about adoption to an adoptive parent. Asking outsiders about their need to search can provide valuable insight and be easier than asking one's own family members. The empathy that one acquires for other triad members can enable the searcher to help members of his or her family cope.

When an adoptee's family members are included in the preparation, they are less likely to be frightened and react defensively. When they understand that there is no desire or need to replace them, and that the motivation for the search is to restore missing pieces of the puzzle, they are better able to put aside their fears to help the person they love. By searching, the adoptee is "risking the exclusivity of the relationship with his or her adoptive family," Demuth explains. This can be frightening, but by doing so, the adoptee is actually expressing deep trust in the relationship. "The willingness to be open is evidence of faith in the family ties that have been established over the years" (Demuth, 1993, p. 7).

"Read, talk to people who have searched, and think about possible responses," advises Barbara Tremetiere. If Jewish identity and the religion of the birth parents are of concern to the adoptee, she recommends learning specifically about religion and ethnicity, the atmosphere at the time the person was born, and similarities as well as differences in culture, race, and economic conditions, all of which can make a difference in the outcome of a search. Adoptees often have little understanding of the pressures that may have been brought to bear on their birth parents because of religious beliefs or cultural expectations, and which led them to choose adoption, Carol Demuth says. Whether or not the birth parents know that the adoptee was placed with a Jewish family can also be significant. It may affect how they react to an adoptee who was raised in a much different environment than their own or the one they imagined.

It is helpful for adoptees to identify and think about their perceptions and feelings about their birth family's possible history, Linda Yellin says. Are they uncomfortable or do they have negative images about lifestyles other than the one with which they are familiar? Or have they been raised in an atmosphere of acceptance of and appreciation for other religions and lifestyles? A Jewish adoptee should be prepared to find Jewish or non-Jewish birth parents, regardless of what he or she has been told.

Encouraging an adoptee to probe his or her own stereotypes about lifestyle, as well as religion, can help the adoptee integrate the new information into his or her self-image. Even if the birth parents turn out to be Jewish, there can still be differences in religious practices and lifestyle. A Jewish adoptee who was raised in a non-observant family, for example, but who finds birth parents who are Orthodox, will encounter major differences and potential conflicts. On the other hand, Yellin adds, an adoptee who was raised in a Jewish family may find non-Jewish birth parents who are very similar in lifestyle or economic circumstances, although not in religion.

What Are You Really Looking For?

A great deal of personal emotional exploration is essential before a triad member is ready to search, Annette Baran says. "They need to explore what they think they're looking for, what they're afraid to find, and how capable they are of braking themselves or the other parties involved if there seem to be problems." That advice applies to any member of the triad who attempts a search.

Some adoptees are not certain when they begin their search what they need or hope to find. "I didn't really know why I was searching or what I was looking for [when I began my search]. It was good that it took two years," says Barbara, an adult adoptee. "You need to be an adult, not young, angry, and having a difficult time. I thought I was looking for a fantastic love. If you are looking to find love, someone to save you, to belong, or to be absolutely loved, those are the wrong reasons to search. The right reason is to discover yourself, to evolve."

"I didn't know what I wanted to do with my life," Julie recalls. "I thought I would find clues if I met people cut from the same cloth."

"My goal," says Amy, "was to find out about myself. Finding out everything about my birth parents was finding out about me.

I was never allowed to acknowledge that I have two families. Any difficulties were always pushed back and suppressed. All that was discussed was that it was wonderful that I had been adopted. My parents just wanted to make me theirs. That worked for them, but I was wandering through childhood knowing I wasn't theirs. Because it was never acknowledged, it was difficult to have questions. I didn't want to talk about it because I didn't have the energy to explain how I felt and I didn't want to hurt my parents, but I always felt like something was missing."

"I had a hard time finding my niche, what I was good at," says Emily, whose birth father, Charles, found her while she was trying unsuccessfully to search. "I didn't want to trade in my family, but I wanted a blood relative to identify with. I wasn't whole and I needed to know."

Birth parents have their own needs and reasons for initiating a search. They may be looking for reassurance that the child they placed is all right, for forgiveness, or for a way to sort out the pieces of their lives. "I think I was going through a midlife crisis," Charles says. "I was in my forties and feeling hyper-nostalgic about the past. I had time off from work and more time to think. It [searching] was on my mind every day; I was fantasizing about the reunion, wondering what my daughter was doing, what she'd look like. I wanted to show her I wasn't a bad guy. She'd matured and we could be friends. My paternal instinct drove me to know."

Many birth parents have been left with a legacy of grief, wondering what kind of person they are, unable to move forward in life, Claude Riedel says. They need to reclaim the emotional part of themselves they blamed for the pregnancy, and honor it as a vital part of their whole being. They have to focus on healing themselves by rediscovering cast-off memories about the reality of their life story, rather than the ones told by family or society.

Adoptive parents may initiate a search for their minor child because the child is requesting it, or because the parent believes there is a compelling need for the child to have certain information. They need to ask themselves whose needs are being served, and as they proceed they must be careful and cognizant of what their child can accept and understand, Linda Yellin says. Some adoptive parents, when they initially learn about searching, may want to "fix" things for their minor—and sometimes even their adult—child. It is not appropriate for a parent to conduct a search for an adult child, she says.

What Are You Afraid Of?

Some of the fears stimulated by a search are obvious, while others may be more subtle and difficult for people to identify. Many adoptees are afraid of yet another rejection, Annette Baran says. Why, they think, would they be wanted now when they weren't wanted before? Or they are afraid of what they may discover. "Why would I want to know her?" Marla asks. "What I know tells me that she wasn't a very good person." They may fear what other people will think. "When I was growing up there was a stigma to being adopted," Brian explains, "and there was a stigma to searching for birth parents. I didn't want people to think I was ungrateful or unstable, or that this meant I had a poor home life." Or, like Stan, they fear adding to the grief of their adoptive parents. "There is a danger of cutting off the adoptive parents while searching," says Joyce Pavao. "Adoptees need to educate their adoptive parents about what they are doing and why."

Some adoptive parents may be fearful of being rejected by the children they have raised and loved, of being replaced by birth parents with whom there are biological ties. That fear may cause them to react in anger, Claude Riedel explains, and they may be tempted to push away from their child, perhaps to avoid their own pain, just when he or she needs their support the most. What many do not realize is that by forcing a choice, or not supporting a search, they may precipitate the very estrangement they

wish to avoid. "Adoptive parents need to examine and acknowledge their uncomfortable feelings," he says, "in order to maintain a loving relationship with their child."

"Adoptees are not looking for a mom and dad," Annette Baran
adds. "Birth parents may be genetically connected, but are
strangers. The parents who raised a person are the parents. If
adoptive parents are open and patient the adoptive family is
strengthened, not weakened, by a search and reunion. Trouble
arises if the adoptive family forces a choice out of fear. It's a no-
win situation; the adoptee will resent this, no matter what happens."

Birth parents may be afraid to search, or to be found, although
they may want both. In fact, says Bradford Blauer Jones, in his
experience 95 percent of birth parents are agreeable to contact.
"They never ever forget," he says. Yet there are many sound reasons for their fear. They may not wish to disrupt their son's or
daughter's life. "I talked to a therapist and put the idea away,"
Sandra recalls. "I felt I shouldn't search. His life could be secure
and happy and this [a reunion] would be something he didn't
need. But I wondered about him every day; he was never far
from my thoughts." Or the birth mother may never have told
her current family about the child she placed for adoption and
may still refuse to tell them, Annette Baran says. "She believes it
makes her seem immoral, and it makes the adoptee feel like a
dirty secret." "My birth mother was afraid to tell her daughters
after our first reunion," Brian recalls. "One of her daughters is an
Orthodox Jew and my birth mother was afraid that her daughter would judge her harshly."

Finally, because there are some things about searching that
don't usually get addressed and that adoptees might find distressing or awkward, they need to be prepared for the possibility
that they'll need or want to slow or even terminate the relationship, Baran explains. "These are complex relationships that call
for a lot of mature judgment, just when people are in a regressed

state," says Marcy Wineman Axness, an adoptee who writes and lectures about adoption and has had a reunion with both of her birth parents. "Boundaries have to be negotiated as you go, so it is very important to take it slow, move away from the process if necessary, and integrate it in little doses. For example, there may be hidden anger on both sides. Because there are feelings that never had an avenue for expression, she suggests that keeping a journal of one's feelings during the process of search and reunion can help people integrate what they are experiencing.

Given these cautions, most adoption professionals, as well as those who have searched, say that the positive aspects of a search and reunion outweigh the negative.

When a Reunion Takes Place

Many triad members are passionate and positive about searching, whether or not it ultimately results in a reunion and/or an ongoing relationship. Searchers benefit from the process, say Brodzinsky, Schechter, and Henig in *Being Adopted: The Lifelong Search for Self* (1992, p. 142), because it can ease their feelings of differentness and isolation and can enable them to gain control over this aspect of their lives. They grapple with universal themes in human development—loss and mourning, envy and jealousy, sexual identity, consolidation of identity and body image—and may resolve some of their issues just by addressing them.

When a search results in a reunion, adoptees discover information. They also discover things about themselves they never knew before. A reunion can change people's perceptions of what they believe about themselves, Claude Riedel says, allowing them to go on in peace. "The reunion brings things to light and fills adoptees with a sense of permanence and belonging. It enables them to relax with themselves and with the rest of the world. The feeling is: If I know where I came from, I can better accept what life brings me," he explains.

Julie found her birth mother, and her birth father's grave.

Although, she says, she and her birth mother "weren't much alike," she recognized herself in her birth mother's tone of voice. "I wouldn't have been happy to leave blankness. I got incredible stories about my birth family, I understand why I was placed, and I realize that it was a good decision for both of us. There would have been tremendous guilt and shame if she'd tried to raise me. She had never looked at me, or she would not have been able to give me up. And she would never have looked for me because she'd promised herself not to interfere in my life. Finding her, I felt I had come to rest on the earth, that I was solid instead of amorphous. I felt peace."

Barbara "felt rejected and lost," and was prepared for rejection and anger from her birth mother who, she'd been told, had never even named her. Barbara had had her own [biological] child, and "couldn't imagine giving up a child," because she "had bonded so strongly" with her daughter while she was pregnant. She assumed her birth mother "would not deal with me." Instead, she found a birth mother who "was totally accepting," and there was "an instant connection with her." Although Barbara is not sure what type of ongoing relationship she and her birth mother will have, she strongly encourages adoptees to search. For the first time, she says, she is beginning to understand herself: "Things have come together and I can stop worrying about the puzzle." But she cautions adoptees that searching can be "a roller coaster from euphoria to depression" and that they "must be open to finding anything."

"I was elated, I felt grounded, centered," Stan remembers. "The empty parts were filled and the anxious parts of myself felt calm and at peace."

The peacefulness that many adoptees find when they make the connection with birth parents can ripple throughout their entire lives, affecting education, career, and other relationships. It is not achieved by all, and for some it can take years, Linda Yellin points out. But for those who find it, it can be significant. Jean recognized the effects in her daughter, Anita, always an angry and troubled person, whom "no one could reach." The reunion with her birth mother "is part of what helped her pull out of her problems," Jean explains. "You can feel the difference. She's friendlier and more at peace; there's an inner peace that wasn't there before. She got a job she likes and that she's good at. Other things make her happy now besides shopping. Before, she was filling herself up artificially; now, she has something real."

After Charles, her birth father, found her, says Emily, she was able to realize some of her inborn talents, because she identified with information she received from him about members of her birth family. "They were very creative and artistic and I always wanted to be like that. Finding them gave me the energy to go for it, knowing it is within me. I've excelled at work since then. It's important to know where you come from; it makes you more secure with yourself." Both Charles and her adoptive mother, Sheila, agree. "I told her that she takes after her [birth] mother, being artistic," Charles says. That motivated her, Sheila adds. "She and Charles compared and found similarities that no one thought about. She found out that people in her family were artistic and it motivated her to be more aggressive in her career."

A reunion can also stir up emotions the adoptee thought were settled. This can be particularly true about religion, although it is difficult to generalize about what birth religion will mean to any individual adoptee. Many factors—observance of Judaism in the home, acceptance of the adoptee in the Jewish community, Jewish education, and the personality development of the adoptee—interact and affect the feelings an adoptee has about Judaism. It can also depend, Annette Baran says, on whether Judaism is "a constricting or freeing identity" to the adoptee. A constricting identity, she explains, "says you're not like we are, so you're not good. Every adoptee has a place within them that tells them they're no good, because they were given up or because they are different." If Judaism feels like a constricting identity, it may be one the adoptee is willing to abandon.

If adoptees discover birth parents who are Jewish, their Judaism "may feel more authentic and more comforting," Baran says. Sandra's son searched for her because, she says he told her, "he needed to know her." Having known from a young age that he was adopted, he had wondered all his life where he came from and where he belonged. Although he'd been raised in a loving and close Jewish family, and was "a very family-minded Jewish man," he needed "to identify his real roots." He was happy to find out that she was Jewish and thanked her for placing him with a Jewish family.

If adoptees find birth parents who are not Jewish, it adds layers to the identity that they must integrate, Baran says. There is a difference between knowing about birth parents and knowing birth parents, Claude Riedel adds. Many adoptees have been told that their birth parents are not Jewish, but experiencing it in person can be "like post-traumatic stress," explains Marshall Schechter. It is much more powerful to meet birth parents than just to hear about them, and can bring up feelings about their past that they thought they'd resolved. "When an adoptee reunites with a birth family that has different customs and a different lifestyle as a result of being of a different religion, the person has to reconcile something internally. Especially because we are a minority and don't find so many people with whom we can match, it can unsettle a stable personality; the adjustment disturbs the adoptee's idea of who he or she is and who has been accepted as a model. Usually, however, the adoptee adheres to the adoptive family's religious values and beliefs; they have taken hold and have primacy," he says.

"I never had any question about being Jewish," Stan explains. "I was Jewish because my adoptive mother said I was Jewish. Even if we were not practicing it, we were Jewish. Feeling Jewish came from being immersed in the Jewish culture; later, when my wife and I were looking for a religious community to be a part of—she wasn't Jewish until she converted—it became very clear to me that a synagogue was the only place I was comfortable. But

I had to come to it on my own, without my adoptive parents pushing me toward it. There had been some rejection of my Jewishness, both because of who I am as a result of my birth and because of my natural adolescent resistance to what my parents wanted me to do.

"But when I came up against the Christian aspect of my history, it threw me for a loop," he continues. "I knew that my birth mother wasn't Jewish, but I hadn't experienced it. I felt that religious belief is what people live; it doesn't have to do with blood. That is what allowed me to feel connected to Judaism. After I returned from the reunion with my birth mother, I went to my Torah study group. Suddenly, as I was sitting there, I could feel the two parts of me meet; I could feel that I was from a Christian mother. I felt disconnected and scared, like maybe I am not who I thought I am. A piece of my unconscious came into consciousness. But I never wavered in my commitment to Judaism in any way."

Immediately following a reunion, some adoptees experiment with a variety of ways of relating to and connecting with their birth family, Carol Demuth says. This may mean exploring different lifestyles, including religion, if the adoptee believes this will facilitate a desired connection with birth parents. An adoptive family that perceives this as rebellion or repudiation will likely be very distressed, especially if the family highly values their Jewish identity. It can be difficult for an adoptive family to understand the pull on the adoptee between birth and adoptive religions, and the complex task of integrating two distinct and disparate parts of oneself that is facing the adoptee, says Sharon Kaplan Roszia, executive director of the Kinship Center in Tustin, California and co-author of *The Open Adoption Experience*. "They weren't raised as who they were; they are someone other than who they would have been. Some, after a reunion, get stuck in between. They can't go back and they can't stay as who they were raised. The way to live with this is to acknowledge it and that it isn't simple. We [Jews] have a rich tradition to share, but we must understand that it will be hard for adoptees."

In a reunion, "adoptees are bringing together what seem to be opposite sides of themselves, and they need to hold and honor both parts in order to feel whole," Claude Riedel explains. Some adoptees feel comfortable with their birth family's religion, and feel that they can connect with it and appreciate the similarities of their two religions, Linda Yellin points out. "I remember feeling that I wasn't really Jewish," Rhonda says. "We weren't observant; Judaism didn't play a big part in my life. I didn't have a conversion, Bat Mitzvah, or Jewish wedding. But it was a strange feeling to be raised as a Jew and find out that I had a Catholic heritage. All my life I felt deprived and struggled with feeling left out at Christmas, and I thought that when I would get older I'd be able to do whatever I want. So I was happy to find that I belonged to it. I'm confused now and I don't know where I belong. My husband isn't Jewish, but we're trying to raise our child Jewish. I think that not belonging is difficult for adopted kids and they need something that says 'this is where I belong.'"

By weaving together the strands of their story, adoptees can recapture a sense of self-value, Holly van Gulden says. This can be difficult, because the lifestyles and religions may seem too different and the dichotomy between birth heritage and current lifestyle too great. It can be distressing to deny either, says Claude Riedel, and people are affected differently, depending on the personality of the adoptee and the adoptive family. The adoptee may also find a birth parent who represents a religion or lifestyle with which he or she is uncomfortable or in disagreement. A Jewish adoptee, for example, may find birth parents who express anti-Semitic views. This can be difficult to accept and integrate, and the adoptee may want to explore issues that seem overwhelmingly difficult or painful with a professional adoption counselor, Carol Demuth advises.

When There Is No Reunion

Sometimes an adoptee's fears are realized and they find a birth parent who would have preferred not to be found, and is unable or unwilling to build any type of relationship or, sometimes, even to meet. Amy's birth mother was "angry to be found and wished that I hadn't found her." She was "negative in general; she had no interest [in me] other than my physical features. And she was shocked that I am Jewish. She had no idea that the man who had placed me for adoption was a rabbi; she only knew that she didn't want me and it didn't matter where I was going." However, Amy still recommends that adoptees search. "I want to tell people that the search is positive, even when it's negative. My goal was to find out about myself, and finding out about her was finding out about me. Anything negative she said wasn't a personal offense."

It is also important to be prepared for what most adoptees who search say is the most difficult and painful scenario of all— not finding anyone. However, most say that the search itself is worthwhile, for the feelings it engenders of taking control of one's life. Maryanne has been searching for well over a decade. She has a name and the location of her birth, but has been unable to find her birth mother. She visited the town where she was born, "which took more courage than anything I've done," met the lawyer who was involved in her adoption, and went to places connected with her birth mother. She even met and formed an emotional connection with a man who may be her birth father, although there is a greater possibility that he is not. As one member of an adoption triad to another, he told her, "I may not be your birth father, but you are definitely my daughter."

"That made such a difference in my life," Maryanne explains. "It was such a healing moment, to meet a birth father. I'd been highly conflicted about doing it. But many of my successes and my personal peace were a result of reaching that crossroads and really taking in what adoption means to my life. It colors my life.

It's not necessarily negative, but it is a part of my life."

Now she asks the question that adoptees who search must resolve for themselves: "Do I search forever, or do I say that it ends?" Then, she answers for herself, and perhaps for many other adoptees who search. "My decision was that to stop searching would be incompatible with my life, with the very integrity of my being. I can never give up and say that I won't find something so vital. Judaism says how vital roots are. So I am always searching, even if I'm not actively doing something."

Search and Reunion: A Lifelong Process

While the actual reunion can be a euphoric and transforming experience, there is intense work that should come after it that can help determine what it means for the rest of the adoptee's life. "Reunion was set as an endpoint for so many years," Marcy Wineman Axness explains. "It is really a beginning point in a lifelong process, one for which there is no model in our social relationships. Reunion is not a panacea, especially for adoptees who have had a lifelong sense of a piece of themselves missing. The reunion, which feels great at first, then begins to feel like it's too little, too late. And it is. People can never go back and fill in, so the reunion doesn't seep down to the depths of themselves."

"People put their energy into the quality of the reunion, the social connection, instead of inward to their own healing," Claude Riedel explains. "They are hoping that the reunion will fill them and heal their wounds somehow. But the reunion isn't going to heal these wounds because people don't even recognize what they are. After the initial euphoria of the reunion, the wounds are still there and need to be dealt with, and the adoptee senses a feeling of 'what now?'"

Because there is no model for this relationship, it can be difficult, yet important, for the adoptee and birth parents to define their desires. "Usually, there is a sort of approach and avoidance, unless they are both in the same place about what they want,"

Holly van Gulden explains. "What they want can be very complex, because of all of the extended family members who may be involved." People who have not done the proper preparatory work probably have little sense of what sort of relationship they need, and how to achieve it. People may find they need to distance themselves in order to determine it.

"In the beginning I was very confused," Sandra, a birth mother, says. "These were uncharted waters, and I was insecure about my place in my son's world. I had to back off, and wear it for a while until I felt secure and fell into a way that felt comfortable."

"The reunion gave me peace of mind and allowed me to put the adoption behind me and move on. It made me feel whole," Brian adds. "But it made my birth mother feel empty. She thought she was getting me back, and she wasn't." "My son made contact, but then pulled back for five years," Janice, Brian's birth mother, recalls. "He needed to sort it out and didn't want to hurt his parents. He was happy to know me and that was enough for him then. I kept in touch, just letting him know that I was interested in more of a relationship, until he was ready." Eventually, her son's adoptive mother encouraged him to reopen the relationship. She and his father were not threatened by it, and told him that they thought it was cruel to have opened that door and then walked away.

After the second reunion, both Janice and Brian are satisfied with the relationship they have developed. "I like to look at it as a unique and close friendship, not a mother-son relationship," Brian says. "We talk on the phone several times a week and see each other several times a year. Janice talks regularly with my mom; they've become friends. I gain support, unconditional love, and caring from her, but my adoptive parents are my parents. I would advise other adoptees to be patient, and understand that reunion goes far beyond the reunion. It's a constant evolution and there are no ground rules. You make it up as you go."

"I had a 'cool' relationship with my birth mother when we first got in touch," Esther remembers. "I finally saw myself reflected in someone else in subtle and unusual ways and it was a heady connection. But she began having mental problems and we became estranged for about ten years. We finally got back in touch and there has been a slow rebuilding of the relationship. She was wary because I was really exploring how adoption had affected me. I'm now able to accept her as she is and enjoy what I can enjoy without nullifying it because she doesn't fill all my needs."

Sometimes, however, the parties discover that an ongoing relationship will not work. "I was close with my birth mother for a brief time after the reunion," Rhonda recalls. "But, as I discovered that there really was no basis for a relationship, I distanced myself." This is not unusual and, Holly van Gulden says, people may feel a stronger connection to their adoptive family after a reunion than before.

Thus, Claude Riedel says, the reunion itself isn't the whole issue. The lifelong challenge is what the adoptee will do to nurture the wounded and missing parts of the self. "Adoptees need to feel an 'inner reunion,' to go into the Pandora's box of unresolved needs and feelings inside them." Marcy Wineman Axness agrees. "They need to look into themselves and ask, 'What haven't I been able or willing to connect with?' This, more than a reunion, is likely to bring about a deep sense of reconciliation. Everyone can have an inner reunion, even if they can't have a real reunion or have one that is unfulfilling."

A successful inner reunion allows the adoptee to integrate both the heritage family and the adoptive family and not reject either one, Holly van Gulden says. The adoptee doesn't have to act on the heritage—"It's not who I am, it's who I would have been," one adoptee explains—but neither does he or she have to reject it. Acceptance of one's past can have a more profound effect on the adoptee's ability to integrate Judaism in his or her life. "If the person can say, 'I came from this, and I've had this other experience, and they are both valuable parts of who I am,' it can be possible to hold on to both the birth and adoptive religion and integrate them into the self," Claude Riedel agrees.

Search and reunion are complex, and are best preceded and followed by thoughtful work on the part of the searcher. This journey of discovery is one that triad members can be proud to have made, Riedel says, because in doing so, they will find strengths in themselves that few people have the opportunity to discover.

CHAPTER 4

Open Adoption: From Secrecy to Full Disclosure

~

Adoption used to be about pretending. People who were unable to conceive adopted a child who was born to someone else and pretended that the child was born to them. The woman who conceived and gave birth to the child pretended that she had not. The man who impregnated her pretended he had not. And, once placement was complete, they both pretended never to think about the child again. The child—if he or she was told about the adoption—pretended never to wonder or worry about the birth family, the unknown past, or the uncharted future. Everyone pretended that pretending was a healthy and appropriate way to arrange an adoption.

The pretending went on for the most positive reasons; adoption solved problems. It provided homes for children who needed them, helped birth parents cope with a difficult situation, and created families for people who were unable to create them biologically. Everyone was supposed to feel good, but it often didn't work out that way.

Adoptees discovered within themselves the need to connect with a biology and a history that belonged to them, even as it was withheld from them. Many were unable to pretend it didn't exist; they could not adopt without question the biology and history of the family that had adopted them. Birth parents recognized that they couldn't forget the children they had placed for adoption. They thought, wondered, and worried about them. Some longed for the opportunity to meet them. Adoptive parents realized that their child's birth parents were, somehow, still always there, an unseen but not unfelt presence in their lives. Pretending and secrecy were not as simple as people had hoped.

Secrecy in adoption is actually a relatively new phenomenon; it began in the late 1930s to avoid the twin stigma of infertility for the adoptive parents and an unwanted pregnancy for the birth parents. There have always been adoptions—by stepparents, foster parents, other relatives—in which contact between the adopted person and his or her birth parents was maintained. As increasing numbers of adoptees and birth parents acknowledged the depth of their feelings and began to search for one another, it became evident that secrecy could lead to complications for all members of the adoption triad. Now the pendulum has swung back in the other direction. Many adoption professionals today believe that secrecy can cause just the type of difficulties it was meant to overcome. Secrecy can leave adoptees with holes in their histories, their identities, and their hearts, which may cause feelings of shame and poor self-esteem. It can leave adoptive and birth parents filled with misunderstanding and fear of one another. Instead of enabling people to move forward, secrecy can hold them back.

Out of this new way of thinking has emerged a different style of adoption. In popular jargon it is known as "open" adoption, and it is defined by both its proponents and detractors in many different ways. Some see absolutes: An adoption is either open or it's closed. Others see a continuum, a process that evolves with the needs and abilities of all the parties involved. It may include sharing information, letters, and photographs, and can extend to contact between members of the adoption triad.

Adoption professionals, triad members, and their concerned family and friends often hold diverse and passionate views on the benefits and challenges of open adoption. While recognizing the pain that can be caused by the secrecy of closed adoptions, some wonder if open adoption will create equally troubling problems of its own. With little long-term experience for guidance, people find that decision making is difficult.

Jewish adoptive parents who explore open adoption may discover additional difficult questions. Because some birth parents are not Jewish, adoptive parents may find a cultural or religious divide that is challenging to bridge. Should non-Jewish birth parents be invited to celebrate Jewish life-cycle ceremonies or holidays with the adoptive family? How will children react when they see birth parents celebrating religious holidays, like Christmas or Kwanzaa, that they don't? What should adoptive parents do if birth parents attempt to include the children in non-Jewish observances? Can non-Jewish birth parents truly understand what it means to be Jewish and support that identity for the children they have placed for adoption? Can adopted children build a strong Jewish identity when faced with undeniable evidence of a different religion of birth?

These are not easy questions. Discovering satisfactory answers demands respect and cooperation. There are no absolutes, no rights or wrongs. The best decisions place the best interests of the child foremost and honor all of the adults involved.

How Open Is Open?

What is an open adoption? How open is open? Misunderstanding this term can be frightening to both adoptive and birth parents, and can cause confusion for the adoptee. If any of them believe that more or less contact with the adoptee is expected or permitted in this relationship than is realistic, or wise, given the participants' comfort levels and maturity, they may find it difficult to forge an open adoption together.

Reuben Pannor, MSW, ACSW, LCSW, one of the pioneers of open adoption as the director of the Vista Del Mar Child-Care

Service in Los Angeles, California, defines open adoption as one in which "the birth and adoptive parents meet, exchange identifying information, and work out a method of ongoing contact that is in the best interest of the child." This may not, however, be the definition that all adoption professionals, adoptive parents, and birth parents agree upon. Deborah H. Siegel, Ph.D., ACSW, LCSW, DCSW, a professor of social work at Rhode Island College, Providence, Rhode Island, and an adoptive parent, began a long-term study of families involved in open adoptions in 1988. She found that "open adoption" means so many things to so many different people that it is difficult to know exactly what it means. While she defined it as any type of direct contact between the birth and adoptive families, she found families whose definitions ranged from living together before the birth and ongoing contact afterward, to simply exchanging letters with all identifying information excised by the mediating agency. Some of the situations that people may consider open include: knowledge of one another's social and demographic circumstances, but not of one another's identities; selection by the birth parent(s) of acceptable adoptive parents; exchange of letters or pictures that is mediated by an agency; meeting prior to or following the birth without the exchange of last names or other identifying information; and knowledge of one another's identities but without ongoing contact.

A semi-open adoption, adds Abby Ruder, an adoptive parent and director of Adoption Information and Support Services in Philadelphia, Pennsylvania, involves only the adults. They choose one another and make an arrangement for future contact among themselves. In a fully open adoption, the adoptee is included in a way that is orchestrated by agreement of the adults, with the child's changing needs and best interests in mind.

The idea of ongoing contact with their child's birth parents may be difficult for some adoptive parents to imagine. If they do not understand the crucial difference between open adoption and co-parenting, they may envision people intruding in their lives, interfering with their parenting, and staking an emotional claim to their child, says Michael Colberg, JD, CSW, an adoptive parent, co-director of the Center for Family Connections in New York, and a member of the Pre and Post Adoption Consulting Team (PACT) at the Family Center in Somerville, Massachusetts, that is led by Joyce Maguire Pavao. Co-parenting, such as that arranged in a divorce, allows both parents to have equal input into raising the child. They both share in making decisions about issues that govern the child's daily existence. In open adoption, on the other hand, there is only one set of parents, the adoptive parents, who are raising the child and making the day-to-day decisions. This requires "an emotional transfer of parenting" from the birth to the adoptive parents, Colberg explains. "The birth parents are there to help the child make sense of who he or she is in the world, where he or she came from, and to know that he or she is loved by the birth, as well as the adoptive parents." But they do not usurp or impinge on the parenting rights of the adoptive parents.

If birth and adoptive parents can define openness together in a way that makes sense to all of them, they will be more comfortable with their choice, Siegel says. Adoption professionals can help them to discover their personal boundaries and desires, rather than working with a preconceived agenda about adoption. "People have to feel it's the right path," advises Linda Yellin, MSW, ACSW, an adult adoptee who has a private practice in adoption counseling in Farmington Hills, Michigan. "Their hearts have to be in it, or it won't be useful to the child."

The most important element in open adoption is the maturity the adults bring to the process, says Dawn Smith-Pliner, director of Friends in Adoption in Middletown Springs, Vermont. "If any one of the adults isn't bringing that [sufficient maturity], it is potentially setting the child up for something he or she won't be able to handle." She is, therefore, rarely in favor of fully open adoption, with participants disclosing complete identifying information, at least at the start.

"There is a reason why adoption is being considered, why the birth parents feel they can't parent. That reason needs to be assessed, so that a plan of action can be determined to best address the needs of all the parties involved," she says. "Some, but not all or many, adoptions lend themselves to full openness, because of the degree of commitment and maturity it takes. Open adoption requires continuity, so the child is always maintained in a stable nurturing position by all the adults involved.

"Closed adoption is potentially harmful," she continues, "but full open adoption can also be potentially harmful. We need to look at each case unto itself. Trust and relationships take time. I would prefer to see people go into a semi-open adoption and allow it to evolve, rather than make the assumption that openness will work from the beginning. There are a lot of components that need to be there to make it safe and comfortable."

While open adoption is not easy or free from problems, there are those who have become convinced it is in the best interests of all triad members. Closed adoption promotes distance from one's own experience, while openness can turn this around, Abby Ruder says. "If people have secrets and lies, they don't have the information they need to have an integrated experience. People deserve to claim whatever is going on for them. For birth parents, open adoption can provide a measure of peace and completion. It allows adoptive parents the opportunity to relate to people from whom they feel entitled to take on the parenting role, rather than remaining fearful of an unknown people and history. It demonstrates to adoptees that their adoptive parents value their birth family and heritage, and helps them acquire a more inclusive sense of self. Closed adoption salts the wounds of the losses of adoption; denying the losses of adoption stunts adoptees' emotional growth. Open adoption makes them more whole, which then gives more of them for both of their families to relate to."

When open adoption is done right, says Michael Colberg, "it is a very powerful experience in which a lot of strength is accumulated over a lifetime." Doing it right requires thought and planning, education and guidance. Primarily, he adds, "it requires a great deal of honor and respect."

The Rhythm of Open Adoption

One of the first things that people need to appreciate about adoption is that their needs will change over time, Colberg says. Adoption isn't static, it doesn't just happen; it is a happening, a process, a way of life. Just as children have different abilities and needs at different stages of their development, so too their understanding of adoption and what they need and want to do changes over time. Birth and adoptive parents experience changes in their lives, some caused by the adoption and some unrelated to it; it is appropriate and natural that their interactions with and relationships to one another can and should also change. But like any change, this can be frightening and difficult if it is unexpected.

Open adoption has its own rhythm, Colberg explains. From the time that the first decisions are made, to adopt and to place a child for adoption, adoptive and birth parents become involved in an intricate process. It begins with education, as they learn what to expect from their new undertaking. A skilled intermediary can help them anticipate and work on issues that arise. The greatest mistake made in open adoption is to proceed without experienced guidance, without a neutral third party who illuminates the issues and helps negotiate how to handle them. While not every intermediary functions in the same way, trained and impartial counsel is essential.

Preparation of all parties is critical, agrees Jim Gritter, MSW, child welfare supervisor for Catholic Human Services in Traverse City, Michigan, who has been involved in open adoption since 1980. "Fear is the major obstacle to open adoption, and it needs to be addressed thoroughly. People need to think about what they are afraid of, which is usually everything, and how they will cope with those fears. The methods of coping are endless, but the major ones are information, support, and reframing the meaning of fear into something motivating. Faith goes a long way, too.

"First, we need to calm people down. Adoptive parents bring a 'get agenda,' an urgency to get a child, no matter what, to the proceedings. We try to shift that, first, to a 'receive agenda.' It's a more patient response, one in which they recognize that the choice of adoption belongs to the birth parents. Then, we try to shift it even more to a 'give agenda,' which is the best remedy for fear. Adoptive parents respect and honor birth parents in a tangible way, as they permit them a continuing role in the life of their family. It enables adoptive parents to adopt in a way that they don't have to sell their souls, and that they will emerge changed for the better."

Counseling for birth parents helps to prepare them for the loss and grief they will likely experience if they choose to place their child for adoption. As they prepare to make that decision, they can be helped to realize the full extent of their feelings, and anticipate feelings they are likely to have in the future. A decision they come to regret may be a bad decision for everyone involved. An adoption counselor can also educate birth parents about their responsibility to their child, Deborah Siegel says. They are forever connected biologically to another human being, who will probably want information about him- or herself at some point. If they understand the adoptee's pain at being forever denied that information, they can better determine what type of access to themselves they want and are able to provide.

Matching birth and adoptive parents who are compatible with one another, people who are able to relate to each other with some rapport, is key to a workable open adoption. This disabuses adoptive parents of their misunderstandings of birth parents and can eliminate the we-they thinking that is common in a closed adoption. In open adoption, birth parents may choose the adoptive parents based on a wealth of in-depth information, Jim Gritter explains. Choice becomes an endorsement of the adoptive parents by the birth parents and can eliminate fundamental disagreements about basic and important issues, be they educational, religious, or lifestyle. This can be extremely affirming to Jewish adoptive parents who are hoping not only to be chosen by non-Jewish birth parents, but to work toward a comfortable partnership.

Once birth parents have made a tentative selection, face-to-face meetings usually follow. A "no obligation" meeting, in Gritter's practice, determines if all parties feel confident enough in one another to move forward. At a second meeting, birth and adoptive parents "iron out" the details of the adoption. "Birth parents need to have role clarity; they need to understand their role in the family and what they will be losing in choosing adoption. They must realize that they will have no legal status, that everything will rely on a handshake, a moral agreement. In doing this, all parties have to have goodwill; they need to be willing not to injure one another—for the sake of the child," Gritter explains.

Adoption professionals can help participants anticipate many of the challenges they may encounter, and may suggest committing some details of their agreement to writing. While they clarify the nature of the understanding, they also help people realize that they can't anticipate everything. Instead, Gritter explains, they work together to develop a value system that outlines how they will proceed with the adoption, emphasizing honesty, courtesy, and working for the ultimate good of the child. Boundaries that are determined in advance may prevent problems and misunderstandings from arising. "I work for openness as a premise of what people deserve, but I also know that complete openness isn't always possible and could be detrimental," says Abby Ruder. "It doesn't work unless everyone has a clear sense of boundaries."

If something about the situation causes discomfort that can't be worked out, people need to be willing to walk away, says Hal, an adoptive father who did just that, not once but three times. "The first time, we had a relationship with the birth mom's mother and everything seemed fine. Just as the girl was getting ready to deliver the baby, we received a call asking for an illegal amount of money. We explained why we couldn't do that, but they insisted. It was dreadful, but we walked away. The second time, we discovered that the birth mom wanted to be involved in our lives in a way that we felt would be pathological. So we walked away. The third time, the birth mom changed her mind right after the child was born." Each of these situations was extremely difficult, he says, but they were eventually paired with two birth mothers with whom they have appropriate relationships.

When a child is born and placed with adoptive parents, it is appropriate that the situation changes, Michael Colberg explains. If everyone has been prepared, this will be neither unexpected nor frightening. Birth and adoptive parents have different tasks that require their attention, so they have less need and ability to pay attention to one another. The adoptive family is becoming a family; they are learning about and attaching to one another. The birth parents' identity has changed; they need to figure out who they are and what they plan to do next. Both sets of parents require space and time away from one another to do this important work. However, they may want to have some contact so that the birth parents will be reassured of the child's well-being.

After everyone has had time to adjust to their new roles, they will again be comfortable with contact with one another, Colberg continues. At that point, they can begin to think once more about the nature of their ongoing relationship, perhaps with the guidance once again of a skilled intermediary who knows what to expect. Later, when the child they share is ready, he or she can and should begin to have input into the nature of the relationship.

Children are not in charge, but can help "fine tune" the situation, Jim Gritter adds. They will often give fairly straightforward messages about what amount and type of contact is comfortable for them. Adults can benefit by listening to these messages.

Open Adoption as Evolution

How do families become involved in open adoptions? For many, it seems to be an evolution, as the initial trust and respect that the birth and adoptive parents have for one another grows. With time and experience, as fear diminishes and comfort increases, they become increasingly willing to open themselves and the adoption to one another.

As an adoptee who had been through her own successful search for her birth parents, Julie knew she "didn't want secrets and gaping holes" in her son Ryan's life. Her husband Todd, however, wasn't as comfortable with openness as she, so their adoption has been a gradual process of becoming more open, in keeping with Todd's comfort level. "It had to do with time and seeing that Helene [Ryan's birth mother] wasn't even remotely considering taking him back," Julie says.

A trusted intermediary took them to meet Helene, Ryan, who was seven weeks old at the time, and Helene's older son, whom she was raising herself. Helene told Julie and Todd to take Ryan that night. "At first, she didn't know our last names, address, or phone number, although we knew hers. We made a commitment to visit a few times a year, but as we got more comfortable we opened things up more. Now we visit regularly."

Jewish adoptive parents may anticipate anti-Semitism and may be fearful of sharing their religious affiliation with non-Jewish birth parents. In an open adoption, however, this basic information can not be hidden, but is best shared early in the process so that everyone involved can determine what it will mean to their relationship.

"We didn't choose open adoption the first time; it evolved," explains Ann, who has two children—Noah and Tovah—and two open adoptions. "We placed ads privately and met with a birth mother. She asked us our religion, and we thought it would be a problem because some of the agencies we'd tried to work with had told us that no birth mother would choose a Jew. We decided, however, that we had to be honest because this had to be a good fit. She said it wasn't a problem, then she asked our last name. We knew hers, and we thought about it and decided to give her our name. In the beginning, we exchanged pictures and letters, but didn't meet again until Noah was about two years old. Once we saw that our fears were unfounded, we opened it more. We're now visiting at each other's homes."

Vivian describes her daughter Shayna's adoption as semi-open and still evolving, with future decisions in her daughter's hands. "Margaret, our child's birth mom, trusted the intermediary, who knew us. Although she didn't want to meet us before placement, she had lots of questions about our attitudes about education, discipline, and religion. Her mother is Jewish and, although she was raised Catholic, she was very close to her Jewish grandmother. So, it might have been a positive thing to her that we were Jewish.

"For four years, we had only nonidentifying information. Then, the intermediary called and said that Margaret wanted a picture of Shayna. As a social worker, I had seen birth parents who wanted to meet the children they had placed, and adoptive parents who were filled with anxiety prior to meeting birth parents but very positive afterward. I didn't feel frightened, although my husband was. We sent a picture, and I wrote a letter with it asking her for information about herself. She wrote back and included a picture, which we didn't give to Shayna for five more years. I was ready, but my husband still had issues. Margaret was leaving it up to us; she'd joined a group for birth mothers and was working through her feelings.

"Shayna now carries a copy of the picture of Margaret in her wallet and has taken her other copy and put it in a magnetic frame on our refrigerator door. Next to her birth mother's picture she has placed a picture of the two of us with our arms around each other. Between the pictures she put a magnet with the inscription: 'Have I told you today that I love you?'

"When Shayna was eleven, she met the intermediary. He suggested that I meet Margaret, which I did. I already admired her courage in dealing with such a major decision at such an early age in her life. I like her very much; she's someone I'd choose for a friend. We'd feel comfortable if Shayna wants to have a relationship with her, but right now Shayna isn't ready. Margaret wrote her a long letter, which we told Shayna she could read whenever she wanted. It took her a while, and at first she denied reading it, but she finally did.

"When I met Margaret, she admitted that she wished she had gotten to know us sooner. But she explained that it was too painful at the time. She'd made up her mind not to like us, or any adoptive family, and was simply trusting our intermediary. Since then, she has told us, 'I made her [Shayna] what she is and you're making her who she is.'"

Open from the Start

Some adoptive parents, because of prior conviction or experience, are ready for open adoption from the beginning. Sharon, herself an adoption professional, had "a strong professional commitment to open adoption." She explains, "I had heard from so many adult adoptees that they felt they had 'a big hole' in their identities. They spoke about emptiness, heartache, and the energy expended on this." Sharon also says, "I believe that information is empowering, and if my children have enough information they won't have the angst. Josh was with us as a foster child, and after ten months he was returned to his birth parents. Six weeks later, we were asked to care for him again and, when the agency determined that his birth parents couldn't care for him, they asked us to adopt him. We were thrilled. So we have known his birth parents from the beginning. They know and respect us, and recognize that this is in their best interest."

"We made an ideological choice to pursue open adoption," Hal explains. "It was not begrudging or a last resort; it was because Rochelle and I believe that children have a right to know their heritage, and part of our job is to keep the door open for them, if possible. Open adoption was certainly not a well-known phenomenon when we started, but we gathered a lot of information—because we knew nothing—by reading and talking to people, and decided we could handle [open adoption] and would feel comfortable with it. We reviewed a menu of agencies, and chose one that had a commitment to both birth and adoptive parents. We had what we thought were normal anxieties, but we didn't see it as risky. We felt we could exercise good judgment and could either pursue it or back off if necessary. Open adoption was appealing on two levels: The birth mother and we would choose one another, and we could then enter into a relationship that would benefit our child.

"The birth mom received a profile on us and we talked on the phone. We were satisfied, but she wanted to interview another couple. It felt funny, but we understood. She then called back and said she'd chosen us. We had regular phone contact and met for the first time at the baby's delivery. Seeing our daughter born was a remarkable experience. We felt overwhelmingly blessed and privileged. In some ways we knew our daughter's birth mother well and in other ways not at all. We feel fortunate that a relationship that started out tentative has grown and matured. We invent the rules as we go, but have maintained a close relationship with phone conversations several times a year and annual visits. She and our daughter have a very nice relationship. It's not daily, but she's in our daughter's heart."

The situation with Hal and Rochelle's second daughter is an example of the need for flexibility and tailoring each situation to the needs of the participants. While Hal and Rochelle were ready for the same type of open relationship they were finding so successful with their older daughter's birth mother, the second birth mother was younger and not ready to have direct contact with them. "We've maintained correspondence with full names and we've exchanged pictures. We're hopeful that someday she'll be willing to meet us. We've worked hard to keep the adoption open, without pushing it, so that if our daughter wants to meet her, she can."

The Challenges

Advocates for open adoption see it as a positive alternative to the old closed and secretive system, which was fraught with problems. They believe, Reuben Pannor explains, that the fears expressed about open adoption, often by people who have had no personal experience with it, have not, in practice, proven to be significant issues or are far outweighed by the positive impact of openness. In order to allow themselves to consider open adoption, adoptive and birth parents need to have their concerns addressed with education and support.

Adoptive parents' primary fear is often that they will be unable to control birth parents' access to and involvement in their lives. They may anticipate that birth parents will not be able to act in what the adoptive parents consider to be the best interests of the child and that involvement may become interference. They may even imagine birth parents attempting to reclaim the child (McRoy, Grotevant, Ayers-Lopez, 1994, p. 14). But while this imagined scenario makes for exciting television, in reality it has not been the experience of families who are involved in open adoption and are working out the complexities their situations involve. Deborah Siegel found that, seven years into open adoptions, birth parents have not interfered in adoptive families' lives. "Because of the people we chose, we aren't concerned that they'd try to enter our lives in ways that are uncomfortable," Hal explains. "If Amanda asks her birth mother something [during a visit], Joan tells her 'Ask your parents.' She's very respectful of us." In fact, Siegel discovered that adoptive parents sometimes seem to want more contact than birth parents can handle. "Birth parents have very difficult lives, or they'd be choosing to parent themselves. Sometimes staying involved isn't really possible for them; they are struggling to survive," she explains.

Moreover, birth families have not tried to reclaim children they placed for adoption. On the contrary, adoptive families who have created a trusting and respectful relationship with their child's birth parents feel reassured that this would never happen. In each case, they have felt comfortable in further opening the adoption. "We have a good relationship with Peter, Josh's birth father," Sharon says. "He doesn't try to undermine us." Ann agrees and says, "Noah's birth mother is very respectful of us and doesn't pry into the details of our life." Adoptive parents' fears are based on a prevailing view about birth parents. "Society has this very pejorative view of birth parents for giving away their own flesh and blood," Siegel says. "This finds expression in these terrible fears about them. But they are choosing adoption because they know they can't parent, and they are willing to take on lifelong loss and grief in order to provide a better life for their child. So why would they show up and do something that could hurt that child, especially when their minds are at ease about the questions that haunt them—whether their child is okay and at peace?"

The other major concern of many adoptive parents is that their child may be "confused" about who his or her "real" parents are, and that this will create difficulty in establishing the primary bond between the child and themselves. They anticipate issues of divided loyalty and that their child may believe that the adoption is not permanent. "It is an emotional challenge for Amanda to figure out who this person is and how she figures in her life," Hal says. "But she says she can handle it, and she seems to be handling it. She knows that Joan couldn't take care of any baby at the time she was born, and understands that we are her family."

Sharon admits that Josh is, sometimes, confused. He misses his birth parents, especially following a visit from Peter, wonders why he can't be with them, and wishes he could. However, she see this confusion as "a trade-off," because "at least he won't have the hole [in his life] that other adoptees have."

At times, Ryan feels torn between his two families and says that he feels he belongs there, Julie says. But, as an adoptee herself, she understands his feelings. "I tell him that he does belong in two places, that he is the child of two sets of parents. This doesn't scare me, because I know that you could never take my adoptive parents out of me anymore than you could take my genes out of me."

The Benefits

Another way to perceive the challenges of open adoption is to focus on the possibilities and benefits of working on issues as they arise. "All adopted children have questions about their birth parents," Julie says. "But in an open adoption, the child doesn't have to deal with them alone. He has the acknowledgment and support of two families who are willing to deal with their reality openly. He feels free to bring up his questions; adoption is not a forbidden topic."

The confusion, she adds, is often felt more by adults than children. "The crux of the question is whether a person can have more than one set of parents. If you have the paradigm that adoptees have and need two sets, then you accept that as reality. It's my reality, too, so it's easy for me to understand it as my son's reality. Children take it for granted that this is Ryan's reality; other adults are frightened by it, don't understand it, and think it must be confusing."

Michael Colberg believes that it is healthier for adopted children to express their confusion directly, rather than to repress it and have it come out in other ways. "Adoptive parents need to understand that their child is still a member of his or her birth family, whether that family is present or absent. They share many things. Our message to children is, 'Of course you are confused; this is confusing.' But in an open adoption the child can address these issues in a safe environment. It's not always fun and it's not always happy, but it is what it is and it can be addressed."

"There are risks and the possibility of confusion and emotional complications," Hal acknowledges. "But given the choices and trade-offs, we think that the path we've taken will minimize the land mines and enhance both of our daughters' abilities to cope with their status as adopted people. Adoption is a marathon, not a sprint. They will struggle with it forever. We think we've given them tools to deal with it."

Jewish adoptive parents may also worry about confusion around religious identity when their partners in the open adoption are not Jewish. They can be comforted by the realization, however, that by choosing a Jewish family and maintaining an open relationship, birth parents are giving the adoptive family permission to parent Jewishly. They need not worry about the reaction of birth parents who reunite with an adult adoptee only to express surprise at finding a Jew. Instead, they may find birth parents who are happy that their child is being given a religious heritage and upbringing and who convey that message throughout the child's life.

"We invited Peter to Josh's naming ceremony, because he is glad that we are giving Josh a spiritual life and teaching him to be a good person, and we are grateful for the opportunity to thank him for entrusting his son to us," Sharon says. Noah's birth mother is a "born again" Christian, who "understands our faith because hers is so important to her," Ann says. "She's more interested that we are giving him strong values and a belief system than in what kind of belief system it is. She thinks that God sent Noah to us, that this match was meant to be. Tovah's birth aunt sent us a mezuzzah for the door of her room as a baby gift. It was the family's way of telling us they accepted us and our religion."

Birth parents can help ameliorate the confusion some adopted children feel about their Jewish identity. Rochelle remembers when nursery-school-age Amanda insisted that she wasn't Jewish because her birth mother wasn't. They talked about her conversion, spoke with the rabbi, and revisited the *mikvah*. Nothing helped. Finally, Rochelle asked whether Amanda would like to discuss this with Joan. On the phone, Joan said to Amanda, "You are Jewish, because I'm your birth mom and I say so!" Amanda was quite satisfied with this explanation, and Joan then sent her a Star of David charm.

"There are highly successful open adoptions between people of different religions," confirms Sharon Kaplan Roszia, co-author with Lois Melina of *The Open Adoption Experience* and executive director of the Kinship Center in Tustin, California. "Jews feel extraordinarily validated because there is no guilt and no hiding; they feel fully entitled to raise the child as a Jew. And the children of open adoption, unlike adoptees who question their Jewish identity, tend to embrace Judaism fully. There is really something to be said for the blessing that the birth family bestows on the adoptive family in an open adoption."

Some birth families have little concept of what being Jewish means, and their unfamiliarity with Jewish traditions and customs can create awkward situations and tension between the families. With some effort and good will, they can learn ways to ease these situations. It is helpful, Linda Yellin says, to discuss religious issues during the pre-adoption process, defining specifically what it means to raise a child in a Jewish family. If religious differences continue to be a problem, adoptive parents may need to discover alternative methods to handle it, both with their child and the birth parents. Leah's birth mother continually sent Christmas gifts, Sharon says, and didn't seem to understand the significance. "We finally had to spell it out very specifically: no sweaters with Santa on them."

Noah's birth mother also sends Christmas gifts, Ann says. "I tell him that people celebrate different things and that we don't celebrate Christmas. We make Judaism positive and focus on what it is, not on what it isn't." Because Ann believes that Noah "needs consistency and to understand his [Jewish] identity," she is thinking of asking Noah's birth mother not to send gifts specifically for Christmas. If Noah's birth mother visits on a Friday night, "we don't say prayers in front of her. We suspend our habits, as does she, in respect for each other."

Open adoption also provides adoptive families with important medical and psychological information that can help them better understand the birth parents. "It makes things make sense to her," Vivian says about Shayna. "I can tell her about her birth mother and she understands where some of her traits come from." The image that adoptive parents have of birth parents in a closed adoption is of a specific snapshot in time, Michael Colberg explains. Without the ongoing contact of an open adoption, "you have no idea of who they [really] are and who they'll become. You make judgments based on that one moment in time and, if you hold a specific image, you'll see those traits in the child. In an open adoption, you see qualities and growth over time." When adoptive families better understand the birth parents they can better understand their child. When they find traits in their child's birth parents to admire, and can convey that admiration to their child, the adoptee is helped to build a positive self-image. He or she can enjoy being like both sets of parents. "We've really come to admire Helene, in terms of what she has done with her life," Julie says. "She has had a really tough time, and she has done really well."

As an adoptee learns about his or her birth parents, understanding about why he or she was placed for adoption can develop. Birth parents have to explain themselves in an open adoption, says Barbara Tremetiere of Tressler Lutheran Services in York, Pennsylvania. Adoptees can then better understand their birth parents as real people who had real problems, but who made a decision for their child's future based on love and caring.

"We've told Ryan that Helene felt she could only raise one child, that she was very sad that she couldn't raise him, but that she felt that the best thing she could do for him was to find him a family that had a dad. He understands that," Julie adds.

When Shayna was eight years old she wrote about her adoption for a school assignment that required her to address something that has been difficult for her. She wrote that "it's hard to know that my sister grew in Mommy's tummy and I didn't," but she also acknowledged that her birth mother cared and was concerned about her: "When I was four years old, my birth mother asked for a picture so she could see how big I've grown."

When situations are painful and the truths unpleasant, families involved in open adoptions may find themselves better able to cope because of the understanding that has developed through open communication. Adults are often tempted to protect children from sadness or unpleasantness, but knowledge is empowering and no reality is as bad as the fantasy children concoct. "Secrets are about things that aren't okay," Abby Ruder says. "Children who know little or nothing about their birth parents may assume that they must be like that part of their birth parent that is so bad that their parents can't even speak about it. Children should know the truth; that there is that of God in all of us and that everyone has something redeeming about them. It is the adoptive parents' responsibility to make the birth parents whole and real, and to find something redeeming about them for their child. They may choose not to have contact, but the child needs to know the truth."

Ultimately, writes Lois Melina in *Adopted Child* (Melina, "Questions Answered About Open Adoptions—Years After Placement," p. 3), when birth parents are not able to maintain an open adoption because they are immature, disorganized, have poor relationship skills, or value alcohol or drugs more than people, the adoptee may get a vivid picture of why they could not raise a child. He or she will understand that it was the birth parents' inadequacies, not their own, that made adoption the best choice. "I used to think that a child in an open adoption, who has contact with his or her birth parents, wouldn't hurt," says Deborah Siegel. "I've learned that it still hurts. The child is still different from his or her peers, and there is still loss. But the pain of not knowing is gone."

Making Open Adoption Work

While open adoption is not easy, those who have experienced it believe the work worthwhile. Each successful open adoption will be different, depending on the needs, abilities, and limitations of all members of the triad. Not every birth or adoptive family is ready for a fully open adoption. It is important, Michael Colberg says, to take people where they are and give them the opportunity and support to move gradually toward openness. He faults adoption professionals who force people into situations for which they are unprepared and, therefore, uncomfortable. People who are anxious to adopt will "get in whichever line is shortest," he says. "Many people find themselves learning about adoption only after they've adopted. As they learn more, they may discover that a different degree of openness better suits their family's needs."

Myra Hettleman, LCSW-C, director of Adoption Alliances of the Jewish Family Services of Central Maryland, Inc., in Baltimore, encourages adoptive parents to be as open as they can. She advises them to know their comfort zones, and not allow themselves to be forced into something truly uncomfortable for them. On the other hand, she says, if people explore the alternatives and find they are able to push their limits they usually end up happy that they did so.

What are some of the ways in which families create open adoptions that work? Children seem able to sort out relationships that appear complicated to adults; many children cope with stepparents, step- or half siblings, and multiple sets of grandparents. As children explore the relationships in an open adoption, they may test to see if the rules are the same in both families, or if their birth parents will become involved in their adoptive family's discipline. Children need consistency, Michael Colberg says. If the adults involved are comfortable with the situation, honest with and respectful of one another, and supportive and loving toward the child, they can create a situation that works for them. Visits with Helene and Dylan, Ryan's biological half brother, aren't very different from visits with other members of their extended family, Julie explains. "They are quite different from us and sometimes there is stress, but we already have a very diverse family so we get together and connect because we have this person in common that we love."

When the adoptive family is Jewish and the birth family is not, children need to learn to respect their birth heritage if they are going to respect that part of themselves that it represents. Adopted children have to be helped to value their identities in both their birth and adoptive cultures, Colberg says. This is simply more obvious in an open adoption. "Ryan thinks his older brother is really cool. Both boys are biracial and he likes having someone who looks something like him. Ryan likes Dylan's music and the things he does as an adolescent. It's special that he knows they're brothers. And he identifies himself as Jewish, even though he knows that he was born to Helene and she isn't Jewish and neither is Dylan," Julie says.

In an open adoption, it is important that adoptive parents acknowledge their child's birth religion, while also educating the birth parents about the importance of Judaism to their family. "I ask adoptive parents to consider what their boundaries are and to dialogue with birth parents about what is and isn't acceptable and comfortable to them," says Abby Ruder. "They can tell birth parents that there are ways in which they want to respect the birth family's heritage, while teaching their child to become a practicing Jew." Ruder suggests that if a child is curious about his or her birth religion, adoptive parents can help them learn about it, may offer to visit the birth family during a holiday, and may consider attending a religious ceremony with them. "Children want to try on different identities, and they'll discard the ones that don't fit. They can be especially curious about identities which might have belonged to them, which are part of their birth culture," Michael Colberg explains.

If the adoptive family has no non-Jewish friends or associates, they may be transmitting the message that they have nothing in common with non-Jewish people. This may indicate to the adoptee that they have nothing in common with a part of him or her, and that it isn't all right to bring that piece of themselves to the adoptive family. "We need to promote inclusion," Colberg says. "We need to teach children not to categorize people. . . . Children ought to be able to see that people can worship differently, but can get along as friends."

When one sibling in a family is adopted and others are not, open adoption can affect those relationships. Vivian says that her biological daughter, Rena, wants her sister Shayna to meet her birth mother; Rena wants her sister to have a biological connection too. "Openness is even more important in a blended family," Vivian says. "It's important to acknowledge the differences; denying or rejecting the losses in adoption isn't healthy. The siblings have different experiences; fair doesn't always mean equal."

It is not uncommon, Deborah Siegel adds, for families to participate in more than one adoption, each with a different amount of openness. It is important not to deprive one child of access to his or her birth parent because the sibling doesn't share a similar situation. Sometimes, the available birth parent even plays the role of birth parent for the sibling. "When Joan gives Amanda a gift, she brings something for Emma, too," Rochelle says. While a sibling's open adoption relationship with a birth parent doesn't create a sense of loss for the adopted sibling who doesn't have contact with birth parents, Lois Melina points out, it can make the absence of contact more apparent. But by observing a sibling's open adoption, the adoptee without contact may realize that birth parents do care, even when his or her own birth parent isn't actively demonstrating it (Melina, 1996, p. 3).

Choosing Other Options

Although not every birth or adoptive family is ready for a fully open adoption, increasing numbers are choosing to have some amount of contact. When the parents have worked out together a situation that makes sense to them, they can feel positive about the experience.

"We met Jason's birth mother several times after he was born," Cindy recalls. "We had also talked on the phone many times during the pregnancy. She wanted us there before he was born, but we chose not to do that. We were working with an agency that provided counseling, housing, and general help to birth mothers, and that was okay. But I didn't want to coach the woman who was having my child. I was afraid the adoption would fall through and that was too much. I grew to appreciate his birth parents and am happy that I can communicate about them to my son. I can say that they are nice people, who have good hearts, and they cared about him. His birth mother told me to tell Jason that if things were different for her she would not have given him up. It was very difficult saying good-bye to her; I wish that we'd had a ceremony for that. I wrote her a letter telling her that she'd given me the greatest gift in the world and that she'd stay in my heart. I promised her that I'd give Jason a better life than she could have."

Marc and Dina met Adam's birth mother several times during the pregnancy, although they didn't exchange last names. They went to the hospital while she was in labor, and Dina saw Adam as soon as he was born. For the first few years, they conducted an annual exchange of letters via the agency, but the birth mother eventually stopped writing. When Adam is an adult, he has the right to contact the agency, which will make contact with his birth mother. She has the choice to see him or not, and the opportunity to contact him the same way. Adam has asked about her, and Marc and Dina are happy that they can explain this arrangement to him.

Ken corresponds with his twins' birth mother through their intermediary. At this time there is no direct contact with the children, a situation with which he is comfortable. "Right now, they don't ask for any contact with her. I send letters and pictures about once a year and tell her how they are doing. But we will let them get in touch with her when they ask," he says.

He did, however, have a unique affirmation from her of raising the children as Jews. He and his wife had previously been turned down by another birth mother when she learned they were Jewish. They were hesitant to share this information a second time, especially since their children's birth mother had made some general comments that they believed were anti-Semitic. After about two months of contact, however, they decided to tell her that they are Jewish. She said little, until a few months later. Then she told them that she had decided to stop eating pork. She explained that she wanted the children to be kosher in utero.

CHAPTER 5

A Jewish Rainbow: Transcultural and Transracial Adoption

Asian, Hispanic . . . and Jewish. Native American, African American . . . and Jewish. As increasing numbers of Jewish couples adopt children from the four corners of the earth, the American Jewish community is becoming a multicultural and multiracial rainbow. We are learning what Jews around the world have always known: that the Jewish people have many faces, many colors, many body types, many names. Transracial or transcultural adoption—the adoption of a child of one race or heritage by a family of another—forever changes that family: It becomes a multicultural or interracial family. These adoptees and their families become part of a rich and varied Jewish tapestry stitched together by choice and love.

For many families, considering transcultural adoption is an evolutionary process. Adoption may not be how they had planned to form their family; transcultural adoption may be an even more novel idea for them. Preparing themselves and learning about what to expect can help them make this choice wisely.

What are the special challenges on this particular path? A Jewish adoptee from another country and culture is a member of a minority within a minority within a minority. If adoption itself presents difficult challenges concerning separation and loss, grief and rejection, and identity with which adoptees and their families must grapple throughout their lives, then transcultural adoption introduces yet another layer of complexity; the adoptee's questions now encompass not only a birth family, but an entire culture. Adoptive parents must become willing and informed transmitters of that birth culture. In order for children to develop a healthy sense of pride in their racial and cultural identity, they need to know where they come from. The message to children who don't receive this information is that there is a part of them that doesn't matter or isn't worth knowing about.

Adoption into a Jewish family adds yet another wrinkle: Historically, the American Jewish community has been rather homogeneous, consisting mainly of Caucasian Jews of European descent. With adoption, all this has changed; the Jewish community is learning to adjust. In addition to knowing about their birth culture, transculturally adopted children need information about their Jewish heritage, and encouragement and assistance in integrating it into their identities. Given the opportunity to live that heritage, they become comfortable and proud of it. They may, unfortunately, also need to learn how to deal with prejudice, both anti-Semitism from outside the community and resistance from inside the community, from people who do not yet understand or accept the American Jewish community's new reality.

Transracial or transcultural adoption is a complicated choice, which brings tremendous challenges and extraordinary rewards. As one adoptive parent said, "The mountain is high and steep, but oh, when you get to the top, the view is incredible."

Medical Challenges

Children adopted internationally may face unique medical challenges, depending on conditions in their birth country at the time of their adoption. They may be at risk for developmental, medical, or emotional problems, some known but others initially unrecognized, that do not generally face children born in the

United States. Although international adoption is not a uniquely Jewish phenomenon, many more Jews are adopting from abroad than ever before. Adjustments in expectations and parenting techniques may be necessary for the family and helpful to the child who experiences delays due to early deprivation. The proper preparation, plus patience and love, can help children make remarkable progress.

According to Victor Groze, Ph.D., an adoption researcher and associate professor at the Mandel School of Applied Social Sciences at Case Western Reserve University in Cleveland, Ohio, inadequate medical care in other parts of the world can have a major impact on American adoptive families. Medical procedures and technology that Americans take for granted are not yet routine elsewhere. Diseases long since conquered in the United States still rampage through many developing countries. A lack of medical knowledge, equipment, and medicine in their birth countries may mean that some children need long-term recuperation for illnesses that would not require hospitalization in the United States. And some of these children have also spent time in less-than-satisfactory substitute care prior to their arrival in the U.S.

These conditions can give rise to four main types of problems, explains Jerri Ann Jenista, MD, of Ann Arbor, Michigan, an adoptive parent and a pediatrician who works with many families who adopt internationally. Chronic infectious diseases, growth and nutrition issues, physical or sexual abuse issues, and delays in cognition and social development are not unusual among children adopted outside the United States. The specific conditions or diseases change—over time, by country, and even by orphanage or agency—and adoptive parents should question knowledgeable professionals about any and all health-related issues at the specific time and in relation to the specific country from which they are adopting. They must also demand of themselves an honest unemotional assessment of the specific situations with which they can cope, the extent of their financial and emotional resources, and the breadth and depth of their support system.

However, even if prospective adoptive parents obtain medical information and prenatal histories from authorities in other countries, such information may be less than completely accurate, agree Victor Groze and David Soule, MD, of Rochester, New York, who is a pediatrician and adoptive parent. Professionals in these countries may use nonstandard medical terminology, which may make information acquired about a child's development confusing or misleading, Soule explains. Doctors and support staff may have little knowledge of child development or disabilities, and are often terribly overburdened with too many children to care for. Inaccurate or nonexistent records can make following a child's progress virtually impossible, Groze adds.

Chronic infectious diseases, such as HIV, tuberculosis, syphilis, hepatitis B, C, and D, and parasitic infections, are found worldwide. Although the incidence of infectious diseases varies by country, the age of the child, and the type of living situation, these conditions remain common, Jenista says. A common battery of tests is not required for visa approval; pre-placement blood testing is only variably administered. In some countries, medical facilities are so limited that they are not able to test for certain diseases, or the results are inaccurate and meaningless. Technicians may be poorly trained, equipment may be obsolete, or the test may have been made before the child could reliably produce antibodies. Some countries fail to acknowledge that diseases such as AIDS are a problem and may refuse to test for it. It is necessary to administer a full battery of tests once the child has arrived in order to evaluate fully the health of any child adopted from abroad (Johnson, 1996, pp. 32–36).

Growth and nutrition problems, such as rickets or hypothyroidism due to iodine deficiency, also affect children in many developing countries. Deficits and general developmental delays are the norm, the severity increasing with the age of the child, Jenista explains. Growth and development should be measured on the basis of biological, not chronological, age. Thus, a child born prematurely is months behind other children of the same chronological age in development. Environmental stresses can also retard growth and development. For example, stress can impede psychosocial growth so that the child fails to grow in height; children commonly fall behind one month in growth for every three to four months of orphanage life. Malnutrition, another common problem, can affect a child's weight. In general, evaluating the growth and development of institutionalized children is difficult because delays can be caused by deficiencies in orphanage care, true neurological abnormalities, or innate intellectual impairment.

The older a child is and the more time spent in substitute care, the more likely it is that the child will have suffered some physical or sexual abuse, Jenista says. Because abuse may be defined differently in other cultures, and because the child may not have mastered enough English, he or she may have difficulty explaining what has happened. But if a child has experienced early abuse, a range of behavior problems may manifest themselves years later.

Fetal alcohol syndrome and the related fetal alcohol effect can seriously compromise a child's mental and emotional development, David Soule says. In some countries, these syndromes are more common than in others. Adoptive parents need to be aware of this and of the symptomology, so that they can make appropriate decisions if their child is affected. (These problems are discussed in greater depth in Chapter 6.)

Delays in cognition and social development also present serious problems. Many children who have spent time in foster care evidence such delays, Jenista adds. If the problems are not too severe, if the children have been adopted early enough, and if they possess certain innate personal characteristics that favor survival, they can recover. Understanding the reasons for such delays, the symptoms, and possible courses of treatment can help adoptive parents plan ways to promote that recovery.

If they have early positive experiences with caregivers who consistently respond to their needs, children learn that they can expect consistent love in future relationships. This in turn helps them to develop an identity, to have a sense of self, explains Terri Doolittle, PA-C, MHP. However, children who are raised in institutional settings, with multiple and inadequate caregivers and shortages of supplies, learn very different lessons from their early experiences. Nothing happens when they cry. They are fed, changed, and bathed on a schedule that suits the staff. No one holds and cuddles them or makes eye contact. They learn to shut down when distressed or to prolong interactions through wiggling and grabbing. They do not learn how to regulate their emotions or their interactions with others.

If adopted at a young age, institutionalized children are often quiet, unemotional, and less reactive than other children of the same age, Doolittle says. They are relatively compliant and cooperative, but when given the chance to act out, they do. Because they have not been taught how to take cues from the environment, to ask for help or to care for others, they become frustrated. Behavior that worked for them in the institution no longer works; they must make a total life adjustment. Frustration leads to tantrums and aggression, or to withdrawal.

Victor Groze found these children at risk for a variety of difficulties. They are more likely to have chronic medical problems, learning disabilities, and delays in fine and gross motor skills, language skills, and social skills. They may have sensory difficulties, displaying over- or underreactions to stimuli. Because they have had little appropriate and personal stimulation in the institution, learning to cope instead with much generalized noise and chaos, they may be overwhelmed when they enter a family setting, over- or underreacting to various normal situations in family life.

Some institutionalized children also suffer from attachment disorder, Groze says. They may show considerable anxiety over any change, no matter how small. Others avoid human contact, pushing people away figuratively and literally, and refusing to engage with them. Having never built stable and lasting relationships with adults, they are unable to trust people, adds Diane Riggs, editor of the newsletter of the North American Council on Adoptable Children in St. Paul, Minnesota. They may be destructive, showing little regard for personal property, or they may steal or run away. Others reach out indiscriminately, exuding warmth and cheerfully attaching to anyone and everyone. This behavior is the coping mechanism of an insecure child rather than an authentic emotion. Such children show no ability to distinguish between a parent figure and everyone else.

Some children recreate situations with which they are familiar and comfortable, such as hoarding food because they aren't certain there will be more and/or bringing others into their bed to recreate the crowded conditions they once knew. These are part of the institutionalized child's normal experiences, explains Abby Ruder, an adoptive parent and director of Adoption Information and Support Services in Philadelphia, Pennsylvania. If adoptive parents understand the conditions in their child's life before he or she came to America, they can work with the child's behaviors and know what to do to help their child feel secure. Some American ideas on childrearing simply don't apply to children who have experienced this level of deprivation.

Howard believes that Rachel, adopted in the early 1970s, was one of the first Korean children placed with a Jewish American family. Told that she was ten months old, he now recognizes that she was probably older. Because she had been abandoned, there were no accurate records. "She had problems from the beginning," he remembers. "She was starving, but had problems adjusting to an American diet; later, she had problems with binge eating.

"She was impossible to deal with. You couldn't hug or hold her. She was violently angry or withdrawn from the time she was small. She had serious problems with trust and with adjusting emotionally to a family. Eventually, she stole everything that wasn't nailed down." When Howard and his wife could no longer cope with her behavior, she was placed in a therapeutic boarding school. Howard recalls that after a few weeks, he called the school to discuss her progress and asked whether the school was having any problems with her stealing. The school's psychiatrist told him that about a third of the children there were adopted—although not all were from foreign countries—and that they all stole. He remembers her saying, "Adopted children have an emptiness inside them that they need to fill, but what they take doesn't fill them because the emptiness directly relates to their adoption and to losing their birth family. When they fill themselves through therapeutic means, they stop stealing."

"Adopted children may feel a lack of connection to their own birth heritage, and this can leave a big hole," explains Ruder, quoting Joyce Pavoa. "If they don't have information about their adoption, they may feel that they were stolen, and their response may be to steal from others. They may be trying to find the part of themselves that is missing. These are behaviors that appear negative and frightening to adoptive parents. But perhaps they can look at them and work with them as part of their child's search for self."

Like most adoptive parents, Howard and his wife were completely unprepared for these types of problems. "No one told us to expect any of this; we had no warning. We searched for answers. And we discovered that there is a pattern among adoptees from similar circumstances; there is a large social and psychological gap."

Jackie adopted her son David from an orphanage in Romania when he was three years old. A medical professional herself, she saw him in the orphanage and realized that despite reports describing him as a healthy, normal child, he was quite ill. She was certain, however, that with the knowledge, support, and desire she and her husband possessed, they could cope with whatever challenges a sick child would present.

"David had kidney stones, scoliosis, malnutrition, perforated eardrums, and tonsillitis. He also had sensory processing problems. New sights, sounds, and smells were confusing and frightening. He had no language at all. He had head-banging tantrums thirty times a day; anything could set him off. It might be a new person, a song on the radio, or a toy that was out of reach. You couldn't hold or cuddle him. And even though we understood the reasons, it was very hard to deal with. You won't know until you have the child home and stabilized exactly what you'll have to deal with. Be prepared for this. You have to realize that this will affect the rest of your life," Jackie reflects.

Arlene says that she didn't have time to think about the rest of her life; she had to immediately claim the child who was offered to her in a Romanian maternity hospital, or leave childless and without the $17,000 she had spent for this adoption. "He was eighteen months old and appeared like a sock monkey. There was no muscle tone, no eye contact; he didn't respond to his name or any language. I was told that all he needed was proper stimulation and he'd recover. I brought him home and put him into an early intervention program. A year later he still didn't talk and couldn't play. He was diagnosed with autism, sensory-integration disorder, and attachment disorder. He has had many years of special education and therapy, but continues to have severe speech and language delays and social and emotional difficulties.

"I was told I was the only person to have a problem [with a child adopted from Romania], but then I met others with the same problems who were told the same thing," she recalls. "Most people are not prepared by their adoption agency, and most American doctors are not equipped to deal with these children once they are home. There is just a wish that everything will be fine. Adoptive parents need to assume their child is at risk and not be lulled into a false sense of security. They should actively seek interventions and not let any time pass while they wait for the child to recover."

Not all stories are horror stories; other adoptive parents have had very different experiences. When Meryl and Jack adopted Talia from an orphanage in the former Soviet Union, she was a healthy three-year-old who was "from the first, full of curiosity and delight," Meryl recalls. "Her intelligence was obvious as she explored every room, every drawer, and every corner of our home. She ate with great appetite, particularly relishing fruit, especially large, juicy strawberries. She was friendly to her [adoptive] brothers, affectionate to us, energetic, and anxious to please. She had little sense of limits and boundaries, which is still something we work on daily, but caught on quickly to what was expected of her.

"To this day, she is known for her warm personality, ready laugh, and delight in new experiences. She sings and dances, loves animals and younger children, swims and plays. People often ask about the treatment she received at the orphanage. From an emotional standpoint, it must have been excellent to have produced such an open and loving child. Her trust level was high from the start. It was a great credit to those who cared for her during her first three years of life."

Children who are older when they are adopted from institutions have often had other experiences that can interfere with their adjustment to family life, Terri Doolittle points out. They may have lived in large groups, in close quarters with others, and with little or no privacy or personal property. Personal hygiene may have been minimal and unpleasant. As older children, they may have been required to help with or control younger children. Corporal punishment was probably frequent, and individual attention infrequent. The social structure of the institution may have been developed by the children themselves rather than by the staff. When they enter their new environment, these children usually experience language problems as their most serious and immediate challenge. Their tantrums may be rooted in feelings of loss, culture shock, loneliness, fear, and bewilderment over the huge changes in their lives. They may be frustrated at their inability to communicate their feelings to anyone.

Sally's two sons are biological brothers, adopted from Korea when one was six and the other was seven years old. They weren't accustomed to being alone at night or to sleeping in beds. They were intimidated by men, even their adoptive father George. And they spoke no English, so the family communicated with them in an invented sign language. They both have been diagnosed with learning disabilities and attention deficit disorder, and English remains difficult for them; as teens, they are only beginning to be able to discuss abstract ideas.

How a child emerges from such early deprivation depends both on the internal makeup and resiliency of the child and external influences, such as the quality of the institutional care, the age at which the child entered the institution, and the length of the stay, Victor Groze says. "Some kids are very resilient; they go into a new environment and rise to the top. Others have delays, but make tremendous gains. Some have delays and don't catch up." Groze estimates that while some children are damaged and traumatized, 80 percent do quite well. In addition to a comprehensive health check upon arrival, he recommends an evaluation of the child's developmental progress a few months later. He also suggests that parents provide as much individual attention as possible before starting a child in group care.

Howard's daughter attended a therapeutic residential school for several years. As she and he became more comfortable with her disability and her adoption, they forged a strong bond with one another. Howard attributes her newfound ability to work her way through a problem by talking about it to the work she did at school. Although he says that she still has some issues that he believes are related to her adoption, such as the need to spend money compulsively as soon as she earns it, she has completed college and holds a responsible job.

Jackie set up a home-based program of progressive desensitization, introducing David to one new thing—a food, article of clothing, sound, or person—at a time. He remained mostly at home for several months, but was eventually able to enter a preschool program for children with disabilities. The tantrums stopped and slowly he began to put two words together. "He's fun now, and 100 percent part of our family, but it was devastating. I had clues, but I thought I was fully prepared [to raise a sick child] and, therefore, immune," she reflects.

Claiming Identities

Jewish parents who are adopting transculturally must recognize that they are creating a family that will forever bring together different cultural identities. They and their child face a lifetime of decisions, some major and some minor, about how to successfully intertwine their child's birth and adopted cultures.

The first time a Jewish adoptive family will encounter such a decision is when they select their child's name. Names can signal origin; they claim a person as a member of a particular group. The child from another country and culture who is adopted by a Jewish family may have three names: the child's birth name, indicating the birth family's heritage; the child's American name, representing entry into one new culture; and the child's Hebrew name, symbolizing inclusion in the adoptive family and a second new culture. The way in which a family handles this first step of what can be a lifelong balancing act can be symbolic of how they intend to negotiate the cultural distance between their child's past and future, explains Cheri Register, Ph.D., in her book *"Are Those Kids Yours?": American Families with Children Adopted from Other Countries* (1991, p. 95). Connecting a child to his or her new cultures, while honoring the birth culture, sends powerful messages to the child and the world.

Many adoptive parents incorporate their child's birth name into the American name they give their child, perhaps as a middle, if not as a first, name. This, Register says, connects the child's birth and adopted heritages in a very specific and tangible way, and indicates the respect that the adoptive family has for their child's birth heritage. A Hebrew name is an opportunity to implant the child symbolically in the family's lineage and the child's second adopted community. Because Jews typically name children for beloved family members, this honors both the child and the person for whom he or she was named. One way to combine the child's multiple heritages is to choose a Hebrew name that means the same thing as the child's birth name.

A naming ceremony is the first opportunity to publicly acknowledge these multiple heritages. Many adoptive parents incorporate symbols, foods, stories, and poems from their child's native culture into a Jewish ritual. The significance of this intertwining of birth and adopted cultures speaks eloquently of their importance to the family and the effort the family plans to make to be sure that both inform their child's life.

Helen's daughter, Deborah, was born in India and came to the United States when she was four years old. In a ceremony at their home, she was given a Hebrew name to accompany her Indian name. A piece of mirrored Indian silk was embroidered with both names and used to wrap the Torah at the ceremony. It now decorates their home and will be incorporated into a huppah when Deborah is married.

Richard and Carol's son, Jeff, is also from India and they chose to use his Indian name as a middle name. They also selected a Hebrew name. The invitation to Jeff's naming ceremony, and the ceremony itself, was designed by Carol and Richard to acknowledge the three strands of Jeff's identity: Indian, American, and Jewish. "We wanted to validate all three as equally important," Carol recalls.

Monica's daughter is Peruvian, and her birth name was maintained as her middle name "as a link to her birth heritage," Monica explains. At the naming ceremony, Monica served a special Peruvian drink that she had discovered during the weeks she spent in Peru waiting to bring her daughter home. She had learned that the beverage is kosher and used it in place of wine "as a bridge between my daughter's background and Judaism."

Jill, a single mother, adopted her daughters from India and Peru. A joint naming ceremony, incorporating aspects of both of their birth cultures into a Jewish ritual, was extremely important to her. "Their heritage is a gift to our family and my Judaism is a gift to them," she explains. The Jewish naming ceremony enabled them to feel part of their Jewish community, and claimed Jewish identity for them in the prescribed ritual, while the portions of the ceremony relating to their birth cultures "made it different and took their unique experiences into account." Each of their names, which incorporate their birth names and Hebrew names with related meanings, also commemorates members of Jill's family.

Straddling Multiple Identities

Jessica, who was adopted from Korea at age two, has three small flags on a stand in her bedroom, one Korean, one American, and one Israeli. By age six, she would look at them and announce: "This is me." She has learned to straddle her multiple identities and knows exactly who she is. Adoptive parents who are confident in and appreciate their own Jewish identity can give their child the gift of their Jewish heritage. If they also respect and honor their child's birth heritage, they can celebrate it as their child's gift to their family.

Some Jewish adoptive parents feel guilty that their child, who would have been a member of a dominant culture, has become a triple minority. They feel guilty when asked by their child, as Judy was by Laura, "Did my birth mom know I wouldn't have Christmas?" Others wonder, as Jane once did, whether Jessica would be "an oddity" who would never fit in anywhere if she were raised as a Jew. They struggle to achieve a balance between offering their children their Jewish culture and their birth culture. "We try to give her as much about Korea as we can, without forcing it; we don't want to separate her from our family. We got a *hanbok* [Korean gown] for Jessica and one for me," Jane explains. "I thought it was nice, but it felt artificial. We joined a group for adopted Korean children and a lot of the Caucasian moms wear them. I wasn't sure how I felt about that."

Some adoptive Jewish parents are not knowledgeable about Judaism or actively involved in Jewish life. Their link to Judaism and feelings for the Jewish people emerge from their ethnicity, from their birth as Jews—something their child, adopted from another country or culture, lacks. Children adopted transculturally need their parents' guidance to help them incorporate Jewish heritage into their own identity. If parents don't actively teach Judaism to their transculturally adopted children, says Sid Katz of Cherry Hill, New Jersey, a psychologist and the adoptive father of two children from Korea, the children may question their connection to Judaism. They may assume that because of their different cultural heritage, they are not welcome in the Jewish community.

Adoptive parents may attempt to achieve that delicate balance between their child's birth and adopted identities by being selective about the components of their child's birth heritage that they introduce. They may feel it appropriate to teach about the language, history, food, holidays, customs, and culture, without teaching a child about his or her birth religion. Lucy Steinitz, Ph.D., former executive director of Jewish Family Services of Central Maryland, Inc., in Baltimore, and the adoptive parent of two children who were born in Guatemala, is one of many adoptive parents and Jewish professionals who believes it is not possible to raise a child in two religions. Emphasizing Judaism by actively celebrating and observing customs and ceremonies in the synagogue and at home will strengthen that identity during a child's impressionable years.

Another way that Jewish adoptive parents may accentuate the Jewish side of their child's identity is by enrolling the child in Jewish day school. Although some parents prefer a public school with a widely diversified population for their transculturally adopted children, others choose a Jewish school to help facilitate their child's integration into their religious community. Judy chose a public school in a very integrated neighborhood so that Laura would be with other children of color and not feel racially isolated. Carol and Richard chose a Jewish day school because they wanted Jeff to have a strong Jewish identity. Both choices have their merits; what matters most is to honor the child's culture of origin while developing his or her Jewish identity.

Other adoptive parents and experts in multicultural adoption, like Abby Ruder, do recommend introducing a child who is being raised as a Jew to the religion of his or her birth, as a part of their culture of origin. Ruder suggests that if children show interest, they can attend religious services with members of their ethnic group, but should be clearly informed that such visits are for cultural exploration, not religious purposes. She believes that children are naturally curious, and may simply want to know more about the religious part of their heritage. They will not reject Judaism as a result of this interest, and may ultimately recognize that this part of their birth identity does not fit them. If forbidden to explore, on the other hand, they may imbue their birth religion with a special attractiveness, Ruder explains.

This does not mean, however, that families should adopt their child's birth religion or celebrate it in ways that cause them discomfort. Parents can be open with their older children about differences between their birth religion and Judaism, and can also explain the similarities, adds Ruder. In adulthood, every person has choices about the parts of his or her family's culture he or she wishes to maintain. The adoptee will also have choices to make, and the birth heritage may influence his or her practice of Judaism.

Some Jewish parents incorporate customs from their child's heritage into their family's practice of Judaism. They research how Jews in their child's birth country celebrate their Judaism. Carol discovered an Indian Jewish custom that she and her husband have added to their seder: They pass the seder plate around over people's heads. Abby Ruder, the parent of a biracial child, incorporates into her family's seder the common experience of slavery and struggles for freedom that African Americans share with Jews. Another family hangs ornaments from their child's Indian culture in their *sukkah*.

Promoting Diversity

In addition to sharing Judaism with their child, it is important that multicultural families learn about and share their child's birth heritage. The extent to which adoptive parents can demonstrate that they value cultural diversity in general, as well as their child's heritage in particular, will help their child integrate these multiple identities. Presenting painful or unpleasant truths about a child's birth country or heritage is difficult. For instance, one adoptee wondered, "If Korea is so great, why couldn't they find a family for me?" Or children may reflect on what they imagine to be the conditions in the country of their birth, as did another adoptee who said, "I wouldn't want to go back and live in a shack in India." Adoptive parents must be careful about making assumptions about the birth culture. It is important that they become familiar with the child's country and culture, and understand the conditions that led to their child's being placed for adoption. They have to be honest, presenting a balanced and realistic picture, advises Rochelle Sanders, MSW, manager of adoption services for the Paths to Parenthood program of the Jewish Family and Children's Service of Greater Philadelphia, in Pennsylvania.

Adoptive parents can help their children understand how the circumstances of the child's birth, such as being born in poverty and/or to a single mother, affected their birth parents' behavior. The society into which a child has been born may have different sexual mores than those in the United States. Options regarding an unplanned pregnancy, which Americans take for granted, may not be available in other countries. In international adoption, it may be difficult for birth parents to divulge their reasons for placement. Adoptive parents should request as much information as possible regarding their child's birth family, the circumstances of their child's life before adoption, and placement. This information can help the child feel positive about him- or herself.

As adoptive parents gain competence from learning about their child's birth heritage, they can communicate and share this information with their children proudly and respectfully, Ruder says. Hopefully, parents began their cultural exploration when they visited their child's country of origin to bring their child home. Many parents bring home slides, videos, pictures, and souvenirs for scrapbooks that maintain their child's connection with his or her birth culture. Some adoptive parents have taken courses about the history, art, language, music, food, customs, and traditions of the child's birth culture. They read books about it, collect objects from the country, and save newspaper clippings of important events in an album for their child. They provide their child with dolls, instruments, books, music, clothing, movies, and posters depicting their culture and/or country. Attending meetings of a support group, either specific to their child's culture or including people from many countries and cultures, can further normalize a family's experience.

Some adoptive parents take their child on a homeland tour to their country of origin, helping them to understand their native country and culture even if they do not actually meet a member of their birth family. They may visit the city, the hospital, or the neighborhood from which the child came. Some adoptive parents have even met their child's birth mother. Monica was able to have a brief ceremony of relinquishment with the birth mother and her parents before leaving Peru. They have agreed to write to one another periodically, and Monica is able to tell her daughter that her birth mother, while Catholic, had no problems with her adoption by a Jewish family. When they were ready to leave, Monica reports, the judge presiding over the adoption hearing wished them "shalom."

Most adoption professionals recommend that parents who adopt transculturally be willing to actively include themselves in a life filled with cultural diversity. Sometimes this requires a very different lifestyle than the one they were living or imagined living before adoption. Many choose to live, work, and play in integrated neighborhoods, and to participate in multicultural events, as well as Jewish events, celebrating many ethnic groups and their unique contributions to the world. These parents emphasize that, as a result of their awareness of the needs of a particular child, they have grown as people, and their families and communities have benefited from the concern and sensitivity they have acquired for all people. "We have become an international family; we are all now a little bit Peruvian," explains Monica, whose oldest child was not adopted and who is waiting for the arrival of her third child from Vietnam. When he arrives, she says, "We'll all also be partly Vietnamese. We see it as an extension of our family tree." Other people are uneasy about this. "I'm not Korean and cooking Korean food won't make me Korean," Donna says. Each adoptive family needs to find its own comfort zone, and its own way to help their child make meaningful connections to his or her birth heritage.

Jews of Color

On the first day of first grade, Korean-born Jessica stood up when the teacher called her name from her rollbook. The teacher promptly told her to be seated, adding that she couldn't possibly be "Jessica Cohen." And, in an experience common to many transracially adopted people, other children ask her whether she is Korean or Jewish, clearly implying that she couldn't be both.

Jewish children of color face some unique and formidable tasks. Not only do they not look like anyone in their adoptive family—an issue for many other adoptees—but they probably do not look like anyone in their extended American Jewish community. They know that when people look at them, they see color first and Jew second, and in some cases, they do not see a Jew at all. They also know, as do teachers, friends, and casual acquaintances, that there are relatively few American Jews of color. They cope with questions, sometimes simply curious but sometimes hostile, regarding their appearance, their birth culture, their adopted culture, their future. Sometimes, they themselves question whether they belong to the American Jewish community, which is still predominantly white. They wonder: Am I entitled to be a "real" Jew? How does my Jewish community see me? How does the secular community see me? How do I see myself?

Too often, people are limited by their experiences. Transculturally adopted Jewish children are often asked questions like, "What are you, Jewish or Chinese?" or "Why are you dressed in a Tinkerbell costume? Tinkerbell is white," or "What color are you?" If adopted children feel positive about themselves and their birth heritage, they might field such questions as Jeff did, with a touch of humor, sarcasm, or disbelief at the question: "Somedays I feel like I'm purple, and some days I feel like I'm green." Other adoptees will answer like Monica's daughter Sophie, who states positively: "I like being Jewish and brown." Matt, who is African American and Caucasian, explains that people often laugh and ask a lot of questions when they first meet him, saying that he can't be both black and Jewish. His best friend, who is also biracial, didn't believe at first that Matt was

Jewish, and needed confirmation from his parents that this was possible. Usually, Matt adds, he doesn't get mad because "it's not their fault if they don't know." Other times, however, he does get angry "because they're trying to tell me what I am."

Some children, however, may react to such questions with pain and self-doubt. If such questions come from within the Jewish community they can become a self-fulfilling prophecy, convincing transracially adopted children that they aren't really accepted and adding to their feelings of displacement and pain. Jessica once wished aloud that she wasn't Korean and didn't have a Korean face. Donna's [Korean] daughter, Carla, has even cried in front of her mirror and asked: "Why are my eyes different from yours? I want my eyes to be like yours."

In contrast to the nurturing other Jews give and get from one another, Jewish children of color may not receive such support. Although Jews as a community despise prejudice and racism, especially in light of their own history, many adoption professionals and adoptive parents have discovered that the American Jewish community does not yet completely and unequivocally include people of color within its ranks. "There is still racism within the Jewish community, and Jews may question whether a person is really Jewish," says Rabbi Michael Gold of Temple Beth Torah in Tamarac, Florida, and author of *And Hannah Wept: Infertility, Adoption, and the Jewish Couple.* This prejudice is difficult for the community to accept about itself; it is something that many members would rather deny.

The Jewish community has fostered an exclusivity that makes it difficult for people of color to feel welcome, Abby Ruder believes. "When we talk about 'we,' the Jewish people, we imply an ethnic connection, that we are one people," adds Karen Rispoli, MSW, LSW, adoption coordinator for Jewish Family Service of East Brunswick, New Jersey. Parents of transracially adopted Jewish children must remind the community that Judaism is not a race; Jews include people of all races and ethnic backgrounds. "We ought to welcome people of all races," says Michael Gold. "Jews are people who share a history and a value system, and you don't need to have the same genes to share that."

Transcultural and transracial adoption is relatively new, and overall the Jewish community has come a long way. However, the degree to which nonwhite children are accepted varies, says Lucy Steinitz. Acceptance may be influenced by the location of an individual family's community, the age of its members, the mix of traditional versus nontraditional families, and the school the child attends. It may also depend on the adoptee's birth heritage. There is often greater comfort, in any community, in welcoming people whose appearance, life experiences, and values are similar to members of the community. In the Jewish community, Eastern European or Asian children, because of stereotypes of their birth cultures, may be more easily welcomed and integrated than African American or other children with dark skin. Richard and Carol, whose son is from India, were cautioned by a rabbi that a dark-skinned child might encounter prejudice from both the secular and Jewish communities. Although Jeff has been accepted at their synagogue and his Jewish day school, older Jews, assuming he's African American and not realizing that he is a member of his Caucasian family, have called him "schwartze" [Yiddish for "black," and often used in a derogatory manner].

Even extended family members may wonder whether a child's appearance will affect his or her acceptance into the Jewish community. One grandmother was concerned about "how slanted" a Korean child's eyes would be and another worried about the darkness of a Colombian child's complexion. Both questions represented only ignorance and a fear of the unknown; once they saw their new grandchildren, both women accepted them unconditionally. Most grandparents and family members eventually love and accept their transracially adopted grandchildren, although some do so without realizing that prejudiced comments about any minority group are hurtful. Ken's mother makes prejudiced comments about gays and lesbians; he wonders what she really thinks about her adopted grandchildren. Richard's father calls African Americans "schwartze," not understanding that the word is denigrating to all people of color. Jeff, however, understands, and asks what his grandfather thinks of him and of people of color. Carol tells him the truth: His grandfather loves him very much, but hasn't had experience with, and therefore isn't very comfortable with, anyone who is different from himself.

Some children of color are more comfortable and identify more closely with people who are racially or culturally like them, Abby Ruder says. Some Jewish parents may find this difficult, especially if they would prefer to ignore the racial difference between themselves and their child. Pat's son, Noam, is a dark-skinned Mayan Indian from El Salvador. In high school, he finds it difficult to find Jewish girls who will date him and his best friends are the only two African American boys in his class. He says he doesn't feel Jewish, which Pat hopes is simply a passing phase. Although Jeff knows that East Indians are Caucasians, he is aware that many people assume he is African American. As the only child of color in his Jewish day school, he has expressed the desire to have a black friend. Carol and Richard want to provide opportunities for Jeff to meet other children of color so that he can also share that aspect of his identity. These are complex issues for adoptive families, and adoptive parents may want to think about discussing alternatives with a trained counselor.

Even as transracial adoption becomes more common in the Jewish community, children of color remain a minority. In some synagogues, there is a single child of color; in large metropolitan cities, there may be a handful of transracially adopted children. There may be tension around their racial or cultural differences which, while usually unaddressed, are often felt. Jill's daughter, Adina, who was born in India, is the only person in their synagogue with black skin. She considers herself black and definitely feels "the odd man out," Jill says. This was reinforced by several young religious school classmates, who informed her that she isn't Jewish because she has dark skin. Upon witnessing the incident, her teacher seized the moment for education, and initiated a classroom discussion about racial and ethnic diversity within the Jewish community. On Purim, another teacher explained that of all the girls in the class, Adina looked the most like Queen Esther.

Searching for Solutions

Because they have adopted a child who is racially or culturally different from themselves, parents will have a shared experience of being a minority family, explains Abby Ruder. Though never wise, it is easier in a same-race adoption to pretend that the child was born to the family. In a transracial adoption, however, it is impossible to hide the family's diversity, which can make it easier to embrace the child's birth heritage. Probably few adoptive parents will have shared Sara's experience. An inquisitive friend, taking her first peek at Malka, newly arrived from China, asked her: "Are you going to tell her that she's adopted?" Sara, incredulous, thought the comment comical, and adds that she plans to share as much as possible with Malka about her birth heritage.

Adoptive parents need to prepare their children for the reality that prejudice exists in the world, Ruder says; children need to know that some people will not like them or will make assumptions about them because of the color of their skin or the shape of their eyes. This is difficult for children to understand, and adoptive parents will have to begin when their children are still quite young to prepare them to fight prejudice and stereotypes. Research has shown that children begin to have racial awareness between ages three and four, and begin to perceive judgments and values associated with racial characteristics by age five. Adopted children of color need to understand that the problem is not theirs; it belongs to those who are prejudiced.

In order to help their child deal with the multiplicity of challenges he or she will face, adoptive parents need to learn what it means to be a person of color in our culture, Ruder says. Although Jews are a minority in the United States, they are, for the most part, a privileged minority. Many are able to control their exposure to prejudice and anti-Semitism, carefully choosing to live, work, and play in places that are comfortable and accepting. Their Jewish heritage is not physically obvious; many have never experienced the true impact of being a member of a minority in the way a person of color does in this society. Adoptive parents who are members of the dominant culture can increase their awareness of their child's experience by placing themselves in situations where they are in the minority and their child is in the majority, Ruder suggests.

Transracially adopted children need to be able to function in the world as people see them; they have to know how to respond as a person of color, she adds. Rare is the child who, like Harvey and Donna's daughter Carla, can announce at her Bat Mitzvah that her goal is to be the first Korean Jewish woman astronaut. The challenge for adoptive parents is to raise children like Carla, who believe they can be whatever they choose.

Ruder believes that this can happen best when a child has frequent opportunities to experience his or her birth culture, sometimes without the buffer of the adoptive parents' presence. She recommends building strong connections and friendships with members of the child's birth heritage who can assist parents in learning about being a member of a racial minority and model positive aspects of their culture as well as how to deal with prejudice.

Individuals who are stimulating, successful and, therefore, empowering role models from the child's birth culture may also help a child learn about and strengthen the connection to his or her birth identity. Although it may not be possible to find role models from the child's birth culture who are also Jewish, Ruder says that members of many cultural groups are often interested in helping adoptive parents who want to strengthen their child's cultural identity. The child can be introduced to professionals and friendly members of his or her birth community. Parents willing to become acquainted with members of other racial and cultural groups learn firsthand about issues of concern not only to their child's cultural group, but to other minorities. Moreover, they demonstrate through their actions that people of many cultures and countries are valued in their family.

Adoptive parents in multicultural families have an added responsibility to teach their children about racial and cultural discrimination, and to model for them rejection of prejudice of any kind, Ruder adds. This includes pejorative comments about their child's, or any other racial, ethnic, or religious group. By emphasizing the value and contribution of minority communities, parents can teach acceptance of people without regard to gender, age, disability, or sexual orientation. Children also need assistance in learning to handle discrimination in safe and empowering ways. They may then be able to serve as role models for others, which can also build a child's self-esteem.

Visiting Israel can also be an extremely positive experience for Jewish children of color. Jeff was thrilled to see other dark-skinned Jews strolling the streets of Tel Aviv, and the family visited an Indian *moshav* near Be'ersheva. This made the connection between his Judaism and his Indian birth very real and very positive, and he left Israel feeling proud of both streams of his heritage.

Sibling Rivalry with a Twist

While adoptive parents are concentrating on the challenges their transculturally adopted child presents, they may inadvertently be ignoring the other children in the family, especially if they either were not adopted or were not adopted transracially or transculturally. They may not be as happy about having a new sibling as their parent imagines or would like them to be. They may resent or be embarrassed at suddenly having a sibling of a different culture or race. Realizing even more acutely than their parents the amount of prejudice in their world, they may be unwilling or unhappy to have to defend the new child in the family. The sibling's culture of origin may seem different and strange, and they may not wish to involve themselves in it or may question why it should be included in their family's Jewish rituals.

Parents can not assume that siblings will bond with one another just because the parent wishes it. Those who are preparing to adopt transculturally or transracially should consider how to ready the other children in the family for the challenges they will face. Discussion of their feelings, questions, and fears prior to their new sibling's arrival can help ease the transition. After a new sibling has begun to settle into the family, ongoing family discussions can be useful to work out acceptable methods of handling any conflicts that may arise.

Some adoption professionals recommend adopting more than one child of color. Biological siblings who are adopted together have the added security of having a member of the family who looks like them, and to whom they are related by blood. They may also be able to bring a part of their early family history to their new family, which can ease their adjustment (Smith, 1994, p. 3). Children from the same country or culture may be able to communicate with one another in their native language, and may recognize comfortable cultural similarities in one another. Children who are adopted from different cultures will become members of a family that feels like an international community in which every culture and every individual is honored.

Still a Minority

Although transracial and transcultural adoption has become more common in the Jewish community, Jewish children of color remain a minority in synagogues, Jewish day schools, youth groups, and camps. There may be only a single multicultural Jewish family in many communities, and some adoptive parents say that their family "just doesn't quite fit." Others have selected their neighborhood and synagogue deliberately, seeking relationships with other Jewish families of color.

While overt prejudice is the exception, adoptive parents fear problems as their children become teens and young adults. Whom will they date? Whom will they marry? Worried that "mainstream" Jewish families will not accept their children, many believe that their children may not marry Jews. Rabbi Gold, however, counsels patience. He believes that, as converts of all kinds are entering the community and the community is becoming more diverse, what it means to look Jewish is changing.

In the meantime, Jewish family service agencies, synagogues, and schools can welcome and work with families as they wrestle with the issues of cross-cultural adoption. Programs highlighting cultural diversity within the Jewish community and post-placement services specifically tailored to their needs and issues can provide a forum for discussing their special challenges and opportunities. Stars of David, a national support group for all Jewish families who have adopted, with chapters in many cities throughout the United States, counts many multicultural families among its members.

With increasing numbers of transculturally and transracially adopted children joining the American Jewish community, the community has the opportunity to recognize and celebrate the value that multicultural diversity can bring to it. "We can create new dialogue with other minority communities, adopting an attitude of discovery and building new bridges of trust and alliance," Abby Ruder says.

CHAPTER 6

Three Times Different: Disabilities, Adoption, and Judaism

⁀

Disability, adoption, and Judaism are all things that make a person different. "Three times different" can present many complex challenges for this special group of Jewish adoptees and their families.

Adoptive families confront issues that families formed biologically do not face, including loss, grief, control, and the search for identity. These same issues also confront people with disabilities. They may have lost some physical or mental ability, which may produce grief or anger. They may have to struggle for control over their daily routine, coping with medical, physical, and educational questions that others don't face.

Certain disabilities, including mental retardation, blindness, deafness, and orthopedic disabilities, are usually known to and accepted by adoptive parents prior to a child's placement. They may feel willing and even eager to adopt such a child, especially because some of these children were born Jewish. Since the 1980s, almost the only Jewish children placed for adoption are those with severe disabilities or other special needs. Some families consider it a special mitzvah to adopt Jewish children who might otherwise be placed outside the Jewish community. Once such children are adopted into the Jewish community, their parents must face, in addition to the daily challenges of living with a disabled child, the challenge of refusing to allow their children to become invisible to their spiritual community or their community to become invisible to them.

But what if the disabilities themselves are "invisible" and unexpected by adoptive parents? Lacking medical and genetic information about their child's birth family, many adoptive parents believe they are adopting a healthy child. But this may not be the case. Professionals in the fields of mental health, education, and adoption now recognize that adopted children, even those placed as infants, are at risk for a variety of psychological and learning problems, many of which may not surface until the child starts school. Then, caught by surprise and unprepared for the special challenges facing them, adoptive parents may find it difficult to accept their child's disability. The discovery that their child is not "healthy" may reopen old wounds from their unresolved struggle with infertility. They may be confused, wondering what happened to their "perfectly normal" baby. They may blame themselves, believing they were not meant to be parents after all. They may be angry or grief stricken at yet another surrender of control. They may feel cheated yet again, by fate and the loss of the dream this child was meant to fulfill. Or they may be in denial, refusing to acknowledge problems and to seek help for themselves and their child. The adoptees themselves may not have the psychological capacity or coping skills to enable them to fully understand the complex issues involved in adoption. Instead they may believe that their disability was the reason their birth parents "gave them away."

Is it any different for Jewish adoptive families? Is Judaism a source of strength or a source of additional pain? In the Jewish community, among the "People of the Book," who so highly prize learning, children with disabilities may have to struggle for acceptance if they can not achieve academically. As one boy explained, "First, I had to be adopted. Then, I had to have a disability. Being Jewish is different, too. It's hard."

Joining a Different Club: Adopting a Child with a Visible Disability

"You join a different club when you adopt a child with a [visible and severe] disability. It isn't less fun or less *nakhus* [joyful], it's just different," explains Vicki Krausz, the adoptive parent of a child with a disability and the founder/director of the Jewish Children's Adoption Network in Denver, Colorado, an adoption exchange that specializes in finding adoptive Jewish homes for Jewish children. This club is small and exclusive, because few people begin the adoption process with the intention of adopting a child with a disability. "Parents who adopt a disabled child are probably not adopting for the first time, Krausz says, because "people usually want to get through adoption the kind of child they assume they would have gotten through birth." The second time people adopt, they may be more relaxed, having found one child to "fulfill the dream," and therefore, they may also be able to be more giving. They may also be more realistic about the difficulties in finding a child to adopt.

Eighty-five percent of the children Krausz places have a disability or other special need. Although some Jews would like to believe that Jewish people don't place their children for adoption or face the termination of their parental rights, they do, she says. Sometimes, a family is under stress before the birth of a child with a disability. Parents may be ill themselves or there may be drug or alcohol abuse. Parental rights may be terminated because of incompetence, abuse, or neglect. Other children come from married, middle-class Jewish couples who place their child for adoption because the child has a disability, such as Down's syndrome, hydrocephalus, or minimal brain damage. Because of the widespread use of birth control, prenatal testing, and abortion, fewer children are born with severe disabilities. However, a child with such a mental or physical disability may not fit into what some Jewish parents envision as the ideal, or even acceptable, family, report many Jewish adoption professionals. "Some mem-

bers of the Orthodox community [which does not accept artificial means of birth control or abortion] have an inherent inability to accept anything less than perfection, since they believe we
were created in the image of God," says Rabbi Eliezer Goldstock,
national director of Heart to Heart, The American Jewish
Society for Distinguished Children in Brooklyn, New York, a
transition agency that works mainly with Orthodox children
born with Down's syndrome. This organization attempts, first,
to encourage the birth parents to keep their child and to help
support them if they do. If this is not possible, the agency will
find an observant Jewish home. "If a child isn't perfect, these
families can't accept and embrace him or her. I find this tragic,
since I never thought of *Yiddishkeit* as requiring a minimum level
of intelligence."

Yet there are Jewish families who are willing and happy to
adopt children with special needs. Ruth's adopted daughter,
Deborah, was born with cerebral palsy. Although her Jewish
birth parents kept her for approximately a year, they were unable
to cope with the demands of a severely disabled child. And in
their close-knit, religious community, Deborah's presence was a
source of tremendous shame and embarrassment. They told
everyone that she was "a vegetable," and placed her in a home for
children with disabilities, Ruth says. "I feel sorry for her parents.
Had they allowed themselves the time and serenity, they would
have discovered that she was a thriving beautiful flower who
needed hothouse care to blossom. But you can't judge others;
everyone has limitations and being able to care for Deborah was
theirs. Their loss was our gain."

When Deborah was about six years old, the home arranged for
her to visit Ruth's family for Passover. By the time the holiday
was over, Ruth and her husband knew they wanted to adopt her.
They already had two biological children, and although they had
not even been thinking about adoption, they responded immediately and emotionally. "We saw a little girl who needed a fam-

ily and we reacted with our hearts, not our intellect," Ruth remembers. "We fell in love with her and she with us. I can't imagine not having adopted her.

"We knew we wanted her and wanted to do our best for her, but we had no idea what that meant," Ruth says. "We were novices; we felt so lost and no one knew how to help us. We had her IQ tested, and she tested as marginally retarded. But in terms of being astute and perceptive about people, she's very bright. We went from place to place and got her enrolled in a special school, which was a wonderful experience. We got some therapy and some surgery, and we wish we could have done more."

The usual keys to parenting a child with a disability are appropriate preparation and expectations, a lot of the first and a limited amount of the second, says Peggy Soule, an adoptive parent and the executive director of Children Awaiting Parents, Inc., in Rochester, New York, which recruits adoptive families for "the most difficult-to-place children" throughout the country. It is important for parents to know as much as possible about the child and the diagnosis. They need to do their homework, learning about the disability as well as both the short- and long-range prognosis. They should ask detailed and explicit questions of doctors, therapists, educators, and social workers about the specifics of the child's condition. They can also learn by reading, observing, and talking to other parents of children who have the same or a similar disability. They can then approach adoption with a realistic idea of what they will be able to give and what can be achieved by the child.

It is not helpful for adoptive parents to harbor illusions about the child's abilities and recovery, agrees Vicki Krausz. "People need to come to grips with the reality of the child. Some people believe they can 'fix it all.' But some things can't be fixed, and parents need to be realistic about the diagnosis and prognosis. They need to be able to feel good about doing the best they can, and not blame themselves for not doing what they can't do."

Adoptive parents should scrutinize themselves, their experiences, and their responses to people with disabilities to determine how they are likely to respond as a parent of a child with a disability, recommends Barbara Tremetiere, Ph.D., adoption specialist and consultant for Tressler Lutheran Services in York, Pennsylvania, and the parent of fifteen children, twelve of whom were adopted. "When people adopt children with significant disabilities, they know what they're in for and the adoptions usually don't disrupt."

"Expectations of children with disabilities must be measured with a different yardstick," Peggy Soule adds. "These parents may not get the rewards they wish for, or the rewards they get may come much later. They need to be able to reap their rewards in other ways, take satisfaction from small steps. If parents can do this, the rewards can be incredible. The joy is in trying to provide a better quality of life and in knowing you are making a difference in a child's life."

"Don't put pressure on a child with a disability for genius, education, or success," adds Rabbi Eliezer Goldstock. "An adoptive parent should have three standards in mind: good character and ethics, a pleasing personality, and the tenacity to complete what is begun." If the child accomplishes these things, the parents can be pleased.

Sometimes, however, people are not as well prepared as they think they are. Joyce and Alan were not prepared for the severity of their son Mark's problems, and did not, at first, appropriately adjust their hopes and expectations. "We knew he had developmental delays, that his mother was an addict, that he was in foster care because she'd abused him, and that he was in a special class when we adopted him at age three," Joyce says. "But there was such symbolism in adopting a child with special needs. We were given the impression that we were wonderful, that we were doing a mitzvah by saving a life. There was also the tremendous burden and expectation that we would perform a miracle.

But we couldn't and didn't. We were in over our heads and got no help from the agencies. It was supposed to be like a fairy tale, and this was reinforced by the Jewish community."

The reaction of the Jewish community to people who adopt children with severe disabilities is mixed, Goldstock points out. "A segment of the population looks at us as *tzaddikim* [righteous people]; a segment thinks we're fools; a segment despises us because they didn't manage the same challenge as well, and so they are taking out their anger at themselves on adoptive parents; and a segment thinks they can do it and they do."

People who adopt children with significant disabilities need to learn a great deal about special education, disability law, therapies and treatments. They learn to be advocates for their children in all of these spheres. They also need to know how to take care of themselves, as individuals and as a couple, Peggy Soule emphasizes. Families and friends can act as a support system for them by providing a much needed respite when overworked parents need a break; they can also help the family to feel good about itself. Support groups, whether focused on adoption or the disability, Jewish or secular, can offer helpful information, useful suggestions, or just a friendly ear.

Does it matter to the Jewish community whether or not severely disabled children are adopted within the community? Some argue that religion should not be a priority when searching for an adoptive home for a child with severe disabilities. Others, however, believe that Judaism makes a difference in the child's life, and that the child, in turn, makes a difference to the community. As in any adoption decision, the best interests of the child must be the deciding factor.

"We don't know what goes on in the mind of a disabled child," Ruth says. "Although my daughter's body and mind might be afflicted, her soul isn't handicapped. When a child with special needs sees Sabbath candles, the same warmth and feeling that is transmitted to other Jews is transmitted to her. She might not be able to verbalize it, but the same manifestation of spirituality that exists for me exists for her."

A strong positive identity can be important and comforting to adopted children who have a disability. "Judaism is wonderful for helping to build identity; it is very symbolic, very ritualistic, and very evident in the home," Ruth says. "The child with special needs can participate on an equal footing with everyone else. Her *berakhah* [blessing] is the same as the *berakhah* of a person who doesn't have a disability. Judaism is an equalizer, an identifier, a self-esteem builder; she knows that God made her a member of this people, so she is necessary."

Invisible Disabilities: Unexpectedly Joining the Club

When adoptive parents discover that their child has a disability that is not immediately obvious and initially went undiagnosed, they find themselves unexpectedly joining a club with a different and unique set of challenges. Most often, this invisible disability is attention deficit disorder. ADD, often accompanied by hyperactivity (ADHD), is the most common childhood psychiatric condition, accounting for half of all referrals to mental health clinics for children. It is even more common among adopted children. Children with ADD are easily distracted, have difficulty following rules and directions, demonstrate poor impulse control, and often have boundless undirected energy. This condition may also be accompanied by learning disabilities, Tourette's syndrome, obsessive-compulsive disorder, and oppositional defiant disorder. An inherited condition, ADD occurs in approximately 3 to 5 percent of the general population; among adoptees, the incidence has been estimated as high as 20 to 40 percent (Melina, 1990, p.1).

"While the vast majority of adoptees do well in all ways, adoption puts some of them at risk for certain psychological problems, even with an infant placement," explains David Brodzinsky, Ph.D., associate professor of Clinical and Developmental Psychology at Rutgers University. He is co-author, with Marshall Schechter, MD, and Robin Henig, of *Being Adopted: The Lifelong Search for Self.* "Mental health professionals see adoptees at a much higher rate than they would expect; it is quite statistically significant and important to know about. Although adoptive parents are probably quicker to use support services because they've had experience doing so, that doesn't account for the higher incidence of referrals."

"I see many patients who are adopted and have ADD," says Dr. Arthur D. Sorosky, clinical professor of psychiatry at the University of California and one of the authors of *Adoption Triangle.* "The population of birth parents is at high risk for having attention and impulse control problems. ADD is a highly hereditary problem, so their children are more likely to have ADD."

The consequences of having ADD and learning disabilities include poor self-esteem, immaturity, trouble with cause and effect connections in daily life, deficits in social judgment and peer relations, poor impulse control, and difficulty modulating emotions. According to Sorosky, Brodzinsky, and Schechter, these personality traits often account for an unplanned pregnancy, and so the birth parents may pass on a genetic predisposition for these problems to their children.

The nature of such a pregnancy itself also increases the chances for problems, they add. When the birth mother is quite young the intrauterine environment may be less than optimal for neurological development. In trying to hide an unplanned pregnancy, she may avoid or delay obtaining prenatal care or making lifestyle changes that would benefit the fetus. Poor nutrition, drugs, and alcohol increase the risk of central nervous system damage. The high stress of such a pregnancy may also be detrimental to the fetus and can alter its neurological development.

"Enormous strain can produce certain chemicals which the child receives in utero from the birth mother. The child comes into the world sensitized to various stresses and with the potential to react to anything that, after birth, produces stress. The child is then placed in a different environment, with parents who aren't aware of the child's general reaction capabilities, as they would be with blood relatives, and who may react inappropriately, as far as the child is concerned," Schechter says.

Gordon and Marlene tell a story similar to that of many adoptive parents. "When our adoption counselor asked if we would adopt an older child or one with mental, emotional, or physical disabilities, we said 'no.' We both work with children with disabilities, and we wanted to come home to a normal healthy infant. That is what we thought we got," Marlene recalls. "When Danny was placed with us as an infant, we received virtually no information about his birth parents. Nothing was available, other than that they were teenagers who had dropped out of school."

By the time he was three, Danny had begun to display problems that would later be diagnosed as attention deficit disorder [ADD]. He wouldn't follow directions and couldn't play appropriately with other children. He was so disorganized that in kindergarten the teacher emptied his desk onto the floor and made the whole class wait while he cleaned up. Still, diagnosis took several more years and many doctors. "When we adopted, nothing indicated problems to us; no one talked about any problems," Marlene adds. "Maybe we were naive, especially given our careers, but even when Danny started having problems, no one ever told us about the connection between attention deficit disorder and adoption. We were idealistic and operating on denial. We would have liked to have known about the genetic connection; maybe we could have gotten him the right help sooner. I feel guilty, yet I know we've done everything possible.

"We know a whole group of parents—we had a support group—who adopted babies from the same agency—a well-known, reputable national adoption agency—at about the same time. All of the boys have significant problems, yet none of us knew anything about their histories or about ADD. We adore our son, so it's not that we wouldn't have adopted. But maybe we could have done better for him—and things might have been easier on us, too."

Because the child's temperament will be more like that of the biological parents than the adoptive parents, there is greater likelihood of a "mismatch" between them, adoption experts agree. In intellectual potential, personality, interests, and talents, a child is likely to resemble the birth parents. And he or she is likely to have inherited the very traits—impulsivity, low self-esteem, deficits in social judgment, poor impulse control—that may have led to the unplanned pregnancy in the first place. Adoptive parents, on the other hand, are likely to be organized, focused, and methodical, just the sort of people who can persevere through the difficult process of adoption. This particular mix of parent and child can create a certain level of tension in the home, Arthur Sorosky says. Although "poor fit" can occur in biological families as well, there are usually recognizable similarities that link a biological child to a relative. But in adoptive families, such behavior can seem foreign and strange.

"My [adopted] daughter had learning disabilities and she hated school. My [adopted] son, too, had learning problems, was very negative and didn't want to study," Philip recalls. "I'm a doctor, so there was a lot of pressure on my kids, even though I tried not to pressure them. It was clear that we valued education."

"My older son once told me that he wished he was my biological child because then he'd have our brains. He said that we're smart and he's not," Marjorie remembers. "The younger one's birth parents were alcoholics and did drugs. He has an intolerance to alcohol. He's dropped out of college—although he could learn, he never seemed to try or to live up to his ability—and he's been in trouble with the law."

"I found my birth parents, and feel I have more in common

with them than with my adoptive parents," Larry says. "My dad and I are both alcoholics, we're impulsive, and we've both been married and divorced several times."

Nature Versus Nurture

The debate over the influence of nature and the power of nurture has touched adoptive families as long as families have been adopting. Adoption professionals used to inform adoptive parents that nurture was everything. They told them that their baby would come to them a blank slate on which they could inscribe the past, present, and future of the child's life. Parents did not need to know or worry about the child's birth family because environment was the all-important influence. "We used to think that you could wipe the slate clean, so you shouldn't taint a child's development by giving a full history," says Myra Hettleman, LCSW-C, director of Adoption Alliances of the Jewish Family Services of Central Maryland, Inc., in Baltimore. Other than serious and obviously inheritable diseases that often made a child ineligible for placement, nothing else was researched or reported.

For their part, adoptive parents were more than ready to accept the primacy of environment, especially as fewer and fewer infants became available for adoption. Jewish families, especially, prided themselves on their ability to provide not only an adequate but an excellent environment, providing their child with every opportunity. Love, they believed, could conquer all. On the other hand, some people argued that nature was ultimately the determining factor of a child's success, a rationale usually embraced when an adoption was disrupted for some reason. In such cases, blame could be placed on "the bad seed" from which the child had come, and about which the adoptive parents could do little. Some adoptive parents selectively accepted both positions, crediting environment for everything they liked about their child and blaming genetics for everything they didn't.

In our own day, we have come to recognize the different contributions that both nature and nurture make to human development. Adoption professionals now counsel adoptive parents that biology and environment influence and interact with one another to create each unique human being. As science has expanded our understanding about how much and what kind of personal abilities, disabilities, attributes, and behaviors we inherit from our biological relatives, we have come to recognize that heredity is more important than we once thought. Because adoptive parents are only able to influence the nurture portion of the equation, it is important that they understand what role nature has played in forming their child.

"There is an interface between biology and the environment," explains David Brodzinsky. "There is a distinct benefit to knowing what influences a child's development, since knowledge gives power. A parent is able to have more realistic expectations about him- or herself as a parent and about his influence on a child's life. With a better sense of who a child is, the parent has a better chance to meet the child's needs."

"Today, we know that adoptive parents should find out as much as possible about their child's history so that, if necessary, they can intervene early and effectively," Myra Hettleman says. "However, they must not be frightened or imprisoned by negative information. Rather, they must balance responsible paying attention with not overreacting. They should assess [the child's development] and consult a professional if it seems indicated."

"Long-term beliefs about adoption—that one can just love the child and deny the birth family—plus the highly tuned hopes of adoptive parents handicap the adoptive family if they are unable to look at a child realistically," agrees Sherry Anderson, MSW, program director of Family Connections, run by the Three Rivers Adoption Council in Pittsburgh, Pennsylvania. "Adoptive families are extremely vulnerable; we need to get them the help they need."

What precisely do adoptive families need? They need to develop a realistic picture about the ramifications of nature and the curative power of nurture. Adoptive families do best when they recognize both and don't feel guilty or defeated by either. "You have to work with who the child is," explains Barbara Tremetiere. "Children will be themselves and environment can help them, within the parameters of who they are, be the best they can be." That, of course, is all any parent can hope for. With an adopted child, however, it's hard to know what those parameters are.

Learning the Parameters

Adoptive parents can understand their child better by obtaining as complete a history of their child's birth family and genetic background as possible. In contrast to past practice, most adoption professionals now inform adoptive parents of the importance of acquiring such information. The guidebook *Medical Genetics Services for Adoptive Parents: A Guidebook for Adoptive Parents*, one in a series of booklets for adoptive parents, explains that: "Every child's medical history begins long before birth. It includes not only the circumstances of that pregnancy, labor, and delivery but also the health and habits of both biological parents. An individual's history is also related to the lives of other members of the immediate family and more distant relatives. A family history can provide information that makes a diagnosis possible, and a diagnosis leads to appropriate treatment and services" (Shryer, Lawry, and Kepple, 1991, p. 1).

"Everyone may find a time when they need birth family genetic information," agrees Joan Burns, MS, MSSW, director of the Genetic Counseling Training Program and clinical professor in the Department of Medical Genetics at the University of Wisconsin-Madison. Burns chaired the Council of Regional Networks of Genetics Services (CORN) Genetics and Adoption Subcommittee, which developed one of the first comprehensive medical/genetic family history forms intended for use in adoptions. The CORN form consists of a one-page pregnancy care form, a one-page delivery and birth information form, and two seven-page medical/genetic family history questionnaires, one to be completed by each birth parent with the help of a trained professional counselor. The forms, generated by professionals actively participating in genetics clinics, request information on all blood relatives. Recognizing that a wide variety of medical, mental, and emotional conditions, as well as characteristic traits and habits, are inherited "helps explain developing problems that an adoptee might be having, helps avoid the consequences of a genetic predisposition to a condition, and helps in an adult adoptee's own reproductive planning," Burns says. She trains genetic counselors to gather the necessary information from birth parents and to act as a support for adoptive families, explaining and clarifying the information they have acquired.

Explaining often complicated, newly available scientific information to adoptees can have a significant impact on their lives. It has been shown, for example, that heredity is the number one determinant of osteoporosis, but without proper diagnostic procedures a woman might not realize she is at risk. If an adoptee is aware that her birth mother and grandmother had this condition, she can take preventative steps. Certain cancers can also be linked to genes; it is not unusual to see more than one family member with colon cancer, ovarian cancer, or a certain type of breast cancer. Early detection, more likely if one's history is known, is critical and can offer prevention options. Other diseases, such as hemophilia and Duchenne's muscular dystrophy, are carried by the mother but affect only a son. Endometriosis and polycystic ovarian disease, which causes irregular periods and sometimes excessive hair growth, may also have a hereditary component. Diabetes and heart disease run in families, but aren't directly inherited. (Linda George, "Like Mother, Like Daughter . . . ", *Jewish Exponent*, July 25, 1996.)

Medical records can also reveal such conditions as fetal alcohol syndrome (FAS) and fetal alcohol effect, which can cause many more problems than adoptive parents ever imagined possible, says David Soule, a pediatrician and adoptive parent. Fetal alcohol syndrome can usually be recognized by classic facial features that include a long narrow upper lip, a small head, small eye openings, a short turned-up nose, and no groove between the nose and lip. Generally, these children demonstrate at least mild mental retardation, but that's only the tip of the iceberg, according to Soule.

Although children with fetal alcohol effect lack the telltale facial features of FAS children, they do display a spectrum of cognitive delays. The nature and extent of these delays are dependent upon when during her pregnancy the birth mother used alcohol: The face develops early in a pregnancy; the brain develops throughout. These children may be socially adept, but they usually do not mature emotionally, and their mental processes do not progress. They are very concrete; they do not abstract, learn from experience, conceptualize, or plan for the future. In other words, Soule explains, "they don't grow up. . . . They can be exceptionally difficult to deal with, but because they don't display the characteristic facial features, people don't recognize the problem and expect them to be okay. They may look and act normal until later; they are a time bomb waiting for their teen years."

It seems clear that adoptive parents have a compelling need to obtain their children's medical records. If this is not possible, they should familiarize themselves with medical/genetic history forms and be prepared to ask appropriate questions. It is important to know if an adoptee may develop or pass on genetic diseases such as sickle cell anemia, Tay Sachs, cystic fibrosis, or Huntington's chorea. And should an adoptee develop such a disease, the biological parents should be informed, for the sake of any future children they might have.

Adoptive parents need this information to do their best—

medically, educationally, emotionally, environmentally—for their children. Adoptees will want to know their medical and genetic histories in order to guard their own health and that of their future children. Both must remember, however, that possibilities and probabilities are not certainties. Adoptees are neither doomed to develop a certain disease or characteristic because a biological family member had it, nor guaranteed to remain free of it because they didn't.

Painful Questions . . . Difficult Answers

When an apparently healthy child, adopted as an infant with no obvious genetic abnormalities and no history of health problems, does develop an invisible disability, the issues they and their families confront are painful, says Sherry Anderson. Some of these issues may even be unfamiliar to many mental health professionals.

Adoptive parents who are completely unprepared for and unaware of the possibility that their child might have invisible disabilities face stress beyond that normally involved in adoption. In addition to the profound loss of their fertility and their dreams, they sustain additional loss and compounded grief when the child is revealed to have a disability, says Lois Melina. When these problems are unexpected, perhaps even unexplained, that grief can be coupled with anger, frustration, a sense of betrayal, and guilt.

"If the pain of infertility is not acknowledged, adoptive parents may face it when their child is diagnosed with ADD," adds Robin Allen, MSW, executive director of the Barker Foundation, an adoption agency in Cabin John, Maryland, which studied the overlap of adoption and ADD. "There is a complex interaction between the parents' experience in dealing with the adoption process and the child's dealing with ADD. We found we could point to several components of the adoption process that were permeating the process of dealing with ADD. The diagnosis of a disability repeats and recycles the old infertility issues; all of the original feelings and doubts reappear. Adoptive parents are, once again, dealing with systems—medical, educational, and psychological—whose jargon they may not understand. They are, once again, confronting decisions that their peers don't have to make. They are, once again, facing isolation, even from other adoptive parents. They may ask themselves why this had to happen to them, what their biological child would have been like, and why parenting seems so much easier for other people. And, once again, they may not be able to share these feelings with anyone, or even admit them to themselves."

Simultaneously, their adoptive children are articulating similar feelings, Allen says. Children may wonder whether they were placed for adoption because there was something wrong with them, whether one of their birth parents has a similar disability, whether their birth parents would understand better than their adoptive parents how difficult school is, whether their [adoptive] parents will be disappointed if they don't go to college, and whether they have [biological] siblings with the same disability. Anger at having been "given up" and at having a disability blends with the fear of failure and of disappointing parents they love, yet they may not feel comfortable sharing these feelings with their parents.

"These [adoptive parents] are competent folks and proud of it; they are survivors of the adoption process. They were told they could be whatever they wanted to be, but what can they tell their children?" she asks. "This is an attack on their sense of being a good parent and on their child's sense of self. Parents may need to revise their expectations and decide where their values lie. They can decide that their goals in life are being a good person, having loving relationships, and that academic success may or may not be as important as they thought. They will feel the loss, but a healthy relationship with their child and their child's emotional health is paramount."

To reach that point, adoptive parents must grieve the loss of their fantasy child, the one they had expected when they adopted, explains Sharon Kaplan Roszia, director of the Kinship Center in Tustin, California. This unexpected loss is additional, an overlay on top of the loss of infertility. It is the loss of a dream—for the second time. "Alan wanted a son who would sit beside him in synagogue, hide under his *tallit*, and play with the fringes. He wanted a certain kind of Jewish son, and he's dealt with a lot of loss," Joyce says. "It hasn't been quite as severe for me, but I've dealt with a lot of loss, too."

"Parents of adopted children with disabilities have to totally remove from their hearts the child they thought would grow into a certain kind of adult," Roszia suggests. "This will create a space in their hearts for the child they actually have. It may feel like a betrayal to the actual child, but they are betraying that child every day that they aren't wanting him for who he is. We get our packages in life in ways we didn't expect. But we can't open the new packages until we set aside the ones that weren't for us."

Adoptive parents may not feel supported by a Jewish community that is all too willing to accept the fiction, however inaccurate, that "Jews don't have these problems." As an especially family-oriented people, the Jewish community rejoices with the family who has successfully adopted. However, few outside the adoption circle realize that there is also loss and pain associated with adoption; they see only a family living "happily ever after." They do not expect and, therefore, do not know how to deal with problems that arise in what is supposed to be a happy situation. In addition, adoptive parents may be too embarrassed to admit they need help, ashamed that they are once again having problems in an area that their friends and colleagues are handling so well. "Shame was the biggest problem," admits Joyce. "The Jewish community is into denial. Maybe it's because, as a vulnerable people, we always had a stake in putting on a good face."

A further complication is the extent to which education and

career are barometers of success in the Jewish community. The "People of the Book," with their great admiration for learning and their strong emphasis on education, create the expectation, whether spoken or silent, that Jewish youth should excel academically, attend college, and walk an auspicious career path. Many adoptive parents embrace these expectations and thus may find it difficult to nurture a child who may not follow them down that path. When parents are faced with a child who does not meet the traditional definition of success they can experience embarrassment and denial, frustration, futility, and fear.

Myra Hettleman has worked with a group of Jewish adoptive mothers who spoke with difficulty about their children who were not achieving in the same way as their peers. Because these women were unprepared for this, they felt a sense of betrayal. They were also, they finally admitted, hesitant to turn back to the Jewish agency [which had placed their children with them] for help. They believed that the agency expected them to be perfect parents, not to have any problems. "We had no idea parents felt this way; we need to make adoptive families more comfortable," Hettleman says.

Mental and emotional preparation can help adoptive parents whose children may have an invisible and unexpected disability. "Intellectual ability was always a very valued and important attribute to me and my family," says Roger, a college professor whose adopted son has a learning disability. "However, I came to an emotional acceptance when we had our first child, who isn't adopted, that my role would be to love and nurture as best I can. This included the possibility that my child might not be academically oriented. I had this mindset for parenting, so in a sense, I was already psychologically prepared for my [adopted] son's problems."

It can be difficult for adoptive parents to achieve this level of acceptance. "People are so threatened; they want to make adoption into a perfect union. But adoption comes out of painful situations. We are trying to be realistic, not to attack adoption," Robin Allen says. "The beautiful picture of 'happily ever after' didn't serve us as well as the way we're training and preparing adoptive families now. We tell them that we see a higher incidence of disabilities in children who are adopted, and that they need to be even more responsible in dealing with their own feelings and getting help for themselves and their child." Adoptive parents may be resistant to this information, not wanting to believe it. Other families, however, have been angry that an agency did not properly prepare them. Allen believes it is important to tell people about these risks, to plant the possibility in their minds just in case.

Increasingly, as the unique and complex challenges facing adoptive families are recognized, adoption counselors are recommending that they seek professional support. They encourage adoptive parents to see such a step not as a sign of weakness, but as one of strength and flexibility. However, not all therapists have experience in working with adoption issues; even fewer recognize the overlay of disability issues and Jewish identity as significant factors. Finding an appropriate therapist or counselor can require some work, but some adoption agencies can help.

Parents can become advocates for their child within both the secular and the Jewish communities. They must educate themselves regarding their child's disability, treatment options, and legal rights. Within the secular community, the law provides for a free appropriate education for all children. Although the Jewish community provides no such guarantee, the leaders of synagogues and religious schools throughout the country have begun to recognize the needs of people with disabilities and these institutions are becoming more welcoming and accessible. However, some adoptive parents worry that there is a negative stereotype surrounding adoption, and fear that all adopted children are automatically seen as having problems. They hesitate to discuss their adopted child's disability for fear of confirming this view.

To prevent such stereotyping, adoptive parents can work with adoption professionals to sensitize rabbis, cantors, teachers, and others to an accurate picture of the relationship between adoption and disabilities. They can work together to make Judaism a source of comfort and strength to adoptees with disabilities and their families.

CHAPTER 7

One Plus One Equals . . . A Family: Singles Adopting

≈

A family used to mean a mother, a father, two children (preferably one of each sex), and either a cat or a dog. Not anymore. Nowadays, a family can consist of a single parent of either sex, one or many children of either sex, and it may or may not include the cat or dog. Unlike in the past, adoption agencies are not automatically refusing to place children with single parents. Adoption professionals have learned what singles have known all along: They can make very successful adoptive parents.

Because of the growing number of single-parent households, due to divorce and to unmarried women choosing to parent their children, as well as the large number of special needs children waiting for adoptive homes, adoption professionals have become increasingly willing to accept singles as adoptive parents. And single people are ready, willing, and able to adopt; many are anxious to share their lives with a child. Just because they have not found a partner with whom they choose to share their lives does not mean they lack the instinct or ability to parent. Studies have shown that children in single-parent families can do extremely well.

Single adoptive Jewish families share all of the same parenting issues and all of the adoption issues that other Jewish adoptive families face. They are as well equipped as couples to handle these issues. In fact, with their undiluted attention, energy, and love directed toward their child, they may be better prepared to cope with certain children's needs. Yet these parents face several issues that other adoptive parents do not.

First of all, although there are a large number of single-parent households, those formed by adoption remain a minority, a difference that may be distressing to children in these households. Also, both adoptees and single parents confront significant issues around loss and grief. Adoptees face the lifelong challenge of integrating the loss of their birth family into their identity. They may blame themselves for having been placed for adoption, wondering what they did to make their birth parents "give them away." When adopted by a single person, they may wonder about the absence of a mother or father in their adoptive family and worry that they did something to cause that. And single adoptive parents have experienced loss as well. They have lost the partner they may have expected to have, and the opportunity, whether or not they are infertile, of producing a biological child. While sharing the mutual sense of loss can be a common bond, helping the parent to understand the child's pain, it is still a loss. There remain difficult questions to confront.

Single adoptive parents experience the satisfaction and sadness of carrying out one of life's most complex challenges on their own. The demands of childrearing can be daunting even for two people; these solo parents are managing everything by themselves. And their accomplishment is even more impressive when they adopt children with special needs, such as learning, social, or emotional disabilities that place them up against the complexities of medical, educational, and legal systems with which most parents are unfamiliar. In addition, the parent-child relationship in a single-parent household, unbuffered by another close relationship for either party, can be extremely intense. It is important for single parents to arrange a helping network that can provide mental, emotional, and physical relief.

Within the Jewish community, singles may not receive much support when they express the wish to adopt. The expectation in the Jewish community, for the most part, remains traditional: that people will form heterosexual two-parent families. Most of the community's institutions still function that way. Their families and friends may also have difficulty understanding and accepting their desire, and may try to discourage them. Segments of the community that still retain circumscribed ritual roles for men and women, fathers and mothers, may give such unconventional families a hard time.

Thus, it may be more difficult for single-parent families with an adopted child to find their niche in the Jewish community. They may feel that they do not fit with singles who don't have children, nor do they quite fit with two-parent families. Yet these families need and want the support of a warm and accepting spiritual community. If the Jewish community can offer such families welcome and support, they can become full participating members.

The Decision to Adopt

Why would a single person, unattached and unfettered, want to trade his or her unlimited freedom for the responsibilities of raising a child? The answer, most single adoptive parents say, is easy. They want children for the same reasons most married people do. "Not getting married doesn't mean you forfeit the instincts to be a mom or a dad," says Elmy Martinez, president of Adoption Resource Exchange for Single Parents, Inc., in Springfield, Virginia, and adoptive father of five. Singles who adopt are mature, responsible people who have achieved success and stability, and recognize their own needs, says Hope Marindin, director of the National Council for Single Adoptive Parents, editor of *The Handbook for Single Adoptive Parents,* and the adoptive mother of three. And their need, she says, is to have a child.

"I always knew I wanted to raise a child. Giving birth was not important, so I easily decided to adopt when I didn't have a partner," says Shirley, who has an adopted daughter. Another adoptive mother, Gerrie, recalls that "as I approached my mid-forties, I was doing a great deal of self-exploration and I recognized that part of my feeling of incompleteness was my great desire to be a parent." Now the adoptive parent of a son, she says she realized that not all singles had this feeling and it made her think seriously about what she wanted out of life. Carlene, who has an adopted daughter, says, "I have a lot of friends, but I realized that I wanted to be more than a friend; I wanted to share my life with someone as family."

For singles who decide to adopt, the desire is often very intense. "Singles come to the decision to adopt later in life, when they realize they are not going to find a mate," says Marilyn Lustig, ACSW, adoption assessor for the Jewish Family Service of Dayton, Ohio. "Most who decide to adopt feel a calling; they say, 'I need to be a parent,' and that's what I need to hear. It isn't enough to want to 'save' a child; this isn't a job for a martyr." Adoption is not about saving a child, says Elmy Martinez. It changes the parent for the better, too. "I adopted for a very selfish reason: I wanted to be a dad. And I'm a very different person, a better person, than I was before I adopted. Sure we make a difference in our kids' lives, but they make a difference in our lives. It is wonderful to feel my kids' unconditional acceptance of me. You see, adoption has a special meaning for singles. Couples can survive without kids; they have each other. But singles are alone and our kids become everything for us."

Within the Jewish community, families are so important that "it is hard not to have children. It is what is expected for us to do," Lustig adds. There is almost a sense of communal obligation to fulfill the biblical injunction to "be fruitful and multiply," and to provide future generations of Jews. Singles who have the desire to parent realize that they can be a part of that. Through adoption, they can participate in what they have been missing. "I'm connected to the Jewish community, and there is a lot of communal energy spent around valuing family and raising children," Hilary explains. "I realized that I was missing something, and decided that if I wasn't married by a certain age, I'd have a child on my own. I wouldn't have chosen the situation I was in, but given the situation, I decided I would fulfill all the dreams I could and not wait for life to happen. I decided that I wanted my cup to be half full rather than half empty. I didn't feel like adoption was second rate. I wrestled with doing it on my own, and decided I felt strongly about it and capable of it."

Once singles make the decision to adopt, the process is easier and more successful than it once was. Prior to 1970, it was almost impossible for a single person to adopt. Since then, the number of single-parent families has ballooned and the number of children who are waiting for homes has also increased, and most agencies have realized that singles are a wonderful resource. However, many singles still think that they can't adopt, and agencies have not made recruiting singles a priority, Elmy Martinez says.

While there is less bias against singles than there once was, that does not mean that all obstacles have disappeared. After a home study, singles may be told that there are no children available, or that the only children who are available have a great many special needs. Ironically, Hope Marindin points out, single parents have traditionally been given older children, those with a disability, those who are part of a sibling group, or children with some other special need that makes them more difficult to place. And so, paradoxically, those adoptive parents who supposedly have the fewest resources are offered the most demanding children. Often, however, singles do adopt these difficult-to-place children, and create happy and stable families. Research shows that children raised in single-parent families "compare favorably with other adopted children and show a healthy involvement with friends and family, as well as in the activities of their age group. It is the instability of broken homes, rather than the absence of a parent that causes difficulty for a child." (Shireman and Johnson, 1985, pp. 332–333) This same study reported that although the single parents led busy lives, their parenting was consistent and of high quality, and they successfully managed the demands of jobs, home, and child care. The researchers also concluded that single-parent homes may be particularly well suited for children who need intense and close relationships, and thus particularly appropriate for many children with special needs for whom such a close bond may be a path to normal development.

How High Are the Hurdles?

Perhaps the highest hurdle and the greatest reward for single parents is the intensity of their relationship with their child. Everything, good and bad, is magnified. "Being a single adoptive parent, one on one, is a very intense relationship. It's wonderful, and it can sometimes be a tremendous strain," says Barbara Stern, CSW, a psychotherapist specializing in adoption and single-parent issues, the president of New York Singles Adopting Children, and the single adoptive parent of a daughter. "There is more tension because everything rests on you alone, and you are obligated to take on every issue," says Carlene. Hilary agrees: "You are aware that no one else in the world loves this child the way you do. When you are out in the world, you have to make all the decisions and speak for this child. You have both the limitations but also the strengths of your own decisions. It's clear that the decisions are yours. It's an excruciatingly lonely way of parenting, in both the good and the painful moments. But," she adds, "there are special and wonderful things about being single. There is the strong and special connection between us. When my daughter learned that I would be getting married, she said, 'These five years with just the two of us have gone so fast.'"

One way to ease this intensity is for single parents to identify a strong support network. An essential part of their preparation for adoption is finding people who can and will assist, both routinely and in emergencies. While high quality, paid child care is essential, it can only go so far. "The main thing I want singles to have is backup," says Marilyn Lustig. "It is hard to raise a child completely on one's own, because no one is prepared for that time when a child just cries and cries, and there's no one to turn to. Singles need to have someone who will drop everything and be there for them."

Single parents also benefit from a more extensive group of people who will be routinely involved in their child's life. "Singles need a broad group of people involved in their child's life," says Barbara Stern. "We need to have our own breaks, with and from our children," Elmy Martinez agrees. "You have to keep your own mental health in order to be there for your children. And sometimes, you need to be away from them."

Some singles have extended family to whom they can turn for help; others find that their family is less than fully supportive. The family may fear the unfamiliar territory that its loved one will be exploring. Such an attitude can be painful and discouraging to the single adoptive parent. "My family was nervous, but supportive," remembers Hilary. "They'd seen other successful adoptions, so they didn't think I was doing something freaky that no one else had ever done." "My parents retired and moved to my city to be a resource," Carlene says. "We lived together and they were wonderful with my daughter." However, Zelda's father stopped speaking to her for three months when she announced her plan to adopt. "He was worried about all of the practical issues," she says. Shirley faced a similar situation. "My mother cried for three days when I told her that I was going to adopt. I didn't understand her resistance, but she finally told me that she never knew a single parent and didn't know what it would be like for me. I told her that, now that I understood, we could work with this, and then I introduced her to other single parents."

Singles may want to wait to tell family members their plans until they are sure in their own minds what they want to do, says Barbara Stern, because "resistance can set you back." But once their decision is made, she advises taking the time and energy to educate them and "bring them along. . . . You can't expect them to be overjoyed immediately; they have a process to go through, too. If you know family members are going to be absolutely impossible, don't include them. If you can work with them at all, it's important to do that."

Jewish families may have special biases to overcome. They may not have accepted the idea that their son or daughter is not married, still a common expectation within the Jewish community. Adopting may seem to finalize that situation, and may even feel like an untenable burden. If the child has special needs, is older, or of a different race or culture, they may worry that the child will not comfortably fit into the community, as well as the family. Carlene recalls that her mother "saw only negatives and tried to discourage" her from adopting at first. "She worried about the child's background and health, the level of acceptance she would feel as a non-Caucasian in our family, and our ability to make her feel good about herself. She also worried about my ability to cope by myself."

Singles who don't have a support system agree that it is important to create one. After Carlene's parents died, she found the lack of support "the most frightening thing. It worries me that I might get sick. I've been trying to do everything myself." Hilary agrees and says that "making the logistics of daily life work is the hardest part about being a single parent. It's very stressful." Singles say that there are many places and ways to build a supportive network. "Because we are already a nontraditional family, we can more easily bring other people into the family," Elmy Martinez says. "They don't have to be blood relatives, because none of us are blood relatives. And it adds a richness to the family."

Adoption support groups specifically for singles are the best source of outside support, most singles say. "Other single friends are busy with their own lives and careers, and you can't rely on them. In most cases, like at work, you are a trailblazer," Gerrie explains. "You create a wonderful cocoon of singles in the early years," adds Zelda. "But when you have a child you are in the minority, both with the singles and with the parents of your child's friends, who are couples." In a singles' adoptive parent group, "you are all in the same boat, so people are a real source of help and comfort," Gerrie adds. "There is so much about parenting to talk and think about that it is really important to have someone to talk to. We run our meetings in a way that makes it safe for people to open up, bare their souls, and get support. It's not superficial," says Barbara Stern. "And it's real important for our kids to get to know each other and know that they are not alone in their situation." Rarely, however, are singles' adoption support groups Jewish, and the Jewish members usually find themselves in the minority. There are only about six Jewish families within Gerrie's group, so, she says, they are encouraging people within the group "to be like a *havurah* [a group of people who come together around a common interest] and do things with people who have the same special interest."

The Jewish Community and Singles

Many singles do not feel that they receive much support from the Jewish community. Hilary is one of the few to have a strong Jewish communal support group. She has belonged to a large and strong *havurah* for over twenty years, and has religious, cultural, and political roots in the group. Another family of *havurah*-members adopted a child from Peru, where Hilary's daughter, Rosa, was born, and gave her hope and support. "I was one of the few singles in the group and it gave me the opportunity to feel connected to families with children." After she adopted, the *havurah* remained, and continues to remain, a strong force in

Hilary and Rosa's lives. "I'm sympathetic to single people who feel shut out, but I think you have to make things happen for yourself. You have to validate yourself," she says.

"I do see a desire to be part of the Jewish community, but I also see some alienation from the community," says Lois Samuels, MSW, adoption coordinator for the Jewish Children's Bureau of Chicago. "Most singles have adopted transracially, and they are concerned about how their children will fit into the Jewish community." Jill, who is involved in her synagogue, explains that she knows very few Jewish single adoptive parents, mainly because "many who were Jewish joined other religions when they adopted their children, especially if the children were adopted from other countries or are biracial." They worry, she explains, about the response of the Jewish community to their children.

Many of these Jewish single adoptive parents emphasize how important support from the Jewish community is, or would be, to them. "Family tradition, community, and religion are anchors, additional ways of connecting to something," says Laura Zuckerman, co-president of the Single Adoptive Parents Support Group in the Chicago area, and the adoptive parent of a son. "I really value a Jewish connection. It adds richness, roots, meaning to a child's life. I see that my son hungers for it and responds so well." A connection to spirituality and community can greatly benefit an adopted child, who is searching for the missing pieces of him- or herself. And when the Jewish community fully accepts his or her child, it can help bond the parent to the community. Sometimes a bond that has been weakened over the years can now be reformed. "Synagogue was very important to me when I was growing up, but I left when there was no Bat Mitzvah available and I thought that was terribly unfair," Shirley, an adoptive parent, remembers. "Judaism remained important to me, and when I adopted my daughter it was imperative that she be converted and named in our synagogue. It was a major statement for me, a symbolic reentry into the community, and a way to make up for what I didn't have."

Single adoptive parents may have to work harder than others to find their place in the Jewish community. "I'm not the only single parent or the only adoptive parent," Jill says. "But I am the only single adoptive parent. And I'm older than other moms with children my daughters' ages. So it took some time for us to find our niche and be accepted, and there were still aspects of the synagogue, like the Mom-Tot Group, where I felt out of place. We were not openly rejected, but we didn't fit. The rabbi and the educational director were very helpful and supportive, but in general, synagogues are not very good at viewing singles as part of the community. Either people are matchmaking, or they treat us as if we are not quite grown-up. We are not treated as real members of the community, and the community doesn't have many structures for accepting singles, single parents, adoptive parents. There needs to be more sensitivity and ways to integrate people."

"Especially if you grew up in the synagogue, don't assume that all needs can be met in the traditional way if you are a nontraditional family," Carlene advises. "Be prepared that the Jewish community isn't always as open to nontraditional families as you would expect. Everybody talks about being supportive, but they don't do anything. There are not many single-parent families, and my daughter is the only transracial child. It has not been a welcoming place for us, and we don't feel like we're part of the synagogue community. The result is that my daughter is Jewishly identified, but not synagogue identified. We've had to find other supportive, nurturing communities."

Gerrie has had a positive experience in one Jewish community, and a negative one in another. She attributes it, as do other singles, to geography. "This community is so homogeneous and traditional, and we don't fit. Singles need to be very careful where they live." Barbara Stern agrees, and counsels singles that

geography—a place where there are a lot of single-parent families—makes a difference. She also suggests that attitude is important. "If you feel uncomfortable, people pick up on it. If you feel
confident, people pick up on that. Just jump in and do things,
and you'll just feel like a parent, rather than focusing on being a
single parent."

"I would like to see the Jewish community do more for singles," Zuckerman says. "Synagogues could sponsor groups for
singles and adoptive families, and members of the community
could be more sensitive to family diversity when they are talking
to children."

Where the Buck Stops

No matter how reliable and comprehensive their support system, singles are parenting alone. The parenting buck stops with
them. The lack of a role model of the opposite sex in the family
can be a compelling issue in any single-parent family. Because
the Jewish community continues, in many ways, to support traditional gender roles, single-parent households confront an additional burden. There may be no father to chant the *kiddush* or
mother to bless the candles. While many modern Jews have
moved beyond these stereotypes, their influence may remain
subtly present. For many single adoptive parents, such a role
model is a pivotal person to include in their support network.
Many feel the need to discuss with their child the absence of this
person in their lives and what it means to them. "The effect this
has on the children depends on how the parents handle telling
their children that their family is different. Usually, parents are
very aware that they're going to have to speak to their children at
a young age about the differences," Marilyn Lustig says. "Then
they're going to have to build their child's self-esteem, so that he
or she can handle whatever comes at them. They can read books
about adoption, have contact with other adoptees who have
nontraditional families so that it will be seen as normal and

good, and talk about their pain and their losses together."

"My daughter does feel the loss [of a dad], and that makes me sad, even though she has people in her life, both men and women, who love her," Shirley says. "We never say that someone is 'like a father,' because you can't replace a father. But she's created her own way of handling it. She calls the day care provider's husband 'dada,' even though she knows that he's not. But we talk about what parents do and who does those things for her. I do feel twinges sometimes and think that wouldn't it be nice if she didn't have to invent a father, but we all have some losses."

Gerrie says that her son really struggled with feelings that their family was somehow "incomplete, and that he wasn't getting the same thing as other kids . . . He was talking about not having a dad and was acting out in school. We had to deal with what a family is and that we are a family, and what adoption means to him. I went for counseling and got him counseling, and it was an enormous help to get support. He's trying to make a story for himself, so I get him to talk about his feelings on a regular basis and I write down what he says in a diary. We also role-play his feelings with dolls. I think these struggles are normal for what he had to deal with and I'm glad he could articulate his feelings. The more connected we became, the more the need for a dad has faded." Gerrie says that she has also provided her son with male role models: a male relative who lived with them for several months and the husband of a friend who spends some time with him. She recognizes that this kind of contact remains important to him, and she continues to seek it for him.

Carlene says that she and her daughter don't discuss the absence of an adoptive father, but that her daughter was always much more curious about her birth father than her birth mother. The presence of a male role model is important, Carlene believes, and a grandfather and male friends have filled that place in her daughter's life. "She has adopted friends who also have single mothers, which has helped her feel less alone or different. We have talked about adoption and I have allowed her to be very angry that she was abandoned, but have told her that I'd never do that." It is also important how the birth family is discussed, Carlene points out, because "a single parent can't say that a single parent can't take care of a child." It can be extremely difficult for children in single-parent families to understand why their single birth mother placed them for adoption.

Kids Who Remember

Single adoptive parents face additional challenges because they so often adopt children who are older or who have disabilities. This can be difficult in the Jewish community, because it is an additional way in which the child is different. "These children come with baggage; they've been rejected, sometimes several times, and they have emotional issues," says Gloria Hochman, communications director of the National Adoption Center in Philadelphia, Pennsylvania. "Parents will need patience to sort through the issues and the testing, and realism about the child's potential. You can't erase the past, so there may be limits to what adoptive parents can do." It is important, Elmy Martinez adds, to be especially willing to accept these children as they are. "They are open to learn and you can introduce things to them, but you have to remember that they have personalities. They will accept some of your values, as you accept them. There has to be mutual acceptance; I consider adoption a two-way street. We adopt our kids and they adopt us. Older kids have to consent to being adopted and have to want to accept us as their parent." He also tells single adoptive parents that they have to put aside their biases and misconceptions about children with special needs, gather information about their child's abilities and disabilities, and empower themselves to deal with them. He says that many children want a home so much that they'll make the best of any opportunity that they are given.

Information about the child's earlier life experiences can tell adoptive parents a great deal about what the child is doing currently. Gloria Hochman suggests that parents learn the details of their child's life and encourage their child to talk, since different children perceive experiences differently. It can be more difficult to integrate an older child who remembers his or her birth community, with its customs and traditions, into the Jewish community. However, some Jewish parents are able to create bridges between their child's birth heritage and adopted Jewish heritage. It may be possible to see similarities of customs and values that allow the child to integrate these pieces of his or her past identities into a complete and satisfying whole. "Rosa was three when I adopted her and we lived in Peru together for six weeks," Hilary says. "This opens the door for us to share memories back and forth. I weave together a whole story and a whole identity for her and she values it a great deal. We have a picture of her with her birth mother and grandmother. It's in the background of her mind, but important to her. She has experienced the trauma of separation and of dire poverty, and that has informed who she is. She has a lot of conscious and unconscious memories. I talk to her about *tikkun olam*, saving the world, and try to tie her experience to our role as Jews in making the world a better place. Adoption has made the world a very small place to me. I realize how much the same we all are and I think about how many other little gems there are, languishing in poverty, waiting to be adopted. The gratification of adoption is immense."

CHAPTER 8

The New Jewish Family: Gays and Lesbians Adopting

~

Today when a family gathers for its seder, it may have a very different look from that of Jewish families a generation ago. The new Jewish family may be headed by two Mommies or two Daddies, surrounded by loving children and supportive relatives. And in increasing numbers, those families are formed by adoption.

As gays and lesbians become more visible in society, their status as parents—both biological and adoptive—has also become more visible. The number of families led by gay and lesbian biological parents has increased because formerly married gays and lesbians are raising their children on their own or with their partners. And as gays and lesbians recognize and act upon their desire and ability to parent, they are adopting in ever greater numbers. It still remains difficult for openly gay men and lesbians to adopt, but once the legal hurdles are surmounted, they can create successful, functional families. Such families, while not without some special challenges, are headed by people who may be uniquely well prepared to meet them.

Gay and lesbian parents confront the usual parenting issues that all parents face, from treating diaper rash to arranging play dates to supervising homework. They also face the special challenges inherent in adoption: Their adopted children struggle to create integrated identities from whatever knowledge they may have of their past and the experiences of their present. And still other challenges can arise because of society's views about homosexuality. If gays and lesbians find it necessary to hide their sexual orientation in order to adopt, such a cover-up can have negative effects on them, their parenting, and, if they are in a partnership, their relationship. On the other hand, if they openly acknowledge their homosexuality, their parenting skills may come under attack since myths and stereotypes about gays linger. Insensitive people may question or tease children about their nontraditional family. Children themselves may sometimes feel embarrassed or defensive that their family is different from other families. Yet because visible gays and lesbians have learned to cope with society's prejudices, they may be well equipped to help their children do the same. Their awareness of sensitive issues can help them effectively communicate about these issues with one another and their children.

Jewish gay and lesbian adoptive families are a minority within a minority within a minority. Although the growth of gay and lesbian synagogues provides families with a supportive and comfortable place within the Jewish community, they may find only limited acceptance from the mainstream Jewish community. Their lifestyle may be condemned outright by traditionally religious Jews; even some liberal communities struggle to be as welcoming in deed as they may be in principle. When the Jewish community accepts all of its members equally, it can truly give these children a message of love and acceptance of diversity.

A Decision with Far-Reaching Effects

"Why?" Barry's mother asked when he and his partner, Mel, decided to adopt. "She thought we had the perfect life, and wondered why we'd want to give it up to sit up at night with a sick child," Barry remembers. And although he thought that he and Mel would make excellent parents and enjoy having a child, her questioning helped him to explore his feelings and doubts about parenting and feel secure in his decision.

Gays and lesbians who adopt do so for the same reasons that straight people do: They believe that they would be good parents for a child who needs a family and that they would enjoy being parents. For some, parenting has been a long-held desire, while for others it is one only newly recognized. "It was there all the time for Rick, but not for me," Lee says. "Then we became alternative parents for a homeless gay boy, and all my parenting urges came out and I realized what I was repressing. The year that he was with us gave me a better understanding of myself, and my ability and desire to parent." A specific event may help people realize what they are feeling. "Deep down, I always knew I wanted a child, but my partner Molly wasn't as sure," Alexis recalls. "When we attended a huge family gathering, with multiple generations of her family, her maternal instinct kicked in, too." Sometimes one member of a couple feels strongly, while the other has either not thought about it or has not thought it possible. "Penny and I both always knew we wanted kids, but didn't know that lesbians could adopt," Martha says. "We tried donor insemination for five years, but that didn't work. Finally, we decided to see if it was possible for us to adopt."

When gay men and lesbians make the decision to adopt, they need to realize that they will be dealing with certain losses and vulnerabilities that face all adoptive parents. Although they may or may not have had to deal with the losses associated with infertility like Penny and Martha, they should understand and prepare for feeling the loss of a biological connection to their child, says Abby Ruder, director of Adoption Information and Support Services in Philadelphia, Pennsylvania. For some people, this tie is much more important than for others. It can be helpful to examine one's feelings on this issue before entering into an adoption. "We tried donor insemination for a year before giving up," Alexis says. "We mourned not being able to become pregnant.

Then my mother suggested being foster parents, and we were approved by the agency for that, but were never called. Finally, we connected with a group of gay and lesbian families and realized that adoption was possible."

Jewish gays and lesbians may also find the pull of their family-oriented heritage tugging them toward adoption. "There is nothing more appropriate than to bring new life into the Jewish community. We are continuing a tradition we learned from our families of birth: to carry on the heritage. But we have to overcome obstacles that others don't," Lee says. "Judaism resonates very strongly with me," adds Barry, "and I felt that the population battle that Jews are facing is important." Alexis explains, "You do learn as a Jewish girl growing up that you should 'be fruitful and multiply,' but when you make this life decision, no one expects it of you. People assume that gays don't have parenting impulses. Gay women have been given up on; there's no pressure to reproduce. My mom was totally shocked, and thrilled, that I wanted to be a parent."

Sexual orientation affects neither one's desire nor ability to parent. The Child Welfare League of America's policy regarding adoption by gays or lesbians states that "applicants [for adoption] should be fairly assessed on their abilities to successfully parent a child needing family membership and not on their appearance, differing lifestyle, or sexual preference. Sexual preference should not be the sole criteria on which the suitability of the adoptive applicants is based. Consideration should be given to other personality and maturity factors and on the ability of the applicant to meet the specific needs of the individual child. The needs of the child are the priority consideration in adoption. Gay/lesbian adoptive applicants should be assessed the same as any other adoptive applicant. It should be recognized that sexual orientation and the capacity to nurture a child are separate issues."

Despite this statement, myths about homosexuals raise fears

that their children will develop psychological and/or social problems because they have grown up in what some people consider an "unnatural" lifestyle. During the time that they are contemplating their decision to adopt, it can be helpful to consider how they will react to baseless prejudice. "One myth is that our children will become gay," Victor acknowledges. "I have five kids and they are all straight. Even we wish that they'll be straight, because it's hard to be gay. The important thing is that we're willing to accept them as they are." Studies of children of homosexual parents indicate that they are no different from children raised by heterosexual parents. In "Children of Lesbian and Gay Parents," an article in *Child Development* in 1992, Charlotte Patterson states, "Despite dire predictions about children based on well-known theories of psychosocial development, and despite the accumulation of a substantial body of research investigating these issues, not a single study has found children of gay or lesbian parents to be disadvantaged in any significant respect relative to children of heterosexual parents" (Hochman, Prowler, and Huston, 1995, pp. 5–6). Psychiatrist Laurintine Fromm, of the Institute of Pennsylvania Hospital, agrees and adds that "a parent's capacity to be respectful and supportive of the child's autonomy and to maintain her own intimate attachments far outweighs the influence of the parent's sexual orientation alone" (Hochman, Prowler, and Huston, 1995, p. 6). Because they are not ambivalent about their legitimacy as a family, they are able to raise emotionally healthy children, Martha explains. "We believe that we're fine, and everyone who is important in our lives gives us that message."

Family members and friends may or may not be supportive of a gay or lesbian's decision to adopt. Whether or not they actually question a person's ability to parent, they may fear society's prejudices and the impact those prejudices may have on the child. Alexis recalls that Molly's parents objected to their plan to adopt, arguing that they were selfish and would be "ruining a child's life" because he or she "would have to deal with having two Mommies." Says Alexis, "This attitude invalidates our relationship, and we decided to ignore their objections. We told them that we were going to make a child's life great. It was a big issue at the time, but has changed because they now see us as good parents." Whether they faced initial resistance or not, many gays and lesbians acknowledge that once they adopted, their extended family members became extremely supportive. "My mother is totally consumed by her granddaughter, as is my stepfather, who never had children of his own and never experienced the unconditional love that a child gives. It's a new lease on life for them," Barry says.

Making a decision to adopt is also a decision to be open about one's lifestyle, if the person hasn't already done so, Abby Ruder says. People are much more visible when they have a child, and it is important that they decide how they will present themselves to the community. Gay and lesbian parents do not want their children to have to lie, nor do they want the full burden of differentness to fall on their children. They would like their children to be able to be open and comfortable in talking about the members of their family, which will be easier for them if the parents themselves have done some advance preparation and thought about how they will handle this.

As they make the decision to adopt, it is helpful for gays and lesbians to think seriously about the multiplicity of issues facing homosexual adoptive parents. Issues about parenting, adoption, and diversity may overlap, complicating the work that people have to do. "Homophobia still exists, and homosexuals may have to work harder because they are breaking down stereotypes," says Ruder. However, she adds, the majority of the work that gays and lesbians have to do involves preparing themselves to be adoptive parents, which is the same for all adoptive families. "Adoption heightens all your insecurities, and people need to get it together before they adopt and have the added responsibility of a child," Martha adds. "It's not negative, not an issue; it's an additional horizon and an opportunity to explore other dimensions of oneself." Gays and lesbians should not be discouraged by the difficult decisions that face them; they should understand that they can adopt and be successful adoptive parents.

Can We Do This?: The Process and Its Implications

Despite the position taken by the Child Welfare League, there is general agreement that it is more difficult for gays and lesbians to adopt. First, there remain legal constraints to adoption by homosexuals. Prospective parents need to find out early in the process about local custody laws that support or are obstacles to their becoming adoptive parents. Once they know what they are facing, they can make decisions about how they wish to proceed. One of the first decisions may be to whom and what they want to reveal about their personal status.

"Our situation was completely open in the home study [by the adoption agency], and we felt strongly that it should be," Lee explains. "Rick and I make no apologies and don't want to convey to our child that there might be something wrong with our relationship or our family. But the home study took about twice as long as for traditional families. They kept digging, to see if they could find something wrong. In order for us to achieve, we have to give 125 percent. After we were approved and we were free to search for children, we began looking in the books of children who are waiting to be adopted. We identified twenty-four children we were interested in, and were turned down twenty-four times. Finally, our agency offered us a four-month-old girl."

Gays and lesbians have to know which agencies are willing to work with them, says Elmy Martinez, an adoptive father and president of Adoption Resource Exchange for Single Parents, Inc. in Springfield, Virginia, which includes many homosexuals among its members. They can become part of a network of friendly agencies, independent counselors, and adoptive parents who will share information and experiences. In many cases, success can depend upon the caseworker who conducts the home study. Martinez believes that if a caseworker is personally uncomfortable with adoption by a homosexual, he or she should turn the case over to a colleague who can concentrate on the good of the child, not the prospective parent's sexual orientation. However, he says that it is easier to adopt as a single and that being seen as single, rather than as gay or lesbian, improves one's prospects of becoming a parent.

As a single, it is possible to keep one's sexual orientation to oneself, Martinez says. "I don't think your children need to know, if you are discreet about your social life. After you have developed a family life, especially after you have done things to promote diversity and can explain what homosexuality is without scaring a child, it is easier. It's a personal decision people have to make." Victor decided not to tell his children when he was adopting them as teenagers that he is gay. He worried that he could lose them because of the stereotypes they might harbor about homosexuals. His son, now grown, admits that he probably wouldn't have agreed to the adoption had he known beforehand that his father-to-be was gay. He says that he thought gays were bad, but has since learned differently. He credits everything he is today to his father and says that he'd probably be dead if he hadn't been adopted.

The Child Welfare League's policy states that gay and lesbian applicants should know that biological parents will be told about the sexual orientation of potential adoptive parents. Some may choose not to consider gays and lesbians, and agencies usually follow the expressed wishes of the biological parent. However, an agency may have a "don't ask, don't tell" policy, Martha says. When she and Penny began adoption proceedings, she moved out of their home and in with friends, and Penny was presented as a single. The more open the adoption, the more gay and lesbian adoptive parents feel they have permission from the birth parents to parent, the more comfortable they will be, says Michael Colberg, JD, CSW, an adoptive parent, co-director of the Center for Family Connections in New York City, and a member of the Pre and Post Adoption Consulting Team, led by Joyce Maguire Pavao, in Somerville, Massachusetts. If the parents' homosexuality is not disclosed, they are adding pressure to themselves. They may feel less able to open the adoption later for fear that the birth parents will disapprove.

Alexis and Molly adopted privately, with Molly identified as a single parent, Alexis explains. "Our lawyer asked us whether we wanted a baby or to be a test case," she says. "We placed an ad and found someone who clicked with Molly. She assumed that Molly was single, and never asked any questions. We didn't feel guilty about keeping her in the dark; we only felt sad that we couldn't share our long and loving relationship with her so that she'd know what kind of family her child was going to have. Today, I'd want to be out."

Gays and lesbians who need to be secretive about their lifestyle in order to adopt may feel a sense of shame, says Abby Ruder. They may feel that they are not as good as other people, because they do not meet society's expectations. "The culture says you aren't as good as other people, and you shouldn't be parents . . . so you think maybe you shouldn't. There may also be a sense of shame, of feeling that something is wrong with you, connected with adoption, because adoptive parents don't meet the traditional paradigm of how people become parents. When shame is again directed at people who are already vulnerable when they try to adopt, it can be very demoralizing. People begin to internalize it and believe they aren't worthy if they are turned down repeatedly when they try to adopt."

If there is secrecy involving one member of a homosexual couple, that person can become disenfranchised, explains Maureen Kenny, MSW, an adoption specialist in Washington, D.C., who conducts home studies for agencies. When one partner can't be acknowledged, it can be difficult for them to feel positive as a couple. "It can be difficult for them to go from one identified parent to two active parents, and for each to have clear roles. It has to do with power and equity in their relationship. This can set up competition between them as they negotiate about parenting issues. For example, who has the right to discipline their child? Are they afforded equal status as a couple by society? If there is a conference at their child's school, do they both go? If not, there can be further disenfranchisement." That is not healthy for children, who need both of their adoptive parents to be able to claim the parenting role. The most successful situation, she says, is when the couple is open about their status and everyone is accepting of them as a couple. While most gay and lesbian couples successfully resolve these questions, it can be an issue to which they want to pay careful attention. Most gay and lesbian couples, she adds, work hard to maintain communication and are good communicators, because they have had to resolve many issues that heterosexual couples take for granted. "They have the skills and they make a commitment to talk, but the issues can still be painful."

After Adoption: Layers of Diversity

Gay and lesbian-led Jewish adoptive families represent multiple layers of diversity, and their children need to learn to deal with the complex challenges of the many ways they are different from their peers. Gay and lesbian parents may have the potential to be particularly helpful to their adopted children because they have already had the experience of dealing with difference, says Michael Colberg. "These are parents who have already dealt with the complexities of not being part of the dominant culture. The gay culture is not dominant, neither is being adopted. However, most children adopted by gays and lesbians are themselves heterosexual. Therefore, aspects of the child are part of the dominant culture and aspects are not. Gay adoptive parents need to help their children manage this very complicated information.

Otherwise, their children will have to leave one culture in order to explore the other."

Children who are adopted by gays and lesbians may also be part of yet other minorities. They may be transculturally or transracially adopted, and they may have special needs. It is ironic, notes April Martin, author of *The Lesbian and Gay Parenting Handbook,* that the bureaucracies that seem to believe that gays and lesbians are less than suitable parents for healthy Caucasian infants will place children who require the most highly skilled parenting with them. Like Colberg, she points out that gays and lesbians may be uniquely suited for parenting children who require special sensitivity. They are usually able to accept differences, understanding what it is like to be in the minority, and able to model adaptive behavior for their adopted children. People feel good about themselves when they feel that all of the pieces of themselves are valued, not merely tolerated. The more parents help children integrate into their identities their membership in a wide variety of communities, the better off the child and the family will be. It may also be significant to help the child understand what his or her birth culture feels and teaches about homosexuality and Judaism. If there is prejudice, it can be more difficult for the child to accept these pieces of him- or herself. Gays and lesbians have the potential to be especially good at handling such circumstances because they have had experience coping with prejudice, Colberg adds.

It is natural for children to be uncomfortable with gay parents, and parents need to address this with their children, Colberg says. It is important for children to see that their parents feel fine about their lifestyle, even as they learn strategies for dealing with any prejudice or teasing. Children may test their parents, just as they are being tested by their peers. It is helpful when parents teach their children that almost everyone gets teased about something, and that their parents are able to take it in stride. Then the children will be more likely to be able to do so, too.

Adolescents may be especially sensitive and embarrassed about their parents' sexual orientation, says Maureen Kenny. They may want their parents to pretend that their relationship isn't homosexual. It is helpful if parents can be sensitive to the child's feelings, but not overreact to what is a normal stage of development. If the child hadn't been embarrassed about this, he or she might be embarrassed by something else about the parents. "Parents should not change their lifestyle or imply that there is anything wrong. They can show their child that they understand his or her feelings and support the child's right to feel whatever he or she feels, while they give the message that the family is okay. This is also a time that family counseling can be helpful."

Parents can model language and behavior for their children, giving them tools with which to meet the world. Charlotte recalls that just before Yom Kippur her daughter's class was asked by their Sunday school teacher whether anyone in the class had ever been teased. Samantha explained that she had, because "I'm adopted, brown, and my parents are lesbians." The teacher commented that it was unfortunate that people would tease her about things she can't change. When Samantha reported the story to Charlotte, Charlotte added " . . . and things you are proud of."

"Someday, someone will tell our daughter that her parents are perverts," Martha says. "But we think we are raising a healthy child with self-esteem because of our complete unambivalence about our legitimacy and about us as a family. If you feel great about yourself, people will like you, unless they are maniacal hatemongers. If I go about my business and love my kid, people will accept and like me, and my child will know that we're okay. And she'll probably have a greater tolerance for diversity than other children." Barry and Mel live in a straight neighborhood and "no one is concerned" about their sexual orientation, although people know they are gay, Barry says. "We're good neighbors and people judge us as us."

However, many gay and lesbian parents feel pressure to prove themselves to society. They believe that people doubt them, and that there is both increased external and internal pressure to be perfect parents, says Abby Ruder. "We are always under a microscope. People are always watching and waiting for us to make a mistake," Lee says. "It is the ability to be visible and let people know us for who and what we are that lets us be free from discrimination. We come across like anyone else, and for people to label us for what we do in bed is inappropriate. But once people get to know us, they accept us for who we are. So we have to be very open. For example, I was in the market with my daughter and someone commented that my wife must be very proud to have a husband who does the shopping. I said no, that I am gay and an adoptive father."

"You have to be out in order to be true to your child," Alexis says. "People will ask 'who's his real mom?' assuming that one of us gave birth to him. People can be so inappropriate and intrusive, right in front of your child. We are constantly having to explain. You expect it, but are never really prepared. We talk to our friends about how to handle it."

Gays and lesbians who are parenting have to be very involved with their children, says Wayne Steinman, an adoptive parent, co-founder of Center Kids, and president of the Gay and Lesbian Parents Coalition International. If they are a couple, it is important for both parents to go to school functions, explain their situation, give professionals the appropriate semantics to describe their family, and establish a rapport with them, letting them know that the parents want to be informed if anything special comes up. "It is often for lack of information that teachers make mistakes that make children feel less equal. If people are hidden, it creates the possibility for innuendo and gossip. If they are visible, it allows them to answer questions directly."

"There is no discrimination at our daughter's school. On the first day of school last year, we got a letter saying that they were going to be drawing family trees and the teacher wanted to know how we wanted to handle it. They know that she calls us Daddy Lee and Daddy Rick, that she makes two gifts on Father's Day, and gifts for her grandmothers on Mother's Day. Other parents are very supportive and we've been accepted by the families of her classmates as just another family, not the gay family," Lee adds.

It can also be helpful to a child's development to have positive male and female role models, and an integrated group of friends. "We know that a heterosexual family is no guarantee of positive role models for either sex, and we have uncles and friends that are role models for our son and daughter. We know how to create extended family because we've had to," Martha says. "Our daughter, who was adopted transculturally, has started to be racially aware and ask questions about her heritage. I expect fewer problems about homosexuality than about transcultural issues."

In the Jewish Community

Within the Jewish community, gays and lesbians are often labeled by their sexual orientation, a label which may then be used to ostracize them. The Jewish community still strongly supports traditional gender roles, says Abby Ruder, and there are expectations of what men and women are supposed to do and be. These assumptions are upset when two people of the same sex run a family. Many gays and lesbians choose not to affiliate with mainstream synagogues because they feel that they are not accepted or welcome, Wayne Steinman says. "When you superimpose being homosexual on religion, it creates problems. Even when you find a synagogue that seems to be liberal, you are often not embraced. This is a problem because the Jewish community can't afford to get rid of anyone in the family."

"I was raised in an Orthodox synagogue, but I cut it off after my Bar Mitzvah. When I came out, I chose not to be affiliated because I always felt different and not welcome. It felt like us versus them," says Lee. "But when I lost a friend to AIDS, I wanted to say *Kaddish*; it was important to me. I found a gay synagogue, and I finally felt welcome. It was home within the gay community."

"My family was not very observant, but Jewish things always resonated very strongly for me," Barry says. "When I first came out, I thought that these two important parts of me, Judaism and homosexuality, couldn't be integrated. Then I found a predominantly gay synagogue and realized that they could. I found it real and relevant in my life. Once I started attending synagogue on Friday night, it became Shabbat to me."

Like other gays and lesbians, Barry found that it became even more important to be part of the Jewish community when he adopted his daughter. "I always see the world through Jewish eyes, and I want her to have as many Jewish experiences as possible. I'd feel terrible if she didn't ask, 'Is it good for the Jews?' The assimilationist influences are so strong that if we don't make a big effort, she won't feel what we feel."

It can, however, be challenging for gays and lesbians to be part of the Jewish community. "We belong to an adoption support group of lesbian moms, and all but one of us are Jewish," says Alexis. "We talk about it a lot. How do we give our children a Jewish identity? What do we do about religious school? Bar or Bat Mitzvah? I'd like our son to feel Jewish and know he's Jewish because we are. It can be very difficult. He has issues about being Jewish because he's already different; he's got two moms and he's adopted. There aren't many Jews where we live, and he doesn't want to be more different from his friends. On the other hand, he wants to be just like us. So he's very conflicted. He says he doesn't want to be Jewish, but he wants to put a Jewish star on our door. We want, and are trying, to build a Jewish flavor into our home. We celebrate Shabbat and holidays and use Yiddish, but we gave him a year off of Hebrew school because he protested so strongly and we didn't want his experience of Judaism to be hating Hebrew school."

A large number of gay and lesbian couples are interfaith families, which can create strain in the relationship and in the family if both partners want to raise their child in their own religion. It is helpful if the couple attempts to decide how they will deal with this in advance, although people may not understand the true depth of their feelings until they are actually in the situation. "Our daughter was supposed to be raised in Rick's religion, because it was so important to him and not important to me," Lee says. "But once we started doing that, I changed, and it creates problems. When it was time for her communion, I didn't want it to happen and I refused to invite my family. She stopped going to church, but it was so important to Rick that it started to affect our relationship. He took his promise to give her religious instruction very seriously. So she started going again. I would just tell people that they need to think about this very carefully."

Another problem is that it may be difficult to find rabbis to officiate at life-cycle events for gays and lesbians and their children. Although there are increasing numbers of gay and lesbian or straight liberal rabbis, they tend to live in or near major cities. People in other places may not have access to sympathetic clergy. "Some *mohels* won't do a *brit*," says Alexis. "They say we aren't a real family. It's a real turndown by the Jewish community." In other cases, gays and lesbians are able to find people to conduct rituals. "We did a halakhic conversion with three observant men who signed the paper," says Martha. "I felt an unbelievable presence as our daughter was in the *mikvah* and it was very affirming. I'm modeling commitment to the path we've chosen." Says Barry, "We had a *bet din* with gay rabbis who know that we are gay." However, the future acceptance of these ceremonies by traditional Jews may be questionable.

Yet another challenge for Jewish gays and lesbians is that mainstream synagogues may not welcome them, and they may be unable to find a liberal or gay and lesbian synagogue near their home. And since people with children are still in the minority, the gay and lesbian synagogue may not have a religious school or children's services. Barry and Mel belong to a gay and lesbian synagogue in a neighboring city, but it is too far from their home to take their daughter there for religious school. When they went to join the local Conservative synagogue, they were told that they couldn't join as a family because the movement had not taken a position on gay and lesbian families. The rabbi explained that the congregation was grappling with so many issues that this was not yet being addressed. He assured Barry that he was personally supportive of their family and that the school would welcome their daughter. When they have attended Shabbat services, Barry says that people were friendly. He says, "They don't live by halakhah, so why is this a concern? Is it to justify their prejudice and discrimination? Maybe once people get to know us, we can bring this before the board."

It is important for Jewish gay and lesbian adoptive parents to find a community within which they and their children can be comfortable. Maureen Kenny encourages families to find some sort of support because "it is very helpful to children to see other children with families like theirs and know that they are not alone." Groups bring people together and, she says, it is even possible for a child to find a pen pal on the Internet with whom to communicate.

Jewish adoptive gay and lesbian parents have a unique and challenging task, but one that should not discourage them. "Wrestling with these issues is complicated and can bring discomfort, but isn't a sign of failure," Michael Colberg says. As they are grappling with these issues, so too, is the Jewish community. "It is important," says Alexis, "that the Jewish community know we're here in numbers, and could be a powerful and positive part of the community."

CHAPTER 9

Sisters, Brothers, Bubbes, Zaydes, and the Whole Mishpakha

Mishpakha, family, is a word that describes complex webs of interconnecting relationships, elucidates the emotional ties of generations, and expresses otherwise inexpressible experiences. Families wield inestimable power; they are more than the sum of their parts. When a person or a couple has a child, something magical happens: Their status changes and they become a family. When the family is created, or partly created, by adoption, the magic is ever so much more potent. This child has been awaited and wished for, planned for and sought after. Not only parents and siblings, but grandparents, aunts, uncles, and cousins are drawn into this magical circle of family.

Yet adoption presents families with special challenges. Any family with more than one child understands the demands that children make on time, energy, emotions, and intellect. Sibling rivalry, no matter how benign, also produces tensions. Children have individual needs, which occasionally conflict with another's. Birth order, sex, temperament, abilities, and disabilities can affect how children relate to each other in any family. Throw adoption into the mix and the outcome is predictably unpredictable. The only sure thing is that at some time, adoptive families will need to deal with the events and emotions that adoption adds to usual sibling interactions.

The extended family, those relatives near and far that revolve around the family, may offer support and succor, or can exacerbate problems. The manner in which families habitually relate to one another, positively or negatively, supportively or destructively, is likely to be played out in regard to whatever adoption issues the family faces. Although it might be pleasant to imagine a family member spontaneously changing his or her usual style when dealing with adoption, it would be foolish to rely upon such a change. Rather, it is more realistic to expect that the complex emotions stirred up by adoption may intensify any existing difficulties.

In the Jewish community, the family as an institution maintains a position of honor and respect. *Mishpakha* is the keystone of the Jewish people's existence. "Honor thy father and mother" is one of the most famous of the Ten Commandments. "*Shalom bayit*," family harmony, is one of Judaism's most treasured principles. And adoption is highly regarded by Jewish tradition as a way to create a family. The Babylonian Talmud (Sanhedrin 19b) states that "Whoever brings up an orphan in his home is regarded by the Bible as though the child had been born to him." The high status of adoptive parents is suggested in a passage (Kiddushin 31b) concerning Abbaye, one of the Talmud's greatest scholars. His father had died when his mother conceived him, and his mother died when she bore him. Yet the Talmud records that Abbaye used to say, "My mother told me." He was referring to his adoptive mother, we are told.

Still, Judaism presents adoptive families with a problematic double message: Although adoption is valued, halakhah recognizes that joining a family through adoption is not the same as joining it by birth. For a people which places such great importance on *mishpakha*, these ritual strictures emphasize and reinforce the differences inherent in adoption. And for a people which intuitively perceives the importance of generations of connectedness, through blood and mutual history, it can be emotionally difficult to bestow full membership on one who does not share that connectedness, on one whose disconnectedness is made so clear.

Jewish adoptive families experience the same family-related issues as other adoptive families. If they also have biological children, there will be differences and similarities to negotiate, as well as sibling rivalry, and questions about love and fairness. If they have adopted more than one child, the siblings may either form a special bond, or develop a different style of sibling rivalry in which one child acts out, as if trying to prove that his or her birth parents were right to "give him or her away," and another becomes "better than good" in order to show adoptive parents that they made the right choice. As the circle is drawn wider, extended family provides additional relationships that can support or undermine the adoptee and the family. These issues can be exacerbated in a Jewish family both by certain halakhic tenets of Judaism and the emotional reactions of the community. Alternatively, the Jewish family can provide a safe haven, a support system, a *mishpakha* in the fullest sense of the word. Adoptive parents may need to facilitate this process through word and deed, teaching first their nuclear and then their extended family how to nurture the adopted member of the family.

Adopted and Biological Siblings: Acknowledging Differences

Parenting an adopted child is different from parenting a birth child because these children have had different life experiences. When adopted and nonadopted children are siblings, these differences can create complex challenges for adoptive families. Many questions are raised about so-called blended families, says Ronny Diamond, MSW, director of Post Adoption Services at Spence/Chapin Services to Families and Children in New York City. Can parents love adopted children as much as they love birth children? Can siblings who have entered the family in two such different ways bond with one another? Will extended family members accept an adopted child or be partial to the biological child? How will a family address the differences between siblings?

Parents need to realize that parenting any child is different from parenting any other child because each child is unique, says Patricia Irwin Johnston, MS, adoptive parent, adoption educator, and publisher of Perspectives Press. Parents' reactions to those differences often determine how they will affect the family. In *Shared Fate*, his seminal work on adoption, H. David Kirk described two types of families, those that acknowledge and accept differences and openly look for ways to deal with them, and those that reject and deny differences. He found that families that accept differences raise children who grow up dealing more successfully with their adoption, while children whose adoptive parents reject and deny differences have much more difficulty. Adoption expert David Brodzinsky, Ph.D., associate professor of Clinical and Developmental Psychology at Rutgers University and co-author of *Being Adopted: The Lifelong Search for Self*, identified a third type of adoptive family: the family that insists on differences and blames adoption for everything negative that happens. It is important, and tricky, Patricia Johnston says, to acknowledge differences sensitively, but not to dwell on them or feel victimized by them. If parents accept and celebrate each child's uniqueness, children will accept those differences too, she explains.

Acknowledging differences is important in any adoptive family; it is critical in a blended family, adds Phyllis Lowinger, MSW, an adoptive and biological parent and a psychiatric social worker specializing in adoption in New York City. Children are aware of these differences; pretending they do not exist implies that there is something wrong or shameful about them. Such pretense also does not allow children to ask their questions and face their feelings and fears. "It isn't healthy to deny or reject the losses of adoption. In a blended family, the siblings have had different experiences that must be acknowledged," she says.

Feelings of loss and abandonment must be acknowledged and discussed for the sake of the nonadopted as well as the adopted sibling, agrees Julie Bulitt, LCSW, an adoptive and biological parent and a family therapist with the Center for Adoptive Families in Silver Spring, Maryland. "Children know that their sibling had a loss, and little children often wonder and worry whether they, too, could be given away by their parents. What does it mean to one child if another perfectly wonderful child is given away?" Bulitt says. Parents can help children make sense of this with explanations of what happened and why, and reassurances that it will not happen in this family.

"If in a blended family, parents find they are not talking about either biology or adoption so as not to stress one over the other, it should be a clue to them," agrees Ronny Diamond. "They shouldn't minimize either, but should celebrate both. It is important to celebrate each child's uniqueness. Families need to talk about differences openly and allow children to express their feelings. They must not force negative feelings underground."

"We never had any family conversation about adoption," Doug recalls. "I didn't even know my older brother was adopted until I was eight, when my sister told me. She and I are biological siblings, and he was very different from us. He looks very different. He was into very different things. But we didn't talk about it, and not talking was very unhealthy for all of us. It set up the guideline that it was okay to have big things that were unspoken and that it wasn't okay to share. It was not a positive example of how to raise kids.

"I always realized that we didn't talk, and I always realized that I had secrets that weren't okay to share, either. My needs were negated because my parents were protecting my brother and trying to make him feel more equal, but it made me feel less equal. It made me less confident and comfortable to be the person I needed to be. And to this day, my brother has never revealed parts of himself; there are things he hasn't shared. He still never talks about being adopted, even though our sister now has an adopted child. I haven't seen that part of who he is."

"Adoption certainly wasn't a secret, but it wasn't discussed very much either," Susan says. "Both Joel, who was adopted at birth, and Nina, who was born to us when Joel was six, knew what the situation was, but they look so much alike that no one would guess that they weren't biological siblings. Somehow, it seemed that talking too much about adoption wasn't necessary and might hurt Joel. Now, however, I think that not talking about it hurt him more in some ways. Obviously, that is something we never meant to have happen. But he recognized the differences that existed were significant, and there was pain and sadness that he never felt able to talk about, so he acted out instead."

When parents honestly and openly acknowledge both similarities and differences between siblings, they help both adopted and birth children feel comfortable with themselves and each other. Adoptive parents can discuss and praise how an adopted child is different from the adoptive family in both accomplishments and physical traits. Positive comments about differences help the child separate and become an individual. When they also acknowledge that these traits are probably like the child's birth parents, adoptive parents provide their child with a piece of his or her missing identity. These traits can also make connections between the child and the adoptive family, says adoption counselor Holly van Gulden. Commenting on the child's similarities reinforces the adoptive family's claiming of the child and the child's sense of belonging, she explains in *Real Parents, Real Children: Parenting the Adopted Child* (1993, p.151).

The Difference We Don't Discuss

One difference that adoptive Jewish families may studiously avoid talking about is religion. If an adopted child was not born Jewish, parents may want to avoid focusing on a situation that they may have gone to great lengths to change. They may prefer that their adopted child not explore this difference. In a heritage like Judaism that greatly values genetic connection, a difference in religious background can be more difficult to accept than it is in blended families of other backgrounds, says Patricia Johnston. "It can create the feeling of 'second-bestness' that can be troubling."

"A child who was adopted understands that his or her parents wanted a biological child; if they could have had that child, perhaps they wouldn't have adopted him or her," explains Linda Yellin, MSW, ACSW, an adoptee and therapist specializing in pre and post adoption work in Farmington Hills, Michigan. "The adoptee may already feel like a second choice. If there is a biological sibling who is more like the parents, perhaps because he or she has 'Jewish blood,' it may make the adopted child feel even less acceptable."

Traditional halakhah can highlight the differences between adopted and nonadopted siblings. For example, an adopted son cannot join his father and nonadopted brothers on the *bimah* for an *aliyah* as a *kohen* or *levi*, explains Aaron, who has to deal with this situation in his family. Shoshana hopes her daughter Batya will never fall in love with an Orthodox man who is a *kohen*, he could marry one of her nonadopted sisters, but would not be permitted to marry her, an adoptee. Even in the liberal branches of Judaism, a subtle but important difference exists between those who were born Jewish and those who weren't: Only adopted children have the right to reject their Judaism at Bar/Bat Mitzvah.

"The question becomes what makes a Jew: heritage or environment?" Ronny Diamond says. "This is much more complicated when one sibling was born Jewish and one wasn't. It is difficult for children to feel different from their family around this issue and still relate to being Jewish. The child might reject Judaism in order to deal with the question of belonging."

It may be difficult to determine whether an adopted child has targeted religion as a way to express doubts about his or her place in the family, or whether the child actually has not accepted and integrated Jewishness into his or her identity. Some adoptees may use religion as a way of expressing their overall feelings of being different from their adoptive siblings. Especially if Judaism is an integral part of the family identity, the child who is trying to claim his or her own identity may reject that religion to assert his or her autonomy. Others, knowing that Judaism defines them differently because they were adopted, question whether they are accepted by and belong to the Jewish people, and may even reject that people and religion before it and they can reject them. Still others, perhaps because they know that they would not be Jewish except for an accident of fate, seem not to have internalized a Jewish identity, as though adoption grants them permission not to feel Jewish. Although there are certainly born Jews whose connections to Judaism and the Jewish community are tenuous, they at least know that they are Jewish by birth if by nothing else. Adoptees, when their religion creates a schism in their lives, may find that reason enough to reject that identity.

"Jason doesn't want to be Jewish, and my other children never say that," Sheryl says. "We're Orthodox, but he's picked up a sense that his relationship to Judaism is different from that of his siblings. It's internal, not external. And it certainly isn't usual in people who were raised in this environment."

"Carly tells people that she wasn't born Jewish; she's rebellious and feels different. So, for example, her brothers were Torah readers in our synagogue, and she won't participate in it, even though she can read Torah beautifully," Cynthia says. "She knows that it's an adopted heritage for her and she bounces back and forth. She's proud to be part of the Jewish community, but she also points out that she was Christian. There's a question in her mind of who she really is; she's constantly wondering."

How can Jewish parents help their adopted children deal with their experience of being different from their siblings? Although they cannot force a child to embrace any religion, they can talk about the difference religion makes, Ronny Diamond says. They can allow kids to be who they are, but they can be clear about the boundaries that are acceptable in the family. "Parents shouldn't be too reactive about this; don't engage children in an argument about being Jewish," agrees Anne C. Bernstein, Ph.D., family psychologist and author of *Flight of the Stork: What Children Think (and When) About Sex and Family Building*. "Parents can tell children that scholars have been debating the question of who is a Jew for ages. And they can let children know that they understand the need to explore, but that being Jewish is more than birth; it is being part of a community. They can also let children know that they hope that Judaism will be a part of their life in the future, and that they will become a part of the Jewish community."

Most Jewish professionals and adoptive parents agree that they would not offer an adopted child more choice than his or her siblings have about participating in the family's Jewish lifestyle. This would be like saying to the child that he or she is not "really" Jewish or even a "real" part of the family, as opposed to everyone else who is participating fully in something important to the family. Such different treatment can separate siblings.

"We were pretty uncomfortable discussing differences, especially the fact that Joel wasn't born Jewish and his sister was," Susan recalls. "It was as if, if we didn't discuss it, it didn't exist. But of course it did. And Joel was giving us all sorts of clues, saying he didn't really feel Jewish. But we just assured him that he was Jewish because we were. That didn't make it so for him. Perhaps if we could have discussed his feelings about it, while maintaining our family's religious practices, he could have better integrated religion into who he is. Now I worry that what I always feared most, and wanted so much to prevent, could happen: that he really could reject Judaism."

Fair Doesn't Mean Equal

Beyond discussions, there are other appropriate ways that adoptive parents can treat siblings differently, taking into account their individuality and their differing life experiences. This can be unusually difficult in blended families, precisely because parents are trying so hard to be fair. But just as parents don't treat every biological child identically, so too they need not treat adopted children identically, says Julie Bulitt.

"Being fair doesn't mean being equal," Ronny Diamond agrees. "Children, especially in a blended family, will use 'fairness' and parents can get caught. Adoption is not the same as when children are born into the family, because parents will stop and think, and wonder if they are being fair. They don't write off an altercation or disagreement as mere sibling rivalry. But if they can try to meet each child's needs, hopefully, children will understand."

Society's expectations about blended families can also affect parents' ability and willingness to deal with differences, because people may assume that the attachment to adopted children is less intense than the attachment to birth children. How many adoptive parents, who subsequently had a child biologically, have heard, "It's too bad you didn't wait." How many parents, who are considering adoption following a struggle with secondary infertility, have been asked, "Why would you want someone else's problem?" In trying to prove their fairness and love to themselves, their children, and the world, some adoptive parents ignore and deny siblings' innate and acquired differences.

"People may think it, but it isn't about loving one more than the other," Vivian says. Members of blended families attest to the strong bonds they feel for one another. Parents can and do form equally intense and solid attachments with both biological and adopted children, explains Lois Melina (Melina, "Parents with Biologic and Adopted Children May Worry About Partiality," 1996, pp. 1–4). "Loving equally is a common concern," agrees Patricia Johnston. "But parents who have been there say they love 'as much as' but differently, no matter how a child arrived. Each child is, and should be, loved for him- or herself. I point out to people that the fear that they won't love an adopted child as much as a biological child assumes that a genetic connection is what causes people to love. I remind them that the person they love most deeply probably doesn't have a genetic connection to them."

At some point in their lives, however, both adopted and non-adopted children in blended families may, in fact, believe that the other is loved more. "Each of my sons thought the other was the favorite," Estelle says. "One because the other was ours by birth and the other because his brother was 'chosen.'" Marla says that she always felt she was "abnormal, wrong, messed up," and that her parents loved her nonadopted brother, "the real one, the normal one," more. Vivian's adopted daughter, Shayna, was jealous of her sister's biological connection to their parents. "It's hard to know that my sister grew in my mom's tummy and I didn't," Shayna says. She sometimes tells Vivian, "You love her more."

It is important for parents to try to understand when problems between siblings actually relate to deeper issues, like the adoptee's feelings about being loved, and when they are merely sibling rivalry, says Phyllis Lowinger. They should be sensitive to the context and what the child is really saying or asking. Sometimes ordinary sibling rivalry can masquerade as an adoption issue. Siblings always look for one another's weak spots to use as ammunition, agrees Patricia Johnston, and if adoption is a weak spot, someone will use it.

"Rena, for example, has used adoption against her sister with comments like 'Mom's not your real mom,'" says Vivian. "We learned that we had to take a strong stand about what would be tolerated, because Rena's verbal abuse was just as hurtful as Shayna's physical striking out. I'd reflect to Rena that she must be saying these things because she wants my complete attention. And we'd explain to Shayna that her sister wasn't being mean because Shayna's adopted, as she believed, but because it is something siblings do to one another. We said that we'd dealt with it with our siblings even though we're not adopted." Whether a child is teasing or truly angry, "there's a line that can't be crossed," says Julie Bulitt. Parents can be very clear about that when discussing the hurt that teasing a sibling about adoption can cause.

Who Came First?

Parents are sometimes responsible, albeit unwittingly, for creating problems between siblings. If the adoptee is the first child, and the family subsequently has birth children, adoptive parents may feel intense guilt, Ronny Diamond points out. They may wonder if they have betrayed their adopted child, if for no other reason than that society will assume they love the birth child more. They may bend over backwards to equalize the situation, and the result can be that they favor the adoptee. They may also feel like betrayers of adoptive families, especially if they have used reproductive technology to produce subsequent pregnancies. They may worry that others will think that adoption and the adopted child weren't good enough, and that they needed to "have one of their own," she explains.

If the adopted child comes after the birth child, the ground is not as ripe for parents to feel guilty, unless they somehow wonder if they have adopted someone else's problem, Diamond says. But it may be more difficult for the adopted child to feel he or she fits in when the family already has children by birth, says Joan Spector, DSW, a clinical social worker in private practice in Great Neck, New York. The adoptee may recognize the similarities between his or her parents and nonadopted siblings, and wonder what role he or she can play in the family. And depending on the age of the birth child, he or she may be privy to the parents' struggle with infertility, and may wonder why the parent had to go to so much trouble to have another child. "It was very difficult on Danielle, who was two, when we started trying to adopt," Marc reflects. "She clearly saw that we consciously worked to get a baby. I didn't realize it then, but it must have seemed like a clear message to her that she wasn't enough. She was no longer the center of attention, and she hasn't worked it out yet. I think it's at the root of some of her insecurity. I've tried to discuss it with her, but she doesn't want to hear it." This feeling can be common to many first children, but may be intensified by the effort they see their parents exerting in order to adopt.

"My sister was adopted when I was fourteen. My mother called her 'the chosen child.' It was horrible; it meant that she was chosen, but they were just stuck with me," Gail says. "My sister had a lot of problems related to being adopted and Mom wasn't honest with her. So when I adopted my own daughter, I bent over backwards to ensure her emotional stability. I didn't realize it at the time, but I didn't give enough to my son, who was older and wasn't adopted. I didn't realize then how it affected him. My daughter was rebellious and acting out, and was getting the attention because she needed it. But my son feels she was favored and getting more and different attention because she was adopted. Even now, as adults, their relationship is strained."

For all that, most adoption experts find that siblings in blended families can and do form very close relationships. "Young children don't really understand biology and adoption," Ronny Diamond says. "Bonds are formed strongly, as in any family, before children really understand. And no matter how they enter a family, siblings share an emotional environment and a history. That sharing is even more important for an adoptee, who is cut off from birth family."

Although her brother sometimes threw adoption into the usual and ordinary sibling arguments over who was loved more, Marla never felt she "was a mistake to him. . . . He was always really a friend," she says. Vivian has no doubt that, despite occasional conflict, her daughters see one another as "real" sisters. Each truly missed the other when Shayna went to overnight camp, and Rena reflected that it would be no fun to be an only child. Rena wanted to arrange for Shayna to meet her birth mother for a special birthday present, Vivian recalls. "She was really concerned and wanted her sister to have a biological connection." When a friend of Rena's pointed out that they were not "real" sisters because Shayna was adopted, Rena's comment was, "So what? We're still sisters."

Other Constellations

Certain family constellations can increase the challenges for blended families. If there is going to be confusion or struggle in a blended family, it is more likely when the siblings are the same sex, Patricia Johnston says. Different sex children are not expected to be as alike, while same sex children tend to be compared automatically. If this is perceived to be a potential issue, or if [extended] families tend to put certain pressures on children of a given sex, e.g., sons are expected to enter the family business, adoptive parents often know this intuitively from their own background, she finds. They may choose not to adopt a specific child or, if they do adopt, they are aware of this as an issue that needs close attention.

Children who are close in age may also have more difficulty, says Johnston, who is critical of what she calls "artificial twinning." She says that the children themselves are more likely to perceive problems with comparisons because everyone wonders if they are twins. They often feel as though they are on public display, and they lose all privacy. Parents are often oblivious to these issues in their pain over their infertility and their focus on acquiring a baby, and are thrilled to adopt two children if the opportunity presents itself, or to adopt even if they have become pregnant during the adoption process. These children become the root of gossip over their parents' motivations, Johnston says.

They may also suffer terribly in school because there, too, they are treated as twins, with the expectation that they will be alike and have similar abilities, rather than seen as individuals who are not biologically related to one another. It can be helpful for an adopted child to have a sibling, she agrees, but not a "twin." Each child must be wanted for who he or she is, and should be the center of his or her parent's attention, at least for a time. For similar reasons, she believes it is not a good idea to bring into a family a child that is the same age as a child already in the family. "Each child needs his or her own space in the family constellation. Adoption should approximate nature, and that normalizes it," she explains.

Vivian's daughters are only eight and a half months apart in age, and that, plus the personality differences between the girls, has been challenging. "I wish I'd understood how emotionally demanding it would be to have two children of the same sex who are so close in age," she reflects. "By eight months of age, Shayna turned more to her dad, while Rena stayed with me. This went on until we became conscious of it, and deliberately made sure that my husband took Rena and I took Shayna. But I think that in a way, Shayna lost another mother. I couldn't give her as much attention as I would have. Actually, I think each of them was somewhat shortchanged by not having more one-on-one with me. I really think people need to be aware of this and think very carefully about it. They're not in the same grade at school, but they should have been. That only happened because Shayna was pushed ahead to keep her from being in the same class as her sister in a very small school. Because she's not very socially mature, it's been additional pressure on her. We saw her as the older child, but it's really a moot point when they are this close in age."

"My oldest two children are only eight months apart, and the third is only one year younger," says Sheryl. "The oldest was adopted and has a disability, and the situation is very difficult for him. I think now that each child needs the space of at least a year, or it creates too much pressure. There is so much competition for time and attention."

When an adopted sibling has a disability, is older, or is racially or culturally different from the family, there is yet another challenge for a blended family. The greatest challenge may be for the other children in the family rather than for the adults, because children are more likely to be openly cruel to one another, says Molly Wiener, LCSW, supervisor of adoption for the Jewish Family Service of West Hartford, Connecticut. "Especially if the children who are already in the family are older, parents should try to determine what is going on in their lives and their peer group. It can be very difficult to have to defend a new sibling, who will likely be rejected, and it may not be fair to either the adoptee or the sibling. Parents sometimes have lofty ideas, but why put a child into a family or community that can't welcome him or her? The adopted child will feel the rejection and believe he or she is to blame. This is a reality, and it is a lifetime decision."

"There is some resentment from the other children about the attention Joe's disability demands," Elaine says. "One of our nonadopted daughters said, 'He's not really part of our family because he's adopted.'" Sheryl says that her biological children tease their adopted sibling about adoption and are critical of him because of his disability. "His sister indicated that she wished we hadn't adopted him."

Some siblings are angry that they have adopted siblings with special needs, while others are nurturing, says Julie Bulitt. However, once the decision is made to adopt, says Patricia Johnston, siblings need to be well prepared about the reactions they may face from friends as well as strangers. Too many adoptive families are naive, and believe that people will just be accepting. This is not always the case, and the siblings "become part of the display" that the family becomes. If they are prepared early in the adoption process, siblings are more likely to be cooperative and tolerant. Once they understand, they often show great maturity for their age. However, any lifestyle changes that the family needs to make in order to make the adoption work—like a move to a new neighborhood—should occur early in the adoption process, she says.

"We didn't tell anyone about adopting, because we weren't sure it would happen, and we didn't want to set up expectations," Cynthia explains. "We didn't tell our older children until we left to pick up our daughter, and that was an issue for one of our sons. He said, 'Why didn't you ask us whether we wanted another sibling?' Now, however, they really love her."

Bubbes, Zaydes . . . and All the Rest

Extended family—grandparents, aunts, uncles, and cousins by the dozens—can be a welcome and important support to an adoptive family, or may cause untold anguish and suffering. They can provide a sense of belonging to the clan that goes beyond parents, siblings, and legalities (Melina, 1986, p. 36), or they can withhold approval and welcome, cast doubts on the process, and cause irreparable rifts between family members. Although adoptive parents might wish for family members who would offer them support at such a challenging time in their lives, it is they, not their relatives, who have the knowledge and the ability to reach out to their families. If they do so, it can make a difference in their lives and in their children's lives as well.

As difficult as it can be for adoptive parents to relinquish the dream of having a biological child, it can be almost as difficult for their families. There may be several reasons that family members may resist adoption. Although such resistance often diminishes as people get used to the idea, and especially as they get acquainted with the new member of the family, the initial resistance by close family members can be so painful that adoptive parents may not ever reconcile with relatives who were unsupportive at the beginning (Melina, 1986, p. 33).

If adoptive parents can try to understand the resistance, they may better be able to prepare the extended family to accept the adoption, Melina points out. Some people have been so private about their struggles with infertility that their families do not know why they have decided to adopt. They may need to share some of their journey through infertility treatments in order for family members to understand their decision. Grandparents may find this information painful, blaming themselves for a defect that has now affected their children, Joan Spector says. Family members may also worry that their loved ones will be further hurt or disappointed by the adoption experience. Providing information about the adoption process, and about becoming an adoptive family, may help people cope with their fears.

Understanding the dynamics of the extended family can help explain their resistance, adoption experts point out. Some families have very closed boundaries in terms of accepting and welcoming new people and experiences, while other families are very nurturing and open to outsiders, Julie Bulitt explains. It could be that one person sets the tone for the entire family. If adoptive parents know this about their families, they can predict problems, know not to take them personally, and plan how to solve them.

Certain characteristics of the child may also affect family members' ability to accept him or her, Bulitt says. It is often easier to accept a child who looks more like other members of the family or the community than a child whose appearance is very different. Thus, an international adoption may be even more difficult for extended family, says Ronny Diamond, especially for a Jewish family. Adopting such a child may seem to them not only like a second but a third choice, and they may have a variety of preconceived notions about the country and ethnic background of the child. The child may look even more different from how they ever expected a grandchild to look, and they may worry about the child's acceptance into the Jewish community at large.

It is also usually easier for family members to accept a younger child; babies are usually cute and are less likely to have, or to be thought to have medical, psychological, and educational problems. The child's birth story can also affect people's opinions. If, for example, the child was the product of rape or incest, adoptive parents may choose not to share such information with their families. Family members may also have difficulty accepting a child with special needs, especially when the disability was undiagnosed before the adoption. "My in-laws deny the difficulties of both adoption and special needs," Joyce says. "They had a lot of investment in having grandchildren and refuse to understand how hard it is. They were not supportive of the professional help we needed." Finally, if the child's personality, interests, and talents are similar to that of the adoptive family it may be easier for the family to integrate him or her. The child will feel "like one of their own," so it is more comfortable to make him or her one of their own.

The symbolic meaning of adoption to individuals within the family can also determine their reactions, Bulitt adds. Older relatives may have strong feelings about continuity of the family's bloodline, or biases and stereotypes about other ethnic or religious groups. "There is an enormous sense of loss for the [prospective] grandparents when they realize they will not have biological grandchildren," agrees Molly Wiener. "They wonder if the adopted child will carry on the talents, the heart and soul, of the family." They may also have a more difficult time with the religious aspects of the adoption. Even people who are not observant in their own religious practices can revert to strictness around boundary issues such as conversion. Especially in a community that considers heritage as important as the Jewish community does, the stage is set for painful problems if adoptive parents and their extended families disagree on how they will approach these fundamental concerns.

One way to identify potential problems is to look at the relationship between the adoptive parents and their extended family, Julie Bulitt continues. How the family expects the adoptive parent to handle their reactions—rebelliously or compliantly— may determine how and how much they resist the adoption. How close and how often the adoptive family plans to be with its extended family may help determine how much attention the adoptive parents should pay to their relatives' concerns. Ultimately parents need to protect themselves and their children. While most extended family members are eventually able to accept the adoption and the adoptee, adoptive parents may have to make painful decisions about whether or not to continue to include certain relatives in their lives. "Grandparents want their children to be happy, and most simply fall in love with their grandchildren, so they come around," Molly Wiener says.

A few, however, do not "come around," which can cause a great deal of anguish to adoptive parents. "Some people say it outright, while others imply it and just do not treat the adopted children the same as other children in the family," Linda Yellin says. Two of Bruce's four children were adopted and his father "truly doesn't recognize them as his own," Bruce says. "When our first biological child was born my father asked me how it felt to finally have a 'Schwartz.' I even heard him tell someone that two of the four grandchildren are his."

What can adoptive parents do to help their families accept adoption? Three things: predict, understand, and educate, says Julie Bulitt. Adoptive parents know their families and can often predict which members will have a difficult time coming to terms with adoption. The earlier such relatives become involved in and understand adoption, the more likely they are to accept it. "I invite grandparents to be as much a part of the adoption as possible," says Molly Wiener. "During a pregnancy, they have nine months to think about it. The earlier they become involved with adoption, the better they'll bond with the child. Adoption feels alien to them, so I invite them to be part of the home study, if the adoptive parents are willing, and introduce them to the adoption worker, the person who is making decisions about their children's lives. The adoption worker can put them at ease by showing them pictures, talking about the process of adoption, discussing the challenges of raising an adopted child, and helping them understand how they can be supportive to their children and grandchildren."

"I like to suggest to adoptive parents that they give their family members articles, books, and magazines about adoption," adds Julie Bulitt. "I also advise inviting them into the child's life and keeping them up-to-date on what the child is doing." If adoptive parents can reach out to their family members, understanding that adoption may be difficult for them to accept, they can help create warm and loving connections that can be meaningful in their children's lives.

Older family members may have ideas about adoption that are decades old, Ronny Diamond points out. They need to be educated, and brought along emotionally. She believes that adoption agencies can help by providing groups specifically for grandparents. Joan Spector has conducted such a group for grandparents who had a great deal of difficulty accepting their adopted grandchildren as their own. They "felt terrible that they felt this way," but were disappointed that their bloodline would not continue and they admitted they were not able to feel that these children "belonged to their families," Spector says. The group was helpful, she says, because "once they could say how they felt and they realized they were not the only ones with these feelings, they realized they weren't terrible people. Then they were able to get past it."

Education can also teach others the implications of hurtful language, Ronny Diamond says. Jewish family members have been known to describe something as "a goyishe thing to do," says adoption counselor Linda Yellin. Such statements convey the impression that Jews are different from and better than other people. Although they may not realize the message they are sending, their listeners often do. Richard's father's references to "schwartzes" is just one such example. It seems to be helpful to educate the child to understand that these types of comments are usually not intended personally, says Ronny Diamond. Parents may also want to teach their children to confront the person gently and explain that this is offensive; they may be better able hear it from a child than from another adult, she says.

The power of the family to wound or heal, to include or exclude, to build up or destroy, can have a critical and lasting effect on adoptees. Before an adoptee can say, as the bibical Ruth did, "Your people will be my people," the family members must demonstrate to the adoptee that he or she is theirs.

CHAPTER 10

Adoption and the Jewish Community

~

𝒯he branch that has been transplanted does not exist alone; it grows within a glorious garden. To truly thrive, the transplant must become an integral part of the garden, intertwining with the existing blooms, yet displaying its own unique beauty. This demands a special measure of the gardener's care and attention, to provide for the transplant's particular needs as it attempts to root itself firmly in new and foreign soil. So, too, the adoptee, transplanted into a new community, must be integrated into it, even as his or her own special gifts are encouraged to blossom. Paying subtle, but essential attention to the challenges inherent in transplanting can ease the process and enable the adoptee to become a healthy, comfortable, productive, and happy member of his or her new home. For this to happen, members of the adoptive family and the Jewish communal family—the gardeners of this transplanted branch—have a special responsibility to this child. They have an obligation to ready the ground and provide additional nurturing during the growing season.

The community's responsibility to adoptees and their families has not been widely or commonly acknowledged or understood. Unless people have a personal connection to adoption, either through a family member or a friend, they may not understand its special challenges. Few professionals, Jewish or secular, have considered the impact of adoption on Jewish adoptees, their families, or on the Jewish community as a whole; they have also not considered the impact of Judaism on members of the adoption triad. Fewer have received any training about how to approach these issues. Most operate from their own experiences, and may themselves be victims of good intentions but poor information. They may believe that adoption, especially the "benign" adoption of a same-race infant, is no different from giving birth to that child. They may believe that there are no special circumstances to consider. Or they may believe that an adoptee is the "bad seed" of irresponsible, damaged people, and that every adoption brings a package of virtually insurmountable problems. They rarely see adoption as it is: on the one hand, an alternative way for a child to join a normal, functional, loving family; on the other hand, a consequence of loss, which creates unique developmental challenges.

Rabbis, cantors, family educators, social workers, adoption professionals, religious schoolteachers, and principals can play a vital role in helping families cope with the variety of personal, family, and communal challenges that adoption presents. They can educate, counsel, and model their acceptance of adoption to adoptive families and the community. First, however, they must understand the social, psychological, medical, and religious issues. They must identify and discard their own biases about adoptees, biological parents, and adoptive parents. To do this, they need meaningful information about adoption in general as well as within a Jewish context. They can then share their understanding with the community.

Adoption *is* a community issue, especially within the Jewish community. It is estimated that of American Jewish families who have children, 2.7 percent have children who were adopted (1990 National Jewish Population Survey by the Council of Jewish Federations). Adoption is also a sensitive issue as the Jewish community becomes increasingly more diverse through intermarriage, conversion, and adoption. And it is especially sensitive because the Jewish community has a contradictory relationship with that diversity; some members or segments of the community believe that diversity strengthens and enhances the community, while others remain convinced that diversity weakens and subverts it. It is additionally sensitive because, although Jews are proud of their reputation for open-mindedness, tolerance, and acceptance, some segments of the community maintain strong emotional and ritual commitments to legitimizing membership and participation in the community only through genealogical connections and religious rituals. It is also sensitive because Jews are a minority that has often been persecuted or excluded and, therefore, usually attempts to put the best possible face on delicate situations, both for themselves and for the non-Jewish community. Finally, it is sensitive because Jews have strong social and communal ties and are acutely aware of what the community accepts or rejects.

The Jewish community can ill afford to lose any potential participant. Jewish adoption professionals can work with adoptive families to sensitize them to the uniquely Jewish as well as the general adoption issues they will face. Synagogues; Jewish nursery, day, and supplementary schools; youth groups; and family service agencies have compelling reasons to encourage their professionals to become knowledgeable about and sensitive to adoption issues. With common sense and sensitivity, the Jewish community can welcome and support adoptive Jewish families.

Through the Formative Years

As children grow and develop, they need to master certain tasks and milestones on the road to adulthood and maturity. Quite naturally, this development is affected by adoption. However, adoption specialists find that many people—professionals as well as parents of adopted children—are naive about issues connected with adoption. Understanding them can help concerned adults appreciate an adoptee's actions and reactions as appropriate in the context of his or her adoption. Joyce Maguire Pavao, Ed.D., founder and director of both the Pre and Post Adopton Counseling Team (PACT) at the Family Center in Somerville, Massachusetts, and the Adoption Resource Center in Cambridge, Massachusetts, calls these the "normative crises" of adoption. She explains that as children develop and understand more about adoption, they have questions and reactions that can be anticipated. Most of these reactions to adoption are normal for the child's particular age and stage of development. If they are aware of these developmental patterns, parents and professionals can accept these crises as normal rather than pathological. They can be less afraid and more open, prepared to answer questions, share information, and discuss feelings about what the adoptee is experiencing. Jewish parents and professionals should also be aware that specifically Jewish issues may also impinge on these normal developmental patterns.

From birth to three years of age, the adopted child does not yet realize that there is any difference between him- or herself and nonadopted children. Parents can use this window of opportunity to collect information on their child's birth family and develop a "Life Book" for their child. A "Life Book" is a method—usually a concrete visual record—for connecting adoptees with their past. It contains as much information as possible about a child's birth family, previous placements, reasons for moving, feelings that birth parents had that led to their choice of adoption, etc. It changes and grows over time as new information is added, as the child's life evolves, and as earlier information is reviewed and expanded. Parents can begin to become comfortable talking with their child, family, and friends about adoption. If necessary, Jewish parents can conduct conversion rituals during this time so that their adopted child enters preschool "on a level playing field" with his or her Jewish peers. Parents should be certain to include pictures and other memorabilia from these ceremonies in their child's "Life Book."

The preschooler, ages three to six years, is fascinated with his or her adoption story and asks many questions, yet has little real understanding of the concept of adoption. Parents should encourage questions and answer honestly, but can withhold more problematic information until the child is older. Adults need to be sensitive to what children are asking, so that they neither gloss over nor provide too much detailed information too soon, explains Janice Bershad, M.S.O.T., an adoptive parent and director of Early Childhood Education at Germantown Jewish Center in Philadelphia, Pennsylvania. Discussions about adoption should be positive and natural, and can be reinforced with appropriate stories and books so that children associate adoption with positive events and interactions. This is the time to reassure children that they are loved unequivocally and will never lose the adoptive family. If told at this age that their birth mother placed them for adoption because she loved them, many adopted children will conclude that their adoptive parents too might someday "give them away," since they love them.

Bershad recommends sharing with children stories about Jews from other lands and different family constellations, so that children will become accustomed at a young age to diversity within their community. Adults should take care not to present white Europeans as normative Jews. Children are learning to classify at this age, she explains, and it is normal for them to comment about people whose appearance is different from theirs, which may be an issue for families who have adopted a child of color. Parents and teachers can be most helpful when they neither overreact nor underreact, since children are exquisitely sensitive to adults' attitudes about adoption.

Around this time, children may notice differences between their family's holiday observances and those of their non-Jewish friends and call upon their parents for an explanation. Again, it is important that parents not overreact. They can instill positive feelings about Judaism through the example they set in their home, and can explain that their family is Jewish and does Jewish things. Children do not yet understand that they were born into a different religion from their adoptive parents and then converted to Judaism. Parents may also consider sending their child to a Jewish preschool, a choice made more complex when the child was transculturally or transracially adopted. Some families opt for the cultural and racial diversity of a secular school, where the child may be in the minority as a Jew. Others, in order to reinforce their child's Jewish identity, prefer immersion in the Jewish environment of a day school, although his or her cultural and/or racial heritage will probably make him or her a minority there.

During the elementary school years, the child reaches his or her first real understanding of the underlying issues of adoption and, with that, begins the grieving process for the loss he or she has sustained. Birthdays, Mother's and Father's Day, and other holidays can be difficult for adopted children; while everyone else is celebrating, they may become acutely aware of their differences. Judy explains that her daughter Laura becomes very depressed around her birthday. "She goes into herself and doesn't want to socialize. She spends some private time imagining that she is with her birth mother, who she calls her 'born lady.'"

If they are in denial about their loss, adopted children may stop asking questions or, Lois Melina explains, they may wonder what they did to cause it. They may conclude that they are "bad" or "unlovable," which can have a negative impact on their self-esteem (Melina, "Teachers Need to Be More Sensitive to Adoption Issues," 1990, p. 2). Some adoptees try to be the "good" adoptee (their term), to prove their adoptive parents right for adopting them and their birth parents wrong for giving them up, while others act out, trying to discover how bad they have to be before this set of parents gives them away, too. Parents and teachers may see children who are daydreaming, withdrawn, distractible, and conflicted over choosing appropriate friends, says Marilyn Schoettle, MA, assistant director of the Center for

Adoptive Families in Silver Spring, Maryland. Adults can let a child know that they are not threatened or angry, and that the child is welcome to ask questions, even difficult ones, when he or she is ready.

By the time they have reached school age, many adopted children have been asked, sometimes by other children but occasionally even by adults, where their "real" mother is, or why their "real parents" gave them away. Parents and teachers can provide children tools with which to face a world that is curious, but ill informed, about adoption. First, children can learn that how they answer questions about being adopted is up to them, says Julie Bulitt, LCSW, an adoptive and biological parent and a family therapist with the Center for Adoptive Families. "They can tell people about being adopted, they can ignore the question, or they can say that this is private information."

Second, when adults use and model positive adoption language, they teach children to do the same, explains Patricia Irwin Johnston, MS, adoptive parent, adoption educator, and publisher of Perspectives Press. Words and phrases such as "real parents," "natural child," or "children of your own" do not describe the loving quality of family relationships in an adoptive family. To distinguish between a child's two sets of parents, it is preferable to use "birth mother/father/parent" to describe the people who conceived the child. The adoptive parents are simply referred to as "parent/mom/dad." Adoption is not a condition or a disability; when referring to a child's adoption, it is appropriate to use the past tense to indicate the way in which the child entered the family ("Sam was adopted," not "Sam is adopted"). The decision made by the birth parents should be referred to as "choosing adoption," or "making an adoption plan," acknowledging their responsibility for this action. It is best to avoid terms such as "giving up" a child or "putting a child up for adoption," since these are far less positive and more emotionally charged (Johnston, 1996).

Jewish children may begin formal religious training during these elementary school years, which can intensify questions about their birth parents' religion(s). Laura once asked Judy whether her "born lady" knew she wouldn't have Christmas if Judy adopted her. Children may express the desire to celebrate the holidays of their birth religion or attend religious services. Adoptive parents hold widely varying views on how to handle such requests, some believing that they have a responsibility to acknowledge their child's birth heritage, others adamant that their foremost responsibility is to raise their children, adopted or not, as Jews. Parents should try to determine the purpose behind their child's questions or comments, advises Nancy Janus, Ed.D., an adoptive parent and associate professor of Human Development at Eckerd College in St. Petersburg, Florida. Is this rebellion or an honest attempt to understand their origin? She believes that it usually is simply exploration, and that adoptive parents can respect and acknowledge their child's desire to know and understand this part of their background, while maintaining their home and personal practices as they believe appropriate.

Young teens, ages twelve to sixteen, may be angry because of the loss of their birth parents, as well as over the loss of control in their lives, and they may resist authority by trying on new identities, including religious identities. Myra Hettleman, LCSW-C, director of Adoption Alliances of the Jewish Family Services of Central Maryland, Inc., in Baltimore, points out that it is developmentally appropriate for teens to wonder how they are alike and different from their parents. Identity formation can be doubly difficult for adopted teens who have to separate both from parents they know and parents they do not know. It can be triply difficult for adopted Jewish teens, since both Judaism and adoption make them different from their peers, and adolescents do not want to be different. If parents can resist responding in anger to their child's anger, they will be able to be firm in setting and carrying out needed and reasonable limits. They should allow the child as much control and opportunity for decision making as possible. And while continuing to let the child know how much he or she is loved, parents can help their child obtain and accept information about his or her birth and adoption.

Jewish teens may begin to prepare for their Bar or Bat Mitzvah at the beginning of this stage and confirmation at the end of it. There is the potential for these life-cycle events to become the focus of the battle over Jewish identity. They may realize that, had they not been adopted by this family, they would not be involved in these rituals. Some teens tell their parents, "I don't want to have a Bar (or Bat) Mitzvah; I'm not really Jewish." This may be, Hettleman points out, the beginning of an internal dialogue about the adoptee's origins and the beginning of the need to search. It may also be the start of social issues for Jewish children adopted transculturally or transracially. Pat remembers that Noam, who was adopted from El Salvador and has very dark skin, was not invited to many Bar or Bat Mitzvah parties. As he grew older, few Jewish girls were willing to date him. Adoptive parents and Jewish professionals should be prepared to deal with these delicate issues, without becoming angry or defensive themselves.

Older teens, age sixteen to nineteen, may be anxious about growing up and leaving home, which can exacerbate any depression they feel over the losses in their lives. If parents are alert for signs of sadness and depression, they can begin to work with their child on appropriate plans for the future, while reassuring him or her of their love. Other concerned adults may be helpful, if they have developed a rapport with the young adult. If the adoptee has not already done so, he or she may express the desire to meet birth parents, Lois Melina points out. Although reunions during these years are usually discouraged as too difficult, since teens are often struggling to establish an appropriate relationship with their adoptive parents, this can become a control issue between parents and teens. Teens begin dating more seriously and religious issues can be a focus of rebellion or a cause for concern by the adoptee who does not feel accepted by the Jewish community. It can also be a minefield for Jewish parents who prefer that their children date and marry Jews. Conveying that message to a child who was not born Jewish can be difficult. "Aren't non-Jews good enough?" one adoptee asked. "Maybe I'm not good enough either; I wasn't born Jewish."

The Jewish Community's Special Role

Judaism is more than a religion; it is an international community, a civilization with a language, history, food, art, literature, music, religion, and social structure of its own. Jews do more than attend religious services. Judaism's influence can infuse every aspect of its adherents' lives. Jewish families often seek relief from the isolation of modern society within the Jewish community. They search for fellowship, especially if their extended families are not in close proximity, within the comfortable familiarity of the group. This provides a unique opportunity—and responsibility—to welcome and integrate all of its members and to enfold them within the protective arms of the community. Adoptive families, however, sometimes find reason to question the warmth of their welcome and may, therefore, limit the extent of their involvement.

Adoptive parents would like people to be sensitive to and anticipate situations that might be difficult for their children, and to modify their behavior accordingly, explains Lois Melina in *Adopted Child* (Melina, 1990, p. 1). However, they are also concerned that adoption not be the first, last, or only thing people think about in relation to their child. In other words, she explains, adoptive parents want the world to put adoption in proper perspective: It is an event—and only one of many—that influences the way children and parents view themselves, their families, and their place in the world. It is important that people neither overemphasize nor ignore it.

Adoptive parents are often hurt when people, with no bad intentions, fumble, points out Elaine Frank, MSW, director of After Adoption and Parenting Services for Children in Philadelphia, Pennsylvania. Rhona remembers her horror when a casual acquaintance, "a very nice woman," approached her in synagogue as she stood with Lindsey, her blonde-haired, blue-eyed ten-year-old, and jokingly asked, "Are you sure she's Jewish?" Rhona had already initiated a discussion with Lindsey about her birth parents and their religion, and they were able to talk about this incident. Lindsey thought that the woman had made the comment because she knew that Lindsey was adopted and converted to Judaism, and therefore "not really Jewish." Rhona assured her that the woman did not know her story, and had meant only to admire her eyes and hair. She also assured Lindsey that she "really" is Jewish. Adoptive parents wish people were more attuned to diversity in general, and to the feelings engendered by adoption in particular. They want to protect their children, yet worry that people will either assume something negative because a child was adopted, or completely ignore the very real issues that exist.

The Jewish community has a special responsibility to trans-culturally and transracially adopted Jewish children, says Gail Steinberg, an adoptive parent and co-director of Pact—An Adoption Alliance, in San Francisco, California. Although their parents may assume that children will be automatically accepted because it is within the context of a spiritual and religious community, this is not necessarily the case. "My children were always perceived first as black or Asian, and then second—maybe—as Jews," says Reba, who has two transracially adopted and two Caucasian adopted children. "The Jewish community always saw two of them as 'other.' The result is that they always perceived that they weren't full members of the community on their own. While they wouldn't miss a [Jewish] family event, they wouldn't attend a Jewish communal event."

"Parents need to have a realistic view of what their children's experience might be in the Jewish community," Steinberg says. "They have to realize that their child will have a different experience being a Jew than they did. Children are getting the message that they don't belong, not from ill will, but lack of consciousness. This is particularly heightened in a religious context, where the message should be one of acceptance. One can't simply expect the community to understand; families have to be their child's advocate. They have to prepare the child to cope, giving them specific ideas about what they can say and do in a specific circumstance if they are made to feel unwelcome. And they have to educate the community.

"Spirituality is particularly important to adopted children. Those who have been separated from one family and then connected to another have a core issue around connectedness. A belief in and support from a Higher Being is an offer of true comfort in stressful times; it is a healing tool to offer children. It is a built-in framework that parents can transmit aggressively to their adopted children," she adds.

Adoptive parents can help the community help their children. They can learn about adoption's special challenges from those adoption professionals who are doing careful and sensitive work in this area. They can then help to educate family, friends, other professionals, and members of the community about adoption, says Nancy Janus. They can also model a positive attitude. When people see that parents view the adopted child as a gift and a blessing, not as "second best," that is how they will view the child. Those who understand the challenges adoptees face are more likely to be willing and able to help.

Family Service Agencies: Helping Adoptive Parents Help Themselves

The first and most direct opportunity to support adoptive Jewish families may belong to Jewish family service agencies and their adoption departments. "Often, the first phone call a prospective adoptive parent makes is to my office," says Lois Samuels, MSW, adoption coordinator at the Jewish Children's Bureau of Chicago, Illinois. "It is meaningful that the person's first step in exploring adoption is within the Jewish community." In the past, however, there was little training for adoptive parenting and for dealing with the lifelong issues of adoption. Even during home studies, which evaluated the prospective parents' readiness to adopt, little effort was made to educate or prepare people for what might lie ahead. "Adoption was not an open topic and we didn't help parents know how to talk to their children," explains Molly Wiener, LCSW, supervisor of adoption at the Jewish Family Service of West Hartford, Connecticut. "But we saw that even in loving families, adopted children were having a tough time and we realized that love is not enough. Pretending [that everything was the same as in biological families] didn't work."

Many agencies do a better job today of educating adoptive parents about the myriad issues of adoption, although some continue to place children and assume that everyone lives "happily ever after." Parents who adopt privately may receive no preparation or education at all. Pre-placement home studies provide an opportunity to sensitize and educate, to prepare people for the unique challenges they will face. Some agencies conduct seminars that include attorneys who speak on the legal issues, physicians who speak on medical issues, adoption specialists who speak on child development specifically in relationship to adoption, and panels of adoptive parents, adult adoptees, and birth parents who share real-life experiences. Post-placement support meetings enable families to deal with issues as they actually arise.

There was also scant recognition in the past of the impact of Judaism on adoptees and their families. Discussion was limited almost completely to halakhic issues involving conversion. However, the complicated process of becoming comfortable with one's adopted identity must include the role that Judaism plays in that identity. Some Jewish agencies have begun to offer various forums for families to discuss the uniquely Jewish issues they confront. It can be difficult for Jewish adoptive parents to seek or accept that support. Often, they think that they have to be perfect parents, Myra Hettleman says. They are especially loath to turn to the Jewish community for help. They may believe that no one else in the community faces similar problems; they may be embarrassed in front of friends and peers; and they may be unaware of the interaction of Judaism and adoption issues.

Hettleman facilitated a group for adoptive Jewish mothers of teenage boys who were having fairly severe academic and behavior problems. These mothers found it difficult to deal with their sons' problems and to face having less than the perfect family of their dreams. They had not been prepared prior to the placement to expect any type of disability, and felt that the Jewish community expected perfection from its members. They were able to benefit from sharing their concerns with one another so that they realized they were not alone, and to gain perspective from Hettleman's professional guidance. Molly Wiener and Lois Samuels invite panels of rabbis to discuss such common concerns as conversion, as well as other issues that many parents have not yet considered, such as helping their children integrate their non-Jewish birth heritage into their identity. Samuels also pairs experienced moms with new moms who need support, providing another tie to the Jewish community. The goal of these efforts, Wiener says, is to give families a frame of reference so that if questions arise they will call and ask for help. However, not every Jewish parent adopts through a Jewish agency and not every Jewish agency conducts this type of training.

"Our agency did wonderful parent training," Fredda says. "I felt really comfortable with our caseworker, not like I was being evaluated. We had several personal meetings, in which we each talked about our childhood, the type of child we felt comfortable adopting, our family interactions. And we had three group meetings with other couples so that we could talk about the concerns we share. After the placement, we had several informal meetings in our home with our caseworker and a few more couples' meetings. But the agency isn't Jewish, none of the other couples in our group were Jewish, and I do have some concerns. We aren't really religious, but religion is important to us. I worry that since we [Jews] are a minority and there is still prejudice and anti-Semitism in the world, Judaism might be a source of pain to my son someday. He might think it would have been better if we hadn't adopted and converted him. But I don't know who to talk to about that."

Jewish families can take such concerns to Stars of David International, Inc., a nonprofit information and support network for Jewish and partly Jewish adoptive families. The organization was founded by Phyllis Nissen, whose three children were adopted from Korea, and Rabbi Susan Abramson. Nissen was active in an adoption group, but found nothing there that dealt with the Jewish family. She asked for Abramson's support in starting a specifically Jewish group. Their first meeting, a Hanukkah party, was so successful that they knew a tremendous unfulfilled need existed. Today, the organization publishes a newsletter and supports a web page. Local chapters around the country host educational/social/support meetings.

Adoption support groups are an invaluable resource, agrees Susan Freivalds, executive director of the National Adoption Foundation, in Danbury, Connecticut. "They can be a place for a reality check, a place to validate one's experiences, when things don't go exactly as planned. They can be a place to meet other adoptive families and see that adoption does work. And they may be a more comfortable place for adoptive families than returning to the agency that placed the child with them, a place where they may have felt they had to prove what a good family they were."

It is appropriate and helpful to join a group during any phase of the adoption. In the exploratory period, when the couple is just considering adoption, a group can help them consider questions about the types of children that may be available for adoption, their readiness to parent those children, and the types of adoption that are available. Once they decide to adopt, as they begin actual preparations, the group can assist with both technical and emotional issues. During the post-placement adjustment, a support group can help a couple make the decisions that will create a family. And during the post-legalization phase, the group can help deal with the ongoing issues of family life (Piantanida and Anderson, 1990, pp. 6–13).

"People find a real, genuine caring within a group; they are able to talk about the things that are most important to them with people who have had similar experiences," confirms Barbara Stern, CSW, an adoptive parent, a psychotherapist who specializes in adoption and single-parent issues, and the president of New York Singles Adopting Children (NYSAC). "Our meetings include the elements common to most support groups: self-help discussions, educational sessions, social activities, and service activities. Openness is the key to success."

Synagogues and Religious Leaders Offer Important Support

The main connection to the Jewish community for many families is their synagogue. Rabbis and cantors, the first-line Jewish professionals, set the tone for the community, points out Lois Samuels. By modeling acceptance of adoptees and explaining Judaism's positive stance on forming families through adoption, they imprint adoption with a Jewish seal of approval. Using positive adoption language and referring to families formed by adoption, as well as biologically, in sermons and discussions can help normalize adoption and adoptive parents' adjustment to parenting.

Rabbis should be counseling infertile couples to consider adoption, says Steve Freedman, an adoptive and biological father and the educational director of Beth Sholom Congregation in Elkins Park, Pennsylvania. If extended family members are critical of adoption or reject the adoptee, the rabbi may be able to help identify the source of their objection and ameliorate it. People may be able to work through their feelings with a rabbi and come to an understanding of how to support their family members. If not, the adoptive parents, and later their child, may need the rabbi's help to deal with the pain of this rejection. If the adoptive family also has birth children, the rabbi may be able to offer them support as they readjust their position in the family to accommodate their new sibling (Piantanida and Anderson, 1990, p. 11).

Life cycle events—*brit milah, pidyon ha-ben,* naming ceremony, conversion, Bar/Bat mitzvah, and confirmation—are also times when Jewish families rely on their religious leaders for guidance. These professionals must understand the emotional, developmental, and ritual issues in order to provide accurate and sensitive advice. However, many rabbis feel helpless in assisting adoptive families, says Lois Samuels. Although their rabbinical training may have prepared them for the halakhic questions, it probably shed little light on the human concerns. The late Barbara Wachs, D.H.L., who was a Jewish family life educator at the Auerbach Central Agency for Jewish Education in Melrose Park, Pennsylvania, suggested that rabbinical schools include adoption in their practical rabbinics courses and that rabbis' handbooks offer resources and suggestions for programming and handling sensitive issues.

Conversion is an extremely sensitive issue throughout the Jewish community and many adoptive parents struggle with it. Many Jewish adoption professionals decry the divisiveness this issue has produced in the Jewish community. Traditional conversions matter to many people who aren't Orthodox, says Dina Rosenfeld, DSW, director of the undergraduate social work program at New York University. "This is a crucial moment in people's lives, and rabbis who are unaccepting of people who want a conversion, or who keep tabs on other rabbis and call their practices into question, are distancing people at a crucial moment in their lives and this turns them off to Judaism," she says. Rabbis who actively assist congregants in arranging a *bet din* have a prime opportunity for both teaching about the tradition and binding a family to it in the most meaningful way imaginable.

In the context of struggling with identity issues, especially during adolescence, many Jewish families worry that their adopted children may someday question their Jewish identity, confirms Ellen Singer, LCSW, an adoptive parent and clinical social worker in private practice and with the Center for Adoptive Families. "What the children and their families do not need is for a portion of the Jewish community to affirm the adopted child's own doubts by questioning the authenticity of their conversion to Judaism. Rabbis should be very sensitive about how and what they communicate regarding adoption and conversion."

Similar opportunities exist when families name their child within the Jewish community. The rabbi may need to initiate these celebrations; some families are not aware of their options for religious ceremonies following the adoption of a child. Existing ceremonies might be modified or new ones created to mark the family's transition. Depending on the family, such ceremonies might be conducted with only the family and friends, or incorporated within a congregational service. Most families are thrilled at the opportunity to begin their child's life with meaningful Jewish rituals, and many find that this is the first step on a lifelong journey of involvement in Judaism.

Bar or Bat Mitzvah is the next significant life-cycle event in a child's life, and rabbis may be able to help adopted teens prepare themselves emotionally for this rite of passage, suggests Rabbi Philip Pohl of B'nai Shalom in Olney, Maryland. He explains that Bar or Bat Mitzvah has a special meaning for an adopted person, as a way of affirming his or her Judaism. According to

traditional Jewish law, a converted child has the option of rejecting the conversion at this moment. If the young person's journey
has been difficult, a rabbi who has been involved with the family may be able to recognize the problem and help the adoptee
deal with his or her conflicting feelings about adoption and
Jewish identity. The rabbi may also offer an understanding ear to
the adoptive parents, who may have believed that such questions
were resolved at the conversion, and may be particularly vulnerable when adoption affects this core issue.

"I have had adoptees with questions about how to relate to the
non-Jewish part of their identity," Rabbi Pohl confirms. "I don't
disregard what they are feeling; rather, I probe their feelings with
them, about Judaism and about their birth religion. I would not
recommend helping a child explore his or her birth religion.
Rather, I would explain that Judaism is what we practice and
what we live, and that while we can discuss aspects of some other
religion theoretically, we can not explore it. I help them look at
what the issues are for them: what doesn't feel authentic to them
about Judaism, what might feel authentic about some other religion, what Judaism says about this, and what comfortable way
they can find to remain a Jew. I wish I could have such discussions with everyone, because people might have similar issues
even if they were born Jewish. But I can see people having
stronger feelings about it if they were adopted."

Another way for synagogues to support adoptive families is to
provide a home for an adoption support group like Stars of
David. "It is important for all synagogues and Jewish communities to be more openly welcoming to adoptive families," says
Rabbi Abramson. An adoption support group within the congregation transmits the message that adoption is valued by the
community, and that the issues of adoption warrant such a
group. When the congregation's religious leaders lend their support by attending meetings, speaking to the group, and making
it clear that they are interested and available to consult with

adoptive families about any issues that the families face, it empowers the families to face the issues and the community.

Schools Leave an Indelible Mark

Once families have made the decision to become involved in the Jewish community, a child's participation in religious school—either supplementary or day school—can create a lasting impression. Parents and professionals intend that impression to establish within the child a desire to identify as a Jew and to involve him- or herself in the Jewish community. If, however, the school is not sensitive to the unique challenges of adoption, it may alienate the child and the family. Many Jewish educators are not aware of adoption issues or, if they are, do not adapt their teaching or the curriculum in response, according to Barbara Wachs. They can, she emphasized, use the material and their presentation of it to affirm adoption in the Jewish community and to welcome adoptees and their families.

Many adoptive parents wonder whether to inform the school that their child was adopted. Many adoptive parents have heard distressing tales of insensitivity on the part of school personnel, and they are afraid. But when educators don't have needed information, it is more difficult for them to plan appropriately. One solution is for teachers to assume that there are children who are adopted in every class. This approach not only allows for sensitivity to the needs of adopted children, but provides a model of respect and an awareness of diversity to all children.

Most adoption experts recommend that parents do tell schools that their child was adopted. "It [adoption] comes up at various times and in various ways during school, and should not be a stigmatized category; it is one more piece of information about this child that can be helpful," explains Dina Rosenfeld. But how and what they tell is an individual decision, adds Elaine Frank, MSW, of After Adoption, in Philadelphia, Pennsylvania, and the child after a certain age should have some input into this decision, because this is his or her information.

Educators need to be sensitive when discussing adoption with parents and careful not to put them on the defensive. Adoptive parents often feel they must be perfect parents and they often believe strongly in the role of environment in child development. They therefore feel responsible for everything that happens to their children, even if what happens is beyond their control, Lois Melina points out (Melina, "Teachers Need to Be More Sensitive to Adoption Issues," 1990, p. 3). Children's learning styles and school performances are a result of a variety of influences, and it does a disservice to both parents and children either to assume adoption is the primary cause of every problem or to ignore the contribution adoption makes altogether.

Educational directors and principals can help their staff deal with adoption-related concerns through in-service education. Does the school have any policies about how to deal with adoption? Intake interviews, parent-teacher conferences, classroom materials, various aspects of the curriculum, and social interactions can be influenced by adoption, and teachers should be aware of why and how to approach these situations. It is extremely helpful, says Elaine Frank, if "everyone is on the same page," and the faculty has discussed ways to be supportive of adoptive families.

During entrance interviews or parent-teacher conferences, educators can explain why they are asking questions pertaining to a child's birth and developmental history. When educators convey the attitude that they want to understand a child's learning style or plan curriculum more sensitively, parents are more likely to share this personal information. It is also helpful for educators to know whether the child knows about the adoption, how he or she feels about it, and whether he or she is aware that this information is being shared with the school. Educators can discuss with parents how the parents handle adoption with their child and how they would like the school to handle it. If they lay the groundwork for an ongoing dialogue with parents, everyone will benefit, Frank says. If, however, parents become aware that their educators are as yet uninformed about adoption issues, they can offer to help, Marilyn Schoettle says. Parents should request programs proactively and advocate for the environment to improve before problems arise and emotions become involved.

When purchasing materials for Jewish schools and libraries, librarians and teachers should carefully select books about adoption that present adoption in a realistic and positive light. They should also remember that the Jewish community consists of people from many different kinds of families, and with many different backgrounds and physical appearances. Textbooks, library books, dolls, puppets, and posters that present the great diversity of the Jewish community can help build a child's self-esteem. "We have images in our school that reflect the population we have," says Janice Bershad. "For example, we have cut-out people with three different skin tones and we dress them for all the Jewish holidays. It felt forced in the beginning, but it was important to make sure it happened."

Aspects of the religious school curriculum can, if handled traditionally, present problems for children who were adopted. Or they can become an opportunity for teachers to take the initiative and discuss adoption as a normal part of life, says Marilyn Schoettle. Many teachers do a unit on "roots," requiring children to create a "family tree," bring in baby or family pictures, or write an autobiography. Judy recalls that Laura was given a grid to fill in with her ancestors' names, and that her reaction was to wonder what to do with it. They decided to modify the assignment, and made a tree with roots as well as branches so that she could find a place on it for her birth parents. Preferably, teachers will modify the assignment in advance, giving all children options and not singling out those who were adopted. They could put in the "active" people in their lives, whether related by birth or adoption, or not related at all. Or they could trace someone else's family tree, perhaps a famous person's or a hero's. If teachers think about what the task is intended to accomplish, and how it will affect the children emotionally as well as academically, they can develop creative ways to accomplish the same thing, Schoettle says.

Bible stories that touch, directly or indirectly, on adoption issues can also be a problematic part of the religious school curriculum. Each of the patriarchs and matriarchs struggled with fertility issues, and their solutions may not translate well in modern times. The story of Moses is possibly the most difficult for adoptive families, since he, ultimately, became a hero when he turned against his adoptive (Egyptian) family and reconnected with his birth family. "This may stir real feelings in the adoptive child and it's crucial to admit it," says Rabbi Pohl. "I would have a dialogue with the child, outside the classroom, and explain that what Moses felt in Pharaoh's house wasn't authentic to him, and that that is why he turned against it." Rhona adds, "I reconcile this by explaining to Lindsey that Moses needed to be adopted to save his people. . . . However, his adoption was under duress, literally, to save his life. The decision to have him raised as an Egyptian was not a decision freely made by his birth mother." Rabbis and teachers should be sensitive to the feelings these stories might stir up, advises Dina Rosenfeld, and can look for opportunities to open conversations with children about their reactions.

Social interactions are often the focus of a child's world; children view anything that sets them apart from their peers as undesirable. Nonadopted children may question or even tease an adopted child, and too often, Schoettle says, no one is there for the child. She recommends that during in-service sessions, staff members brainstorm responses to these behaviors, which can help normalize adoption and demonstrate that it is viewed as a valid way to build a family. If guidance counselors are available, they can approach children personally to let them know someone is there for them. They can also conduct support groups for the children, to help them realize that they are not alone, and to teach them to advocate for themselves. Given that researchers believe that school failure can contribute to adoption-related problems, while school enjoyment correlates with adoption success, schools are an especially important target for adoption awareness activities. (1996 North American Council on Adoptable Children [NACAC] National Adoption Awareness Month Guide).

Epilogue

~

"The branch You have made strong . . . " The psalmist, of course, refers to God. He might also have been referring to adoptive parents, who have undertaken a great challenge and, in most cases, succeeded admirably. The "branch" that they have transplanted, their beloved child, their adopted child, has become an able and healthy individual, an integral member of their family, and a welcomed member of the Jewish community. They have poured love, energy, time, thought, and care into their child. They have tended the garden diligently throughout the seasons. And they have triumphed; the transplanting has "taken" and their child has been made strong.

Adoption is a miraculous way to form a family. It is a difficult, but rewarding, way—and that is the message of this book. The real work of adoption is not in the act of adopting; the real work is in raising the adopted child to comfortable, self-confident, self-respecting adulthood. Every adopted person, every adoptive family, will have challenges to face arising simply from the fact of adoption. Jewish adoptees and their families have additional and special challenges—but ones from which they should not shrink. They should not doubt themselves. These are challenges that are surmountable, hurdles they can clear, and when they do, the rewards are tremendous. Perhaps the most critical, and first, challenge is to understand and accept that future challenges exist, and then to set out to confront them head-on.

An adoptive family's Jewish identity is, hopefully, a source of joy and strength. Adoptive parents can help make it that for their child, too. But in order to do so, they must realize that grafting that additional new identity onto the transplanted branch will take work and commitment. It will require delicacy and perseverance. Love will be essential, but it will not be enough.

What will be enough? The key, it seems, is honest and ongoing communication. If adoptive parents combine the candid expression of own feelings with respectful listening to their child's, they will create an atmosphere wherein together they will be able to surmount the challenges. Adoptive parents will not have all the answers when they begin, and they will not have them as they proceed. But if they are willing to make the journey and respect the process, the outcome will take care of itself.

Judaism and the Jewish community have much to offer adoptive families. The values and beliefs of Judaism are a wondrous guide to both self-fulfillment and a humane and giving life. The community can be an enriching source of strength and support, enveloping its members in words and deeds of caring and love. Those instincts are there; adoptive parents may have to help the community express them toward their adopted children. This will help those children embrace their adopted community in turn.

My hope is that all members of the adoption triad—adoptees, adoptive parents, and biological parents—as well as all those professionals who work with them, will recognize the wonder of the transplanted branch that has grown healthy and strong, and the beauty that the adoptee brings to the garden. Then they can all grow from strength to strength together.

APPENDIX I

Ametz HaBrit, Adopting the Covenant: Jewish Adoption Rituals

~

The Jewish religion is rich in rituals, formal and symbolic acts that recognize life's meaningful passages. Rituals meet a variety of needs: the need for the individual to be acknowledged by the community, for the community to be acknowledged by its members, and for the individual and community to bond with one another. They provide the authentic stamp of something ancient upon a personal event, and allow those participating in the ritual to reenact, and learn from, the messages of tradition. And they create a predictable structure, which provides a sense of safety during a time of transition (Orenstein, 1994, p. xx).

Transition, even when it involves joyful and eagerly awaited events, can be stressful. Rituals serve an important purpose. "Rituals mark transitions in family life and help families heal," says Lois Ruskai Melina and Sharon Kaplan Roszia in *The Open Adoption Experience* (1993, p. 133). "They create change as well as create an awareness of change, provide a vehicle for people to express their feelings, define relationships, help them arrive at solutions and restore balance to lives that have been disrupted by change or crisis."

Adoption is the very essence of change, and as such, is a life transition that deserves to be acknowledged. It marks the beginning of a new life for the adoptee, as someone other than who he

239

or she would have been. It creates a new family for the adoptive relatives by adding a member who is not biologically related to the rest of the family. And it marks the end of the birth parents' roles as active parenting figures in a child's life. The power of an adoption ritual comes from acknowledging these changes. It explicitly incorporates the new member into the family's and community's past, present, and future, as it implicitly recognizes the losses incurred by all members of the adoption triad and facilitates healing the wounds caused by these losses.

All cultures have their own distinctive rituals, which assign meaning to life transitions and define membership within that particular culture. Tribes, clans, and ethnic groups throughout the world use rituals and ceremonies to designate such events as a child's birth and coming of age, marriage, new parenthood, and dying, explains Mary Martin Mason in *Designing Rituals of Adoption for the Religious and Secular Community* (1995, p. iii). Rituals, she notes, "mark and define us, either by our relationship to God or by our place in the world and among the people around us; comprise our habits in everyday life and thus comprise the fabric of our being; let us know where we are inside our life's journey, marking important life and death passages; connect us to those who came before us and those who will come after us; provide, define, and display membership or inter-reliance within a community; and create understanding and support among those who participate or serve as witnesses to the ritual" (p. 2).

Religious rituals fill a special and unique niche. People for whom religious observance is a familiar and comforting part of daily life feel drawn to express themselves through their religion during times of particular importance to them. Even those who have little regular contact with any religious group seem to sense a need within themselves for affiliation during such times. Some respond to the invisible, yet powerful, lure of not quite forgotten childhood memories imprinted forever on their psyches. Others, even those whose lives hold no such traditions, find they wish to commemorate and mark the importance of the present event. Specifically Jewish adoption rituals can both create and validate the adoptive family's connection to the Jewish community, as well as involve extended family and that community in affirming and embracing the new member.

In Jewish tradition, however, the emphasis is on giving birth; there is no ritual acknowledgment of adoption. A *brit milah* or *hatafat dam brit* for a boy, a naming ceremony for a girl, and even a conversion ceremony, do not specifically ritualize adoption. In years past, because many adoptive parents were advised to behave "as if" their child was theirs by birth, because they didn't know anything else was possible, and because they didn't question tradition, they often participated in ceremonies that did not explicitly acknowledge how their child joined their family. As a result, many adoptive parents, who would have liked to rejoice with their community, felt disconnected from their heritage rather than welcomed by it. "People who missed out on a ritual suffer a profound sense of deprivation; when there is no ceremony, they have feelings of isolation, loss and exclusion. Rituals that are based on the traditional nuclear family, and the assumption that these rituals fit everyone, serve to distance some people from the community rather than bringing them to it," confirms Rela M. Geffen in *Celebration and Renewal: Rites of Passage in Judaism* (1993, pp. 5–6).

With the growing awareness of other new life-cycle rituals, an increasing number of adoptive families desire to commemorate this joyful event with a specifically Jewish adoption ceremony. They yearn to actively write themselves and their children into the community, and to call upon Judaism's vast power to create meaning and facilitate healing. They may not, however, feel entitled or empowered to do so. They may believe that only ceremonies handed down from ancient ancestors or authored by professionals are valid or authentic. Or, they assume that they lack the requisite knowledge to create a ceremony. But rituals are continually evolving to fit new social roles, writes Geffen, because if they fail to do so, "they cease to be the democratic constants that have always undergirded the Jewish community" (Geffen, 1993, p. 6). Thus, with some thought and guidance, adoptive families can create beautiful and meaningful rituals.

Rituals can be created in at least three ways, explains Debra Orenstein in *Lifecycles: Jewish Women on Life Passages and Personal Milestones*. Traditions that have fallen into disuse can be recovered; an existing rite or blessing can be used in a new context, or traditional texts, symbols, images, and ritual objects can be employed to create an entirely new composition. "The first two methods renew the old creatively, while the last creates the new authentically. Thus, they fulfill Rabbi Abraham Isaac Kook's (the chief rabbi of Palestine, 1921) intention that "the old be made new, and the new, made holy" (Orenstein, 1994, p. xxi).

Rituals should be meaningful to each participant, for each person who takes part marks his or her place in the adoption constellation. Adoptive parents, the most likely creators of Jewish adoption rituals, receive empowerment and validation for their new role in their child's life. Children find acknowledgment of where they began and where they now belong. Birth parents, who can be included either actually or by proxy, are affirmed in their decision and released from their role as active parents, while their unbreakable genetic tie to the child is emphasized (Mason, 1995, p. iv). Siblings and other members of the extended family forge, acknowledge, and/or strengthen their connection to the new member of their family. A rabbi who helps create and participates in such a ceremony empowers congregrants, legitimizes both the specific ceremony and the creation of such rituals in general, and serves as a role model of how to welcome into the community families who have not been created in the typical way. Friends and other members of the Jewish community recognize, by their presence and participation, the family's struggle and ultimate success in creating a family, and the individual's right to membership in the group.

Creating Ritual

Because there is no precedent for an adoption ritual in either Jewish law or tradition, virtually everything can be determined by the participants. Those who decide to create an adoption ritual have a variety of things to consider, says Mary Martin Mason (Mason, 1995, p. 10). These include

• halakhah

• the day and time

• the location

• the leader

• witnesses and participants

• symbolic actions or objects

• music

• appropriate readings, prayers, and poems

The child's age and stage of development (especially if he or she is not an infant and is able to participate), culture, race, and history should also be taken into consideration. Blending the child's heritage with the adoptive family's recognizes his or her dual community membership, pays tribute to his or her heritage of origin, and establishes a tone for the years to come (Mason, p. iv).

Halakhah

Although an adoption ritual has tremendous importance for the family, it has no halakhic or legal ramifications. While it may include conversion and naming rituals, it does not replace them, says Rabbi Richard Fagan, an educational consultant at the Auerbach Central Agency for Jewish Education in Melrose Park, Pennsylvania. At the same time, families will likely want a ceremony that is in consonance with their branch of Judaism. If they have family members whose views and beliefs differ from theirs they may want to be aware of the halakhic sensitivities of those involved and prepare them for a ceremony that is different from what they know, Rabbi Fagan adds. If, for example, they create a new blessing, traditional Jews may have a problem with that.

Day and Time

Families usually wait until the adoption is final before proceeding with a formal conversion ceremony. Because this involves immersion in the *mikvah*, many parents like to wait until their child is older and comfortable in the water. Of course, most baby boys will already have had a *brit milah* or a *hatafat dam brit* and many girls will have had a naming ceremony, but the immersion and an *Ametz HaBrit* [Adopting the Covenant] ritual can be combined in a meaningful and beautiful ceremony.

While any time is acceptable, one appropriate time for an adoption ritual is on the Shabbat following the finalization proceedings. The Shabbat is a time of *kedusha* [holiness and sanctity], and adoption rituals are, in effect, sanctifying the nonreligious, legal proceeding. Shabbat is also a sign of the covenant between God and Israel; what more appropriate time to bring a child into membership in that covenant? It might be possible to conduct the *bet din* and visit the *mikvah* on Friday morning or afternoon before sundown, and complete the ritual with an Adopting the Covenant ceremony on Shabbat.

Because adoption is about separation and new beginnings, another suggestion is to have the ceremony during a Havdalah service on a Saturday evening. Havdalah is the service that closes the Sabbath and marks the separation between Shabbat and the weekdays. It treats this separation and new beginning gently, seeing the Sabbath out with a special candle, wine, and sweet-smelling spices. Adoptive parents might wish to create a ceremony that acknowledges the formal separation of their child from his or her birth parents in an equally positive way.

Other families may choose a Sunday for their ceremony; it is a day of leisure that will not present conflicts for those who observe Shabbat in a traditional manner.

Location

It is always appropriate to conduct a Jewish ritual in the synagogue. Families who wish to include an *aliyah,* being called up to the Torah—one of the greatest honors a Jew can receive—as part of their ritual may choose to have their ceremony in the synagogue during a service when the Torah is read. A special blessing giving the child his or her Hebrew name is recited after the *aliyah.* Others might decide to hold the ceremony at their home or outdoors. There is no rule regarding this and families should find a place that is particularly meaningful to them, and that creates for them a feeling of holiness and sanctity.

Leader

A family that belongs to a synagogue can consult its rabbi for advice, or ask him or her to conduct, or help conduct, the ceremony. However, some rabbis may not have had experience with or given much thought to adoption rituals and parents may want to be prepared to share their knowledge with their rabbi. The leader can also be one or both of the adoptive parents, a relative, or a friend. What seems most significant is that the leader be someone who understands the import of this ceremony in the family's life and wishes to help create a special and meaningful ritual.

Witnesses and Participants

"Rituals link people to other Jews across space and time, tying their personal history with that of the Jewish people," observes Rela M. Geffen in *Celebration and Renewal: Rites of Passage in Judaism* (1993, p. 3). That this tie is meaningful to the family that plans an Adopting the Covenant ritual is clear; it is the family's opportunity to officially welcome its child into the Jewish community. The need to affirm family continuity within a public context was understood by the rabbis of old, who decreed that life passages be celebrated in the presence of a quorum or minyan [a group of ten people], the minimum definition of a Jewish community (p. 4). Whether the ceremony is public, within the context of the synagogue service, or private, it is appropriate, but not necessary, to have at least a minyan of people attend.

One of the family's major decisions will be whether and how to include the child's birth parents—if one or both are available and wish to be included. Some families who have open adoptions have invited birth parents to attend, and even to participate. This is a very delicate matter, and it is important that adoptive parents be extremely sensitive to the needs of the birth parents, who may well be grieving their loss at the same time that the adoptive parents are celebrating the new addition to their family.

Beyond that, adoptive parents may wish to include grandparents, siblings, other members of their extended family, and friends. For many grandparents and siblings, this is an important first opportunity to demonstrate a connection to their new family member, and their participation in an adoption ritual can have lifelong benefits.

Music

Music seems to play an important role in spiritual events, both elevating them out of the mundane and allowing people emotional access to them. Making music together also seems to bind people together as a community. There are extensive collections on tape or CD of traditional and modern Jewish music which would provide an appropriately joyous, and specifically Jewish, aura to such an occasion. (The use of instruments and musical equipment such as tape players depends on where and when the ceremony is held. Most traditional synagogues would not permit their use on Shabbat.) Certainly, singing Hebrew songs a cappella is an appropriate addition to any celebration.

Parents of transculturally adopted children may wish to select music from their child's birth country, honoring it as a part of the child's heritage.

Symbolic Actions or Objects

There are a number of symbolic actions or objects, already well recognized in Jewish tradition, that can add meaning to an *Ametz HaBrit*. Families can contemplate the following suggestions and choose those that feel appropriate to them.

Giving tzedakah [a monetary donation] is one way of acknowledging that one's personal happiness is incomplete in a world so badly in need of repair, point out Anita Diamant and Howard Cooper in *Living a Jewish Life: Jewish Traditions, Customs and Values for Today's Families* (1991, p. 249). It is a way that the adoptive family can celebrate how much it has been given and its desire to give something to others in turn. Donating, in the child's name, to a group that represents the family's values graphically demonstrates connection to community and how one supports things that one believes in, and is an example to the child, who will learn about this event as he or she grows up, of an appropriate way to celebrate. Families may wish to choose a cause of Jewish interest, or one that is connected to their child's birth country or heritage.

Lighting candles is often the first act in a Jewish ceremony; light represents both Torah, which is considered a light to the people of Israel, as well as the Jewish people themselves, who have been called "a light unto the nations." In this ceremony, light also represents the divine spark of the new life that is being welcomed into the Jewish community. It is traditional to light two candles for Shabbat; some families add a candle for each child. When the parents light the child's candle, they are symbolically and literally passing on their heritage to their child.

Some adoptive parents may wish to include a ritual washing of the child's feet in their ceremony. This custom, which commemorates the patriarch Abraham, who greeted guests by washing their feet, has become a sign of hospitality and a tangible symbol of welcome into the covenant. Water, a symbol of both physical and spiritual sustenance, is a sign that God sustained the Israelites in their wandering search for the meaning of life, and of Torah, the ultimate meaning of life, and the promise of salvation. It is, therefore, an appropriate symbol for a ritual that welcomes the adoptee, who will be searching for his or her life's meaning, into the covenant. Parents can recite the blessing: "Blessed are You, O God, Ruler of the Universe, who is mindful of the Covenant through the washing of the feet" (*"Brit Milah* and *Brit Banot,"* Laura Geller in Orenstein's *Lifecycles*, pp. 57–67).

The rainbow is the sign of the covenant between God and Noah (Genesis 9:8–17). Jewish tradition holds that children are that covenant's guarantors, a privilege the adoptee assumes with his or her adoption. Adoptive parents might, therefore, select a rainbow motif for decorations or invitations to the event, perhaps accompanied by a verse from Genesis explaining the significance of the rainbow. Reading verses from the Torah or Talmud that refer to adoption also creates a meaningful addition to the ceremony.

The 613 knots on the fringes of a *tallit* [prayer shawl] represent the number of mitzvot [commandments] that Jews are required to observe. When a child enters into the convenant, he or she becomes responsible for obeying these commandments. Wrapping a child in a *tallit* can dramatically and physically symbolize the parents' hope that their child will live a life enveloped in and comforted by Torah and mitzvot, says Shulamit Magnus (Orenstein, 1994, p. 70). This is an especially appropriate honor for the grandparents to perform. If the *tallit* is a gift to the child, he or she can later use it for Shabbat, holidays, and his or her Bar/Bat Mitzvah; if the *tallit* belongs to a parent or grandparent, it reinforces the continuity of the family and the importance of tradition.

Planting a tree in a child's honor is an ancient tradition in the

Babylonian Talmud (Gittin 57a) that is especially appropriate for an Adopting the Convenant ceremony. A cedar, representing strength and stature, is planted for a boy and a cypress, signifying gentleness and sweetness, for a girl. Branches of the grown trees are traditionally used as the poles for a couple's huppah [wedding canopy]. This custom can convey to the adoptee that he or she has been rerooted into the adoptive, Jewish community, which celebrates life and growth, roots and branches. Grandparents can take part in this ceremony too, reflecting the talmudic ideal of planting trees that grandchildren will see grow to maturity (BT Ta'anit 23a) ("Creating a Tree-dition," p. 78, Treasure Cohen, pp. 76–82, in Orenstein's *Lifecycles: Jewish Women on Life Passages and Personal Milestones*).

In the Book of Genesis (48:12), Efraim and Menashe, the children of Joseph, are placed on their grandfather Jacob's knees as a sign that he is adopting them and giving them a portion of inheritance. Adoptive parents may want to hold their child on their knees during the ritual, symbolically acknowledging adoption in this biblical fashion, says Ronald Isaacs in *Rites of Passage: A Guide to the Jewish Life Cycle* (1992, p. 127). They may also wish to recite Jacob's words of blessing (Genesis 48:15–16) or the verses of Psalm 80 (15–16) from which the word, *ametz*, adoption, comes.

Parents of transculturally adopted children may have brought home objects representing their child's birth country that can be used in their ceremony. This could, for example, include a cup (to use as a *kiddush* cup) or material with which to make a *tallit*. They may also know, or research, birth and naming customs in their child's country of origin. For example, there is a custom among Sephardic Jews called "las fadas," which includes passing the child around to everyone present to receive blessings for herself and her family. This ritual may have come from non-Jewish Spaniards who used to have children blessed by fairies, since the word "fadas" comes from "hadas," which means "fairies." However it was derived, the custom of passing a child from person to person to receive their blessings seems an appropriate way to welcome an adopted child into the community. (Ceremony of "Las Fadas" from naming ceremony by Steve and Penina Adelman of Newton, MA for Laura Deetza Adelman.)

A celebration would be incomplete without food, and breaking bread together is a way of welcoming and accepting people, so families may want to host light refreshments or a meal following the service. Hallah is the traditional bread that is appropriate to serve at every Jewish event. Families who have adopted internationally may also appreciate the symbolism of including a food or beverage from their child's birth country. It is customary to close Jewish ceremonies with the *kiddush* [the ceremonial blessing of wine] to celebrate the sweetness and happiness of the occasion. Placing a drop of wine on the child's lips, sharing from the communal cup of life, welcomes the adoptee into the community.

Appropriate Readings, Prayers, and Poems

Because there is no traditional, fixed ritual for celebrating adoption, adoptive parents have the privilege, pleasure, and challenge of fashioning something that meets their needs. That requires finding or creating appropriate and meaningful prayers, readings, and poems. Collected here are a variety of selections, traditional and new, by rabbis and lay people, which adoptive parents may want to include in their own ceremony or which may jog their memories or creative juices. They should also feel free to share their individual thoughts, hopes, and prayers for their child.

An Adopting the Covenant ritual is the perfect time to give the child his or her Hebrew name and to explain its meaning. One new tradition is to create a personal poem for the child by selecting verses from Psalm 119, an alphabetic acrostic containing eight verses for every letter of the Hebrew alphabet. One verse is chosen for each letter of the child's name. Two examples follow, the first for a girl, the second for a boy. (These were created by the author for her own children, Michael and Jessica.)

Naming Poem for *Khana Niza*

The earth, oh Lord, is full of Your mercy,   (Chet)
Teach me Your Statutes.
Your testimonies have I taken as a heritage forever;   (Nun)
For they are the rejoicing of my heart.
Give me understanding, that I keep Your law   (Hay)
And observe it with my whole heart.

Your word is a lamp at my feet,   (Nun)
And a light unto my path.
Your righteousness is an everlasting righteousness,   (Tzadee)
and Your law is truth.
Make me to tread in the path of Your commandments;   (Hay)
For therein do I delight.

Naming poem for *Mikhael Gad*

How sweet are Your words unto my palate!   (Mem)
Yea, sweeter than honey to my mouth!
Your hands have made me and fashioned me;   (Yud)
Give me understanding, that I may learn Your commandments.
My soul pines for Your salvation: (Kaf)
In Your word do I hope.
I will give thanks to You with uprightness of heart,   (Alef)
When I learn Your righteous ordinances.
Forever, O Lord,   (Lamed)
Your word stands fast in heaven.

Open my eyes, that I may behold   (Gimel)
Wondrous things out of Your law.
I will follow the way of Your commandments,   (Daled)
For You enlarge my heart.

When a Jewish couple is married, Seven Blessings are recited under the huppah. They have been adapted and used in several baby-naming ceremonies, for which transcriptions have been found in the Creative Liturgy File of the Reconstructionist Rabbinical College in Wyncote, Pennsylvania, though no author has been identified. Although these were not adoption rituals, the Blessings, nonetheless, seem appropriate.

Blesssed are you Adonai our God, Ruler of the Universe,
Who has sanctified us with Your commandments and
has commanded us to initiate our son/daughter into the
covenant of the people Israel.
Blessed are you Adonai Who makes parents joyful
with their children.
Blessed is Adonai, God of Israel, Who alone does wondrous things.
Blessed are You Adonai our God, Ruler of the Universe,
Who has created all things, for Your glory.
Blessed are You Adonai our God, Ruler of the Universe,
Creator of all humanity.
Blessed are You Adonai our God, Ruler of the Universe,
Creator of the mystery of creation.
May Zion and the land of Israel, so long without children or joy,
now become glad and joyful with children
living happily in the land.
Blessed are You Who makes Zion joyful through her children.

On Bringing a Child Home for the First Time
(author unidentified, Reconstructionist Rabbinical College
Liturgy File)

*With joy and anticipation I/we bring my/our son/daughter
into my/our home for the first time.
How lovely are your tents, O Jacob, your dwelling places, O Israel.
Ma Tovu o-ha-lekha Yaakov.
May my/our home always be a mikdash ma'at, a small sanctuary,
filled with Your presence.
May my/our home be your sanctuary, my/our child,
a place where arms shall cradle you and voices sing you lullabies,
where hands shall uphold you and eyes delight to watch you grow.
In this home may we reach out to each other in love.
In this home may our hearts and those of my/our children
be turned to one another.
In this home may we create bonds of trust and care
that will keep us close as we grow together as a family.
Bless us, Source of Life, all of us together
with the light of Your presence.*

≈

New Genesis, A Ceremony of Identity
(by Rabbi Rami Shapiro, Rabbi of Temple Beth Or, Miami, Florida,
author of *Wisdom of the Jewish Sages* and *Minyan, 10 Principles for
Living Life with Integrity*)

*Long ago our ancestors came to believe
that they were a people apart:
witnesses to the oneness of the world,
and called upon to set the world firmly
upon a foundation of justice and peace.*

This sense of mission
impressed itself deeply upon the soul of our People.
And yet we did not consider ourselves
superior to other nations.
It was not our lineage but our Teaching that made us unique.
Israel gave birth to other religions
and these have brought many to an understanding of Unity;
but our responsibility continues,
for our mission remains unfulfilled.
It will continue until the earth is filled with Wisdom
as the sea-bed is filled with the sea.
It is a mission we are willing to take upon ourselves.
It is a mission worthy of the highest loyalty.
It is a mission demanding true love and deep commitment.
May Adonai, the Way of all Life,
be our guide and teacher,
helping us become ever more worthy of the name Jew.
May we do nothing to disgrace this inheritance,
and may our every act bring honor to our People.
May we ever more deeply appreciate the mission of our
People as repairers of the world, working to bring Light and
Blessing to all the families of earth. . . .

New encounters,
new dreams,
new wisdom
shape us subtly;
altering our being
by encouraging our becoming.

Not that our past need be cut off,
but that our future be allowed to embrace it,
mold it, move it from what was
to what could be.

Choosing to become a Jew,
choosing to stand with a people at the apex
of human horror as well as human triumph,
is to choose a new identity,
to build upon one's past by affirming a new future.

For Our Children
(by Leonard Beerman and included in New Genesis, the previous
reading/ceremony by Rami Shapiro)

We want our children to be at home in their Jewishness,
to have that comfortable sense of belonging
which is such a rarity among us.

We want their Jewishness to be neither a burden
nor a source of shame or contempt to them.
Nor do we want them to wear it too ostentatiously,
to flaunt it before the world,
to insert it clumsily into every situation.
We want their Jewishness to be as natural to them
as their breathing.

We want our children to have a religious attitude toward life,
to have a reverence for all that enhances life;
to develop a sense of awe and mystery about the known
as well as the unknown,
to be warmed by the sun of knowledge;
to have a feeling for beauty and all that issues
from being a part of this earth and this life.
We want life and the religious understanding of it
to be a joyous thing.

We want our children to appreciate the beauty
and the richness of our customs and ceremonies,
and to observe them, not out of a sense of guilt,
not out of a belief in their magical quality,
not even to hallow the memory of an ancestor;
but rather as an expression of their own recognition
that a symbol or a ceremony is a technique
of concretizing certain values,
a way of clothing ideals in flesh.

We want them to understand that the custom or ceremony
is not as important as the feelings which surround it.

We want them to appreciate
that their religion is concerned with all reality,
that it can flourish only when the mind is open and free,
that it can be destructive when it enslaves people
to outworn beliefs and archaic patterns of thought,
and that no religion is worth its salt
unless it can liberate rather than shackle.

We want them to understand
that their religion welcomes all truth,
whether shining from the annals of ancient revelation
or reaching us through the seers of our own time.

We want our children to learn how to love,
to love themselves,
to love humanity
for the world needs so much love.

We want them to sense
their bond of union
with the Jewish people
and with all the children of the world.

We want them to look upon religion
not as something
to be inherited
but as something to be discovered.

~

A Mother's Prayer
(by Rabbi Rami Shapiro)

May the Source of Life, the Fountain of Being,
bestow rest, healing and full blessing upon me and my child.
May the Ineffable Mystery of Life fill us both
with good health, strength of body and character,
happiness, peace and length of days.

May my child grow to discover her/his unique place in the world,
and may s/he find the courage to take it.
May her/his heart come to love the world and may her/his labors
be for the healing of all creation.
May s/he overflow with wisdom, and walk the path of righteousness,
truth, humility and understanding.
May s/he honor both self and other, and bring blessing upon all s/he
meets. Amen.
Barukh ata adonai eloheinu melekh ha-olam, she-heh-kheh-yanu,
v'kee-y'-manu, v'he-ge-anu laz-man ha-zeh.
Blessed is the Source of Life, the Fountain of Being whose power
enlivens us, sustains us, and enables us to reach this moment of joy.

May my child be blessed with health, strength, happiness, peace
and length of days.
May s/he grow at peace with her/himself and her/his world.
May s/he labor for the redemption of all creation, and be filled
with the wonder of Life and Wisdom.

May her/his Path be Right, leading her/him to truth, humility,
understanding and peace.
Amen.

⪥

The *Rabbi's Manual*, published by the Reconstructionist Rabbinical Association in 1997, calls an adoption ritual "an opportunity to embrace adoptive parents as links in the chain of tradition (p. B-1). It contains a sample ritual as well as various readings that can be included in any ceremony a family chooses to create. The following selections have been reprinted, with permission, from the manual.

A Blessing
(by Leila Gal Berner, adapted with permission, p. BP-23; it is an appropriate reading for grandparents)

May the Shekhinah spread her wings over you and protect you.
May you know great joy and fulfillment in your life.
May you walk with your people Israel in pride, and may you
understand that to be a Jew is a source of joy and meaning
and an important responsibility.
May you honor your parent(s), recognizing that
they have welcomed you into the world in love and in hope,
and may you bring them great joy.
May you go from strength to strength, yet always be able to accept
your own weaknesses and those of others.
May you judge yourself and others with fairness and compassion,
without undue harshness.
May you have the confidence and self-esteem to move toward
whatever goals you choose for yourself.
May you have the wisdom and courage to change your mind
as you rethink your original goals.

May you allow yourself to dream your dreams and soar
with flights of fancy and imagination.
May you always keep a precious part of yourself as "Child"
even as you move into adulthood.
May your ears be filled with music of every imaginable kind,
and may the rhythms be of your own making.
Allow yourself to march at your own pace and
dance to your own beat.
May you experience the inevitable moments of sadness and pain
(which are also a part of life) in a way that gives
these moments meaning and adds value to your life.
May you live in a world blessed with peace and harmony,
and may your future be as bright and as hopeful
as the world's first rainbow.
And let us all say:
Amen.

A Public Welcoming Ceremony

(author unknown, combining elements from the Reconstructionist
Rabbinical College Liturgy File and Manual pp. B-28, 31, 36)

Rabbi: Blessed are you, a community of faith.
Blessed is he/she who comes into the presence of God.

Parent(s): This child whom I/we have brought into the covenant of
the generations, past and future, I/we now bring into this community of the people of Israel on Shabbat _____.

May the one who blessed our ancestors, Abraham, Isaac and Jacob,
Sarah, Rebekah, Rachel and Leah, accept and strengthen us on this
Sabbath. May I/we as parent(s) provide the home to nurture my/our
child in responsibility to my/our heritage and my/our people, the larger community in which his/her life will unfold [from the Liturgy File].

Congregation: May you, _____, find support and friendship, warmth and love within our community. May we be your guides along life's journey. We promise to offer you challenge and affection, forgiveness and praise. We will strive to teach you values of justice and compassion, and to share with you our love of Jewish living. May your heart beat with the rhythm of the Jewish people and your eyes be open to the world [from the Manual, p. B-31].

Rabbi: It is good to pause on this Shabbat and to look into the eyes of a newborn child, our tomorrow, and to be at peace on this day, a celebration of renewal and consecration. May this child, _____, grow to enjoy many Sabbaths in a community of loved ones and friends and be inspired by the vision of Shabbat to bring about a world at peace [from the Liturgy File].

Parent(s): This small child, precious in my/our eye(s), is a new beginning, which I/we have long awaited. Now for the first time I/we am/are experiencing the responsibilities and privileges of being (a) parent(s), and I/we face the days and years ahead with joy and confidence, humility and loving enthusiasm.

As (a) new parent(s), I/we am/are like (a) child(ren). Just as this child, new to the world, must rely on me/us for sustenance and guidance, so I/we, having no experience of parenthood, must depend on God, as reflected in the patient support of this community: for wisdom and compassion are needed to raise my/our child in holiness [from the Manual, p. B-36].

⁀

Reading on Adoption of a Child
(Manual, p. B-3)

Parent(s): I/We have been blessed with the precious gift of a child.

After so much waiting and hoping, I/we am/are filled with wonder and gratitude as I/we call you my/our child. You have grown to life apart from me/us, but now I/we hold you close to my/our heart(s), lovingly cradle you in my/our arm(s), welcome you into the family circle and embrace you with the beauty of a rich tradition.

I/We dedicate myself/ourselves to the creation of a Jewish home—a place of generosity, a place of compassion for others, a place of learning—in the hope that you will grow to cherish and carry on these ideals.

God of new beginnings, teach me/us to be (a) parent(s) worthy of this sacred trust of life. May my/our child grow in health, strong in mind and kind in heart, a lover of Torah, a seeker of peace. Bless all of us together within your shelter of shalom.

The community responds: As he/she has entered the covenant of our people, so may he/she grow into a life of Torah, loving commitment and good deeds.

Parent(s): As (a) parent(s) I/we commit myself/ourselves to be my/our child's model and guide. May God's blessings rest on my/our child now and always.
[Parent(s) may invite all children present to gather around the newborn. Say: You are our tomorrow—a new generation. Siblings may be given the opportunity to speak.]

≈)

Ceremony of Welcome
(by Rabbi Lenore Bohm, Encinitas, California)

Parent(s): Welcome sweet daughter/son. I/We rejoice in your presence, in the gift that you are. May love and hope follow you through the cycles and seasons of your life. May knowledge and strength be your companions, and Shekhinah be your guide.

Parent(s): We welcome you, _____, into the circle of our family and community. May sunshine and warmth surround you as you go forth from this day of Shabbat and this place of holiness.

Rabbi: Our God and God of our ancestors, sustain _____ in life and health and let her/his name be known in the household of Israel as _____. Even as _____ now enters the covenant of our people, so may she/he enter into the study of Torah, relationships of commitment and deeds of generosity and kindness.

In keeping with the Jewish respect for and sensitivity to adoption, a number of Jewish adoptive parents wrote a description of their understanding of what it means to adopt a child. This version contains an added verse, in brackets, for a family that has other, biological, children.

We did not plant you, true.
But when the season is done,
When the alternate prayers
For sun and rain are counted,
When the pain of weeding
And the pride of watching are through,
We will hold you high,
A shining sheaf
Above the thousand seeds grown wild,
[Beside our own first fruits.]
Not by our planting,
But by heaven,
A new harvest,
A daughter/son to love.

At the close of an Adopting the Covenant ceremony, it is appropriate to recite the *she-he-heyanu,* the blessing that traditionally celebrates something new and wonderful, and thanks God for permitting the celebrants to reach this special time.

Reading on the Occasion of Placing a Child for Adoption

Placing a child for adoption is, of course, a very painful and difficult time for birth parents. Clergy, social workers, and attorneys who work with them need to be especially sensitive to their feelings. If the birth parents are Jewish and it is felt that a ritual at this time could be a mechanism for healing, the following selection, found in The Reconstructionist Rabbinical Association Rabbi's Manual, is suggested.

On Adoption of a Child
(Manual, p. BP-12)

I, _____, known in Israel as _____, do knowingly and willingly and without reservation give my newborn son/daughter into the care of _____ (name of guardian) of _____(name of institution) on _____(Hebrew date), corresponding to _____(English date and time), for the purpose of placing this child in an adoptive home and in order to fulfill the mitzvah of *pikuah nefesh*, preserving a life. May God grant him/her the wisdom and guidance to find a family who will love, nurture and care for this child as he/she grows in the traditions of Israel and the values of the Jewish people. May the one who blessed our fathers Abraham, Isaac, and Jacob, and our mothers Sarah, Rebekah, Rachel, and Leah, guard and protect my son's/daughter's adoptive parents and may they live to raise him/her in the fear of God, in study of the Torah, and with loving commitment, and for a life of good deeds. And let us say: Amen.

Guardian says: I hereby accept this child knowingly and willingly for the express purpose of placing him/her in an adoptive home and in order to fulfill the mitzvah of *pikuah nefesh*.

Bar and Bat Mitzvah: Reaffirming the Covenant

Because most adopted children become Jewish through conversion during infancy or early childhood, they have the right to reject that conversion upon reaching the age of Jewish adulthood. On the other hand, their Bar or Bat Mitzvah is the first time that they are able to officially and formally reaffirm their acceptance of their Jewish identities. Whether it is mentioned outright, or is a subtle undercurrent to the ceremony, this reaffirmation provides special meaning to the Bar or Bat Mitzvah ceremony.

One of the first ritual acts the Bar or Bat Mitzvah child performs is donning the *tallit*. The child may use one he or she received as a baby at his or her Adopting the Convenant ritual, or may be given one for the Bar/Bat Mizvah. This is an especially appropriate gift for grandparents to give, signifying the continuity of family and tradition. Before reciting the traditional blessing, the following meditation is a meaningful addition to the ceremony. It can be seen as having special significance to the adoptee.

Tallit Meditation
(By Rabbi Rami Shapiro, from his Bar/Bat Mitzvah service,
Toward Autonomy)

A tallit *represents the world;*
its four corners are the outer
reaches of the known;
its fringes are the subtle
teasing of the unknown.
To stand wrapped in tallit
is to take your place in the world;
to stand wrapped in tallit
is to take responsibility for the world:

To take a single life is
to destroy an entire world;
To save a single life is to save an entire world.
May my coming into adulthood
be accompanied by my taking up
the challenge of standing in **tallit**.
May I begin to learn the skills of mitzvah,
the skills of living in harmony with the world.
May I begin to grow in the way of wisdom
that through my life I might save life.

A popular new tradition in many synagogues is passing the Torah from generation to generation. When the Torah is removed from the ark at the start of the Torah service, great-grandparents, grandparents, parents, and the Bar or Bat Mitzvah child stand in front of the ark and hand the Torah from one to the next. This act literally and symbolically includes the adoptee in the line of those who have received the covenant. The following reading, also by Rabbi Rami Shapiro from his Bar/Bat Mitzvah service, *Toward Autonomy*, is appropriate for the participants to recite as they pass the Torah from person to person.

Parent(s) and/or grandparent(s) say(s): Sinai calls to you as it called to Moses: establish mitzvot for your life. Torah calls to you as it called to our people: set yourself firmly on the Way of Harmony. At this time of Bar/Bat Mitzvah you prepare to ascend the heights of Sinai within. The path is yours alone, and alone you must travel upon it. Yet you take with you the love and hope of the past years. They will be your companions forever, as we/I will stand ever beside you.

As we/I now hold the Torah, so we/I once held you. Yet holding on is not the way of Life, and we/I must begin to let you go that you may find your own way. But we/I must give you more than the fact of freedom, we/I must give you the tools that make freedom meaningful. Mitzvot are these tools, the skills you will need to embrace life openly and fully. These, too, we/I must let you discover for yourself. So we/I now hand to you the Torah as a symbol of the power of mitzvah you will henceforth, with ever greater zeal, seek for yourself.

The Bar/Bat Mitzvah child responds: As I have received the Torah from your hands, so do I accept the challenge that comes to me this day. The challenge is one of both freedom and responsibility, calling me to affirm not only my own dignity but the dignity of others as well. It is my destiny on this day to enter into a new relationship with Life, seeking out the mitzvot I need to live in harmony with my people and my world. May my actions bring peace and healing to all who know me, and may my struggles be for the good.

It is hoped that adoptive parents who desire it will use and adapt the material included here or create new rituals of their own to celebrate their child's entrance into the covenant and community. There is no one way or correct way to formulate such a ritual, but there seems to be compelling testimony to suggest that it is an important and meaningful gesture.

References and Resources

Diamant, Anita and Howard Cooper. *Living a Jewish Life: Jewish Traditions, Customs and Values for Today's Families.* New York: HarperPerennial, 1991.

Geffen, Rela M. *Celebration and Renewal: Rites of Passage in Judaism.* Philadelphia: The Jewish Publication Society, 1993.

Isaacs, Ronald H. *Rites of Passage: A Guide to the Jewish Life Cycle.* Hoboken, NJ: KTAV Publishing House, Inc., 1992.

Johnston, Patricia Irwin. *Perspectives on a Grafted Tree: Thoughts for Those Touched by Adoption.* Fort Wayne, IN: Perspective Press, 1982.

Mason, Mary Martin. *Designing Rituals of Adoption for the Religious and Secular Community.* Minneapolis: Resources for Adoptive Parents, 1995.

Melina, Lois Ruskai and Sharon Kaplan Roszia. *The Open Adoption Experience.* New York: HarperPerennial, 1993.

Orenstein, Debra. *Lifecycles: Jewish Women on Life Passages and Personal Milestones.* Woodstock, VT: Jewish Lights Publishing Company, 1994.

Reimer, Seth, ed. *Rabbi's Manual.* Philadelphia: Reconstructionist Rabbinical Association, 1997.

Shapiro, Rami M. *Toward Autonomy: A Service for Bar and Bat Mitzvah.* Miami: Light House Books, 1996.

APPENDIX II

National Adoption Organizations

≈

$\mathcal{A}$ wide variety of local, state, and national organizations serve members of the adoption triad, adoption professionals, and others interested in and concerned about adoption, in several ways. Some provide material about adoption, some of which is free. Some offer regional and/or national conferences. Because funding sources change, some organizations charge a fee and some do not. It is important to inquire directly of the organizations about these and other issues and concerns. This list, as is the case with any list, cannot be comprehensive, but is intended to provide a place to begin—or to continue learning about—adoption.

Adoption Resource Exchange for Single Parents, Inc. (ARESP)
P. O. Box 5782
Springfield, VA 22150
703-866-5577

Educates, advocates, and assists single adoptive parents to adopt primarily older and special needs children. Publishes *ARESP News.*

Adoptive Families of America, Inc. (AFA)
2309 Como Ave.
St. Paul, MN 55108
612-645-9955; 1-800-372-3300

Organization for individuals, families, and parent support groups that educates and advocates for adoptive families. Publishes bimonthly magazine, *Adoptive Families.*

American Adoption Congress (AAC)
1000 Connecticut Ave., NW, Suite 9
Washington, DC 20036
202-483-3399

Umbrella organization for search and support groups that assist in reuniting adoptees and birth families throughout U.S. and Canada. Provides resources, education, and listings of groups.

American Academy of Adoption Attorneys
Box 33053
Washington, DC 20033-0053
202-832-2222

Organization of attorneys who include independent adoption in their legal practice. Provides directory.

Children Awaiting Parents, Inc.
700 Exchange St.
Rochester, NY 14608
716-232-5110

Publishes frequently updated national photo-listing of children who are waiting for adoptive families and can be placed across state lines.

Child Welfare League of America, Inc.
440 First St., NW, Ste. 310
Washington, DC 20001
202-638-2952

Provides consultation and education. Conducts research and publishes books and pamphlets. Advocates on behalf of children. Library Information Service offers films, slides, and tapes on adoption issues.

Families Adopting Children Everywhere (FACE)
P. O. Box 28058
Baltimore, MD 21239
410-488-2656

Adoptive parent organization that provides support, education, and service activities primarily for prospective adoptive families and adoptive families. Publishes the *Face Adoption Quarterly*.

Gay and Lesbian Parents' Coalition International (GLPCI)
P. O. Box 34337
San Diego, CA 92163
619-296-0199
www.glpci.org

Advocacy, education, and support organization for gay and lesbian persons in child-nurturing roles and their families. Adoption is not main focus, although a significant number of members are adoptive families.

Heart to Heart, The American Jewish Society for Distinguished Children
1227 President St., Ste. 1B
Brooklyn, NY 11225
718-774-5712

Organization that finds Jewish homes for Jewish children with Down's syndrome.

Jewish Children's Adoption Network
P. O. Box 16544
Denver, CO 80216-0544
303-573-8113

Jewish adoption exchange that matches home-studied Jewish families with Jewish children, most with special needs, who are available for adoption.

Joint Council on International Children's Services
7 Cheverly Circle
Cheverly, MD 20785
301-322-1906
www.jcics.org

Organization of licensed international adoption agencies and parent advocacy groups. Provides list of agencies and resources.

National Adoption Center
1500 Walnut St., Ste. 701
Philadelphia, PA 19102
1-800-TO-ADOPT

Maintains computer list of children with special needs awaiting families. Provides general information on adoption as well as on adoption of children with special needs.

National Adoption Foundation
100 Mill Plain Rd.
Danbury, CT 06811
203-791-3811

Provides grants and loans to help with adoption expenses. Call or write for an application.

National Adoption Information Clearinghouse
P. O. Box 1182
Washington, DC 20013
1-888-251-0075; 703-352-3488

Compiles and disseminates current information and articles on adoption to researchers, practitioners, prospective adopters, and members of the adoption triad. Develops original publications, maintains library and searchable database, and provides referrals to other sources of adoption information.

National Council for Single Adoptive Parents
Box 15084
Chevy Chase, MD 20825
202-966-6367

Provides information for single people interested in adoption opportunities. Publishes a parent handbook.

National Resource Center for Special Needs Adoption
16250 Northland Dr., Ste. 120
Southfield, MI 48075
248-443-7080

Provides information and resources on special needs adoption. Refers parents to agencies and health professionals with expertise in special needs adoption.

North American Council on Adoptable Children (NACAC)
970 Raymond Ave., #106
St. Paul, MN 55114-1149
612-644-3036; 1-800-479-6665 for adoption subsidy questions

Membership organization of individuals, adoptive parent groups, and adoption organizations that focuses on needs of waiting children. Provides advocacy, education, research and policy analysis, and grants for development of training and support services. Publishes quarterly newsletter *Adoptalk.*

Resolve, Inc.
Dept. GM, 1310 Broadway
Somerville, MA 02144-1779
617-623-0744
www.resolve.org

Provides services for people dealing with infertility. Offers adoption education, information, referral, and support. Maintains list of groups throughout U.S.

Stars of David International, Inc.
3175 Commercial Ave., Ste. 100
Northbrook, IL 60062-1915
708-509-9929; 800-STAR-349

Information and support network for Jewish and partly Jewish adoptive and prospective adoptive families. Membership organization. Local chapters hold social and educational meetings and events, often around Jewish holidays. Maintains resources and articles on adoption and Jewish adoption issues. Publishes *STARTRACKS* newsletter.

[This list was compiled from information provided by Susan Freivalds, executive director of the National Adoption Foundation, and Linda Yellin, MSW, of Farmington Hills, Michigan, adoption and infertility counselor and educator.]

APPENDIX III

Resources for People Touched by Adoption

Books and Magazines

So many informative and sensitive books about infertility and all facets of adoption are available today that it would be impossible to list them all. Following is a short list of books, many recommended by Susan Freivalds, executive director of the National Adoption Foundation. The descriptions of the books are adapted and reprinted with permission from the Tapestry Books Adoption Book Catalog. It contains the widest selection of adoption and infertility material available. Their website is http://www.tapestrybooks.com/

For Prospective Adoptive Parents

The Adoption Resource Book by Lois Gilman

This book covers all aspects of adoption, from preparation to raising an adopted child. It has suggested checklists of procedures and questions for each step of the adoption process, and an annotated bibliography for further reading.

Launching A Baby's Adoption: Practical Strategies for Parents and Professionals by Patricia Irwin Johnston

While prospective adoptive parents are waiting to adopt, this book can help them prepare to make the transition from an adults-only

275

family to one with an adopted child. It examines the many issues that arise in psychologically and practically preparing for a baby, as well as those that arise during the first year.

Adopt International: Everything You Need to Know to Adopt a Child from Abroad by O. Robin Sweet and Patty Bryan

The number of children adopted from abroad has grown dramatically in recent years. Step-by-step advice on everything from selecting an adoption agency to traveling abroad to pick up the child to adjusting to the new life at home is discussed in this book. It also contains stories of people who have successfully adopted from around the world. It includes details of government regulations, complicated forms, and financial issues, as well as facts, regulations, and licensed agency listings for each country that allows foreign adoption.

With Eyes Wide Open: A Workbook for Parents Adopting International Children over Age One by Margi Miller, MA, and Nancy Ward, MA, LCSW

This workbook helps prepare people who are thinking about adopting a toddler from overseas. Such a child has already attempted to attach to a parent figure, experienced pain, learned to recognize language, and become familiar with his or her body. This book will help adoptive parents to reconstruct the experiences they missed during their child's first year.

Adopting the Hurt Child by Gregory C. Keck, Ph.D., and Regina M. Kupecky, LSW

A parent who adopts a child with special needs must be prepared to deal with past physical and emotional trauma, interruptions in parent-child bonding, losses felt by the child, and his or her corresponding inappropriate behavior. This book is a realistic, yet hopeful, examination of the reality of adoption for parents and professionals who deal with special needs children.

And Hannah Wept: Infertility, Adoption, and the Jewish Couple by
  Rabbi Michael Gold

A guide to the Jewish view on infertility and adoption.

Parenting Adopted Children

The Adoption Triangle by Arthur Sorosky, MD, Annette Baran,
  MSW, and Reuben Pannor, MSW

An adoption classic that leads to a better understanding of adoption
as a lifelong process for all triad members.

Shared Fate: A Theory and Method of Adoptive Relationships by H.
  David Kirk

This classic work, based on research on over two thousand families,
was the first to acknowledge that adoptive families are different from
other families, and that, if acknowledged, this difference can be an
asset.

Handbook for Single Adoptive Parents ed. by Hope Marindin

This book is divided into five sections, providing information of particular interest to single adoptive parents: the mechanics of adoption,
managing single parenthood, coping with challenges, adoption experiences, and the way in which professional social workers look at
single person adoption.

The Open Adoption Experience by Lois Ruskai Melina and Sharon
  Kaplan Roszia

An authoritative guide to issues of adoptive and birth families through
all stages of the open adoption relationship, by two leading adoption
experts. It moves from placement and the challenges of the first year
to those experienced during adolescence.

Toddler Adoption: The Weaver's Craft by Mary Hopkins Best, Ed.D.

Today, for a variety of reasons, more children are entering their adoptive families past the age of infancy, although not yet as "older" chil-

dren. This book covers all aspects of adopting and parenting these children, who may bring a variety of unexpected issues with them.

Secret Thoughts of an Adoptive Mother by Jana Wolff

The author shares fears, concerns, and questions common to adoptive parents, revealing the hidden emotions that so many are afraid or embarrassed to admit, believing they are the only ones feeling this way.

Raising Adopted Children by Lois Ruskai Melina

A comprehensive parent's guide, this book examines the physical, emotional, and psychological development of adopted children at every age and stage. It also contains chapters on special topics such as the multiracial family and single parent adoption.

The Whole Life Adoption Book by Jayne E. Schooler

Adoptive families face unique issues regarding attachment, adjustment, and identity. Being prepared for typical crisis points is critical to forming a nurturing family environment. The practical information in this book helps families succeed.

Real Parents, Real Children: Parenting the Adopted Child by Holly van Gulden and Lisa M. Bartels-Rabb

This book offers honest and revealing insight into how adopted children think and feel about being adopted. It explains how and why they grieve for their birth parents and offers practical suggestions for ways adoptive parents can help them come to healthy resolutions for these feelings.

When Friends Ask about Adoption: Question and Answer Guide for Non-Adoptive Parents and Other Caring Adults by Linda Bothun

Friends, family members, teachers, and clergy often have questions about adoption but hesitate to ask. This question and answer guide shows them how they can be supportive of the adoptive family.

"Are Those Kids Yours?": American Families with Children Adopted from Other Countries by Cheri Register, Ph.D.

What is involved in adopting from another country? What is involved in becoming an international family? This book answers these questions and many more.

Talking with Young Children about Adoption by Mary Watkins, Ph.D. and Susan Fisher, MD

Current wisdom says adoptive parents should talk with their children about adoption as early as possible. What is the best way for them to do that? And how do children react? What worries do they have? This book answers these questions for parents of children ages two to ten.

Being Adopted: The Lifelong Search for Self by David Brodzinsky, Ph.D., Marshall Schechter, MD, and Robin Henig

This book probes the complex issues that adoption presents throughout the life span. Five themes are examined: the experience of adoptees, developmental perspectives, normality, search for self, and sense of loss.

Journey of the Adopted Self: A Quest for Wholeness by Betty Jean Lifton, Ph.D.

This book explores the inner psychological world of adopted people and shows that their search for biological and historical roots can be a journey toward wholeness. The book draws on a study of adult adoptees as well as the author's personal experiences to demonstrate how adoptees form a sense of self.

Courageous Blessing: Adoptive Parents & the Search by Carol L. Demuth, LMSW-ACP

This booklet is for adoptive parents who adopted through the traditional system and now find, to their surprise, and perhaps horror, that their child wishes to search for his or her birth parents. How should they feel? What should they do?

The Primal Wound: Understanding the Adopted Child by Nancy Newton Verrier, MA

Using information about pre- and perinatal psychology, attachment, bonding and loss, this book illuminates the effects of separation from the birth mother. It validates adoptees' feelings, as well as clarifies various life experiences.

Perspectives on a Grafted Tree: Thoughts for Those Touched by Adoption ed. by Patricia Irwin Johnston, MS

This beautiful collection of poetry, written by adoptees, birth and adoptive parents, other members of adoptive families, and adoption professionals describes the blend of pain and happiness, gain and loss that are part of adoption.

The Lesbian and Gay Parenting Handbook by April Martin

A guidebook for parenting with a section on adoption.

Flight of the Stork: What Children Think (and When) about Sex and Family Building by Anne C. Bernstein

A family therapist has talked to children between the ages of three and twelve and explains the complex relationships and feelings that arise when a child has both birth and adoptive parents.

Adopted Child newsletter edited by Lois Melina

A monthly four-page newsletter that presents original, in-depth articles on all aspects of adoption at all stages of the life cycle. The information is practical, relevant, and well supported by current research. Subscriptions are available from P. O. Box 9362, Moscow, Idaho 83843. 208-882-1794.

Roots and Wings Adoption Magazine

This quarterly magazine examines international and domestic adoption, parenting issues, etc. It can be ordered at P. O. Box 577, Hackettstown, NJ 07840. 908-813-8252.

For Children and Teens

The Day We Met You by Phoebe Koehler

Using only a few simple words, this book describes the events on the day that parents meet their child for the first time. This book is an introduction to the loving feelings behind adoption. Ages 0 to 3.

Tell Me Again about the Night I Was Born by Jamie Lee Curtis

A young girl asks again and again to hear all the details about the night she was born—the night that her adoptive parents came to bring her to her new home. Ages 2 to 8.

A Mother for Choco by Keiko Kasza

Choco is a bird who is looking for a mother who looks just like him. When he finally meets Mrs. Bear he learns that there is more to being the perfect mother than looks. Ages 2 to 8.

Mr. Rogers—Let's Talk about It: Adoption by Fred Rogers

Mr. Rogers confronts the questions children have about being adopted with sensitivity and insight. This book describes the many ways that children feel close to their families and makes the point that the secure feeling of belonging comes from being loved. Ages 4 to 8.

Did My First Mother Love Me? by Kathryn Ann Miller

Many children fear that they were "given away" because they were unlovable. This book tells of a birth mother's wishes, hopes, and dreams for her baby, and explains why she made an adoption plan. Ages 4 to 8.

When You Were Born in China: A Memory Book for Children Adopted from China by Sara Dorow

This photo-essay provides a child's eye view of the process of adopting from China, including the "whys" and "hows" that brought the child to his or her new family. Ages 6 and up.

When You Were Born in Korea: A Memory Book for Children Adopted from Korea by Brian Boyd

This book answers all of the questions children ask about life before they were adopted. Ages 6 and up.

Why Was I Adopted? The Facts of Adoption with Love and Illustrations by Carole Livingston

A humorous look at the basic facts about adoption, this book uses informal language and encourages children to ask questions. Ages 4 to 12.

The Mulberry Bird: Story of an Adoption by Anne Braff Brodzinsky

This is the story of a mother bird who decides to place her baby bird for adoption. The book explains, in a nonthreatening manner, using birds instead of humans, why a parent might make an adoption plan. Ages 4 to 12.

How It Feels to Be Adopted by Jill Krementz

This book presents nineteen stories, told by teenagers, about the good and bad sides of being adopted. Ages 12 and up.

Filling in the Blanks: A Guided Look at Growing Up Adopted by Susan Gabel, M.Ed.

Many teens have questions and concerns about adoption that they hesitate to express. This workbook helps them learn about adoption. Its four sections—My Birth Family, My Adoption Process, My Adoptive Family, Myself—contain text, definitions, fill-in-the-blanks, and space for pictures. Ages 12 and up.

Why Didn't She Keep Me?: Answers to the Question Every Adopted Child Asks . . . by Barbara Burlingham-Brown, MS

This book presents a selection of firsthand narratives by birth mothers who candidly discuss the rational, practical, and emotional motivations that led them to place a child for adoption. So many different situations are involved that the book is appropriate for all members of the triad. Ages 10 to adult.

On the Internet

There are so many interesting and informative sites on the internet dedicated to adoption that it would be impossible to mention all of them, and one can gain access by simply typing in "adoption" or "adoption resources" and allowing the browser to do its work. One site links to the next and it is possible to spend hours exploring. Many sites provide articles, book lists, mailing lists, etc., which can be printed out.

In order to get started, following is a list of a few of the largest and generally most informative sites.

- **Stars of David International, Inc.**—http://www.starsofdavid.org/
 A nonprofit information and support network encompassing every branch of Judaism for Jewish and partly Jewish adoptive families. The Jewish Adoption Information Exchange provides general and Jewish adoption resources, articles, and books; links to other Jewish sites; and a list of events.

- **Internet Adoption Resources**—http://www.adopting.com/
 One of the largest adoption resources indexes on the net. It contains links to agencies, letters to birth parents, names of support groups, adoption information, photo listings of waiting children, e-mail lists, newsgroups, lists of other adoption websites, and more.

- **Adopt: Assistance Information Support**— http://www.adopting.org/
 An extensive website that contains articles, both personal and professional, a Q & A column by Patricia Irwin Johnston, links to other sites, search assistance, a support forum, a book list, and more.

- **AdoptioNetwork**—http://www.adoption.org/
 A volunteer operated information resource that contains online doc-

uments from the National Adoption Information Clearinghouse,
articles, a book list, an organization list, and links to other sites.

• **Special Families Support Site—**
http://comeunity.com/adoption/listservs.html/
This site provides a summary of mailing lists for adoptive families
to discuss adoption issues, provide mutual support, and use as a
clearinghouse for information.

• **Internet Sources for Adoption—**
http://fwcc.org/internetsources.html/
This site contains a list of general resources as well as resources
about China. It includes personal stories and links to other sites.

• **The Adoption Web Ring—**
http://www.plumsite.com/adoptionring/ring.shtml/
This is a public service ring of over one hundred pages that allows
surfers to visit not-for-profit adoption sites. It provides access to a
wealth of free adoption related information for search, support,
and activism for all members of the triad.

• **Adoption Information, Laws and Reforms—**
http://www.webcom.com/kmc/
This is a comprehensive collection of information relating to adoption law. It contains links to other sites and description of usenet
newsgroups.

• **Perspectives Press**—http://www.perspectivespress.com/
This site contains a book list, a list of speakers and conferences
which is updated regularly, links to other sites, and fact sheets and
articles on adoption which can be printed out.

• **Adoptive Families of America**—http://www.AdoptiveFam.org/
This comprehensive site contains articles, resources, and links to
other sites of interest to adoptive and perspective adoptive parents.
It contains the online version of the organization's *Guide to*

Adoption, as well as information on books, videos, multicultural resources, and its own magazine.

• **Adoption Options**—http://www.gapeach.com/~moj/Adoption/ This web page is dedicated to promoting adoption awareness, resources, information, and support for all members of the triad.

• **Adoption Puzzle Pieces**—http://home.earthlink.net/~tacallen/ Searching adoptees and other members of the triad will find links, databases, and other valuable information on this site.

• **AdoptionQuest**—http://www.adopt.org/adopt/adoptqst.html/ This resource listing of information and support is provided by the National Adoption Center, a nonprofit organization whose mission is to expand opportunities for children with special needs and from minority cultures.

Bibliography

Alexander, Julie Brook. *Contemporary Adoption: Reform Jewish Perspectives.* New York: Union of American Hebrew Congregations (Committee on the Jewish Family) and Women of Reform Judaism, 1993.

Brodzinsky, David, Ph.D., Marshall Schechter, MD, and Robin Henig. *Being Adopted: The Lifelong Search for Self.* New York: Anchor Books/Doubleday, 1992.

Commission on Gerut. "Standards for Conversion and Adoption." New York: Rabbinical Council of America, 1994.

Demuth, Carol L. *Courageous Blessing: Adoptive Parents and the Search.* Garland, TX: The Aries Center, 1993.

Doolittle, Terri. *The Long Term Effects of Institutionalization on the Behavior of Children from Eastern Europe and the Former Soviet Union: Research, Diagnosis, and Therapy Options.* Meadow Lands, PA: The Parent Network for the Post-Institutionalized Child, 1995.

George, Linda. "Like Mother, Like Daughter." *Jewish Exponent,* 25 July 1996.

Gluskin, Shai and Yael Levy. *A Reconstructionist Conversion Manual.* Philadelphia: Reconstructionist Rabbinical College, 1993.

Gold, Michael. "Adoption: A New Problem for Jewish Law." *Judaism* 36, no. 144 (1987): 4. American Jewish Congress.

Harnack, Andrew, ed. *Adoption: Opposing Viewpoints.* San Diego: Greenhaven Press, 1995.

Hochman, Gloria and Anna Huston. *Parenting the Adopted Adolescent.* Rockville, MD: National Adoption Information Clearinghouse, 1995.

Hochman, Gloria, Mady Prowler, and Anna Huston. *Working with Gay and Lesbian Adoptive Parents.* Rockville, MD: National Adoption Information Clearinghouse, 1995.

Johnson, Dana, MD, Ph.D. "Evaluating the Health of Adopted Children." In *The FACE Adoption Resource Manual,* edited by Clyde Tolley Clyde and Shaw Michie. Baltimore: Families Adopting Children Everywhere, 1996.

Johnston, Patricia Irwin. "Speaking Positively: An Information Sheet About Adoption Language." Indianapolis: Perspectives Press, 1996.

McRoy, Ruth G., Harold D. Grotevant, and Susan Ayers-Lopez. *Changing Practices in Adoption.* Austin: Hogg Foundation for Mental Health, 1994.

Melina, Lois Ruskai. "Parents with Biologic and Adopted Children May Worry About Partiality." *Adopted Child* 15, no. 3 (1996).

Melina, Lois Ruskai. "Adoptees May Be at Risk for Hyperactivity, But No One Knows Why." *Adopted Child* 9, no. 1 (1990).

Melina, Lois Ruskai. "Teachers Need to Be More Sensitive to Adoption Issues." *Adopted Child* 9, no. 8 (1990).

Melina, Lois Ruskai. "Questions Answered About Open Adoptions—Years After Placement." *Adopted Child* 15, no. 12 (1996).

Melina, Lois Ruskai. *Raising Adopted Children: A Manual for Adoptive Parents.* New York: Harper and Row, 1986.

Michelson, Roseann P. "The Challenge of Judaism to the Adoptee." Master's thesis, Hebrew Union College-Jewish Institute of Religion, School of Education, 1993.

Piantanida, Maria, Ph.D., and Sherry Anderson, MSW. *Creating and Using Life Books: A Guide for Prospective Adoptive Parents.* Pittsburgh: Three Rivers Adoption Council, 1994.

Piantanida, Maria, Ph.D., and Sherry Anderson, MSW. *Focus on Adoption: The Role of Clergy and Lay Parish Workers in Supporting Adoptive Families.* Pittsburgh: Three Rivers Adoption Council, 1990.

Register, Cheri, Ph.D. *"Are Those Kids Yours?": American Families with Children Adopted from Other Countries.* New York: The Free Press, 1991.

Reisner, Rabbi Avram Israel. *On the Conversion of Adopted and Patrilineal Children.* New York: Rabbinical Assembly, 1988.

Shireman, Joan F. and Penny R. Johnson. "Single Parent Adoptions: A Longitudinal Study." *Children and Youth Services Review* 7 (1985).

Shryer, Beth, Sally Lawry, and Richard Kepple. *Medical Genetics Services for Adoptive Parents: A Guidebook for Adoptive Parents.* Pittsburgh: Three Rivers Adoption Council, 1991.

Silverstein, Deborah N. "Identity Issues in the Adopted Adolescent." *Journal of Jewish Communal Service* 61, no. 4 (1985).

Smith, Debra Goldstein. *Searching for Birth Relatives.* Rockville, MD: National Adoption Clearinghouse, 1995.

Smith, Debra Goldstein. *Transcultural and Transracial Adoption.* Rockville, MD: National Adoption Information Clearinghouse, 1994.

van Gulden, Holly and Lisa Bartels-Rabb. *Real Parents, Real Children: Parenting the Adopted Child.* New York: Crossroad Publishing Company, 1993.

Index

religious issues, 83, 99–100
semi-open, 84
Organizations, 269–274
Orphanage, adopting children from foreign institutions, 111–117
Orthodox Judaism
acceptance of special needs children, 138
adoption, views on, 3–5, 197
conversion, 12, 14–17
gays and lesbians, 186–187
illegitimate children, 4–5
marriage, 20–21, 197

℗

Parenting
books for adoptive parents, 275–280
training, 225–228
Parent-teacher conferences, 233–234
Patrilineal descent, 3, 13
Perspective Press (website), 279
Physical abuse, transcultural and transracial adoptees, 109, 111
Pidyon ha-ben, 6, 229
Planting a tree, as part of adoption ritual, 248–249
Poems, for adoption rituals, 251–266
Power issues, adoptees and, 32
Prayers, for adoption rituals, 251–266
Pregnancy
ADD and, 143
birth parent search motivated by, 59
Prejudice
anti-Semitism, 91
derogatory remarks about non-Jews, 40, 42, 108, 128, 129, 132, 134
gay and lesbians adopting, 178
Jews of color, 127–131
transracial and transcultural adoption, 108, 130–131, 132
Psychological problems, transcultural and transracial adoption, 112–117

ℛ

Rabbis
adoption ritual, 242, 245
support for Jewish adoptive families, 214, 228–236
Racism, Jews of color, 127–131
Readings, for adoption rituals, 251–266

Reconstructionist Judaism
adoption ritual, 258
conversion, 13–14
patrilineal descent, 3, 13
Reform Judaism
conversion, 12–13
patrilineal descent, 3
Rejection, adoptees' feelings of, 31
Religion
of birth family, 35–36, 41–43, 57–58, 65, 196
discussion of, 196–199
Religious leaders
adoption ritual, 242, 245
support for Jewish adoptive families, 214, 228–236
Religious ritual *see* Life cycle rituals
Religious school, 232–236
Religious training, adoptees, 220
Resolve (organization), 273
Resources, books, 234
Reunion, with birth family, 70–76, 77–80
Rickets, in transcultural and transracial adoption, 110
Ritual immersion, 10–11
Rituals *see* Life cycle rituals

𝒮

Same sex partners *see* Gays and lesbians adopting
Same sex siblings, 204–205
Schools
guidance counselors, 236
informing of adoption, 232–233
Search for birth parents *see* Birth family search
Secrecy, in adoption, 82, 101, 181–182, 194
Semi-open adoption, 84
Separation issues, of adoptees, 30
Sephardic tradition, naming a child, 18
Seven Blessings, adoption rituals, 252
Sexual abuse, transcultural and transracial adoptees, 109, 111
Sexual orientation, *see also* Gays and lesbians adopting
Jewish community and, 186
parenting and, 165